THE SOCIAL AND POLITICAL THOUGHT
OF KARL MARX

Cambridge Studies in the History and Theory of Politics

THE SOCIAL AND POLITICAL THOUGHT OF KARL MARX

BY

SHLOMO AVINERI

*Professor of Political Theory
and Dean of the Faculty of Social Sciences,
The Hebrew University of Jerusalem*

CAMBRIDGE
UNIVERSITY PRESS

Published by the Press Syndicate of the University of Cambridge
The Pitt Building, Trumpington Street, Cambridge CB2 1RP
40 West 20th Street, New York, NY 10011-4211, USA
10 Stamford Road, Oakleigh, Melbourne 3166, Australia

© Cambridge University Press 1968

First published 1968
Reprinted 1969, 1970, 1971, 1972, 1975, 1976,
1978, 1980, 1987, 1988, 1990, 1993

Printed in the United States of America

Library of Congress Catalogue Card Number: 68-12055

ISBN 0-521-04071-X hardback
ISBN 0-521-09619-7 paperback

CONTENTS

Contents

PREFACE

Any discussion of Marx's thought is still suffering from the absence of a comprehensive critical edition of his works. The Marx–Engels *Werke* edition, now being completed in East Berlin, is despite its shortcomings the most comprehensive effort to collect Marx's and Engels' writings. Occasionally, however, it has to be supplemented by references to other editions, especially Riazanov's superb *Gesamtausgabe* which was discontinued during the Stalin purges.

In the present work, every effort has been made to refer to English translations of Marx's works. In cases where no such translation exists, I have rendered my own translation and referred the reader to the German edition I have used. Loyd D. Easton's and Kurt H. Guddat's selection *Writings of the Young Marx on Philosophy and Society* (Garden City, 1967), has unfortunately reached me too late to be used for this book.

Anyone who adds another volume to the already prolific literature on Marx can be expected to be accused of either repetitiveness or immodesty. I would not have presumed to write this book had I not been convinced that the discussion of Marx's political and social ideas has suffered from a double distortion conditioned by the intellectual history of those ideas themselves. Seldom has the debate about Marx been successfully divorced from explicit or implied political objectives; and the rediscovery of Marx's earlier writings has created an imbalance in most prevalent views about the nature of Marx's thought. It is the intent of this book to emancipate Marx from both his disciples and his enemies and to conduct the discussion with an eye towards restoring the inner balance of Marx's thought as a political theory. It seems a truism, yet it has been repeatedly overlooked, that Marx's political theory should not be judged by Lenin's or Stalin's policies any more than Mill should be judged by Gladstone's performance. The dialectical relations between theory and practice have to be predicated upon a prior autonomous understanding of theory. It is the aim of this book to emancipate the discussion about Marx from the aftermath of the Cold War which is still lingering in many of the writings about Marx in the West. To

vii

Preface

hope that a comparable emancipation would occur in the East may perhaps be naïve: I would still like to voice it. There may actually be signs that such an emancipation is slowly getting under way in at least some Communist countries.

I have been privileged to prepare the first version of the study that ultimately turned out to be this book under the supervision of Professor J. L. Talmon. His inspiration, erudition, understanding and tolerance constituted the ingredients of a relationship I deeply cherish. To Professor Nathan Rotenstreich, now Rector of the Hebrew University of Jerusalem, I owe my awareness of the inseparable link between Marx and the Hegelian heritage; his friendly advice has been of invaluable help. Sir Isaiah Berlin encouraged me in a difficult time during my work and has been a constant stimulus towards self-criticism.

While preparing the final draft of this book during the year I spent at Yale University I have been greatly stimulated and challenged by discussions with several colleagues who shared on various levels an interest in Hegel, Marx and social change: Kenley Dove, William McBride, Roger Masters and Sidney Tarrow will, I am sure, still disagree violently with much that is contained in this book. I do, however, owe them more than they probably realise.

For research and travel grants I am greatly indebted to the Hebrew University, the British Council and the Academic Research Committee of the Israel Federation of Labour (*Histadruth*). For their valuable bibliographical help and research facilities I would like to thank the National and University Library, Jerusalem; the British Museum Reading Room; the British Library of Political and Economic Science at the London School of Economics; the International Institute for Social History in Amsterdam; the Hegel Archives in Bonn; and the Istituto Giangiacomo Feltrinelli in Milan.

My debt to my wife Dvora is greater and more profound than can be expressed in words.   S.A.

October 1967

TO THE MEMORY OF MY FATHER

INTRODUCTION

It is only a few decades ago that some of Marx's most important theoretical writings were discovered and published. Marx's *Critique of Hegel's Philosophy of Right* was published in 1927; the full text of *The German Ideology* was printed for the first time in 1932; the same year saw also the discovery of the *Economic-Philosophical Manuscripts*. The draft manuscript of *Das Kapital*, known as *Grundrisse der Kritik der politischen Ökonomie*, was printed for the first time as late as 1939.

A considerable gap exists therefore between the interest and discussion evoked by Marx and a real acquaintance with his writings and his theory. Most of the controversies in the Marxist movement raged while the protagonists did not know Marx's own views on the relevant subjects: Plekhanov wrote *The Monist View of History* without being aware that Marx had covered much of the same ground, though in a different fashion, in *The German Ideology*; and Lenin wrote his *Materialism and Empirio-Criticism* without knowing about the existence of the *Economic-Philosophical Manuscripts*. It sometimes happens that much of what traditionally passes for Marxism is directly contradicted by some of Marx's own writings.

The recent discovery of Marx's earlier writings shifted much of the emphasis in the discussions of Marx's theories. Until this discovery, discussion about Marx was largely limited to a political and ideological debate between various schools of socialists or between Marxists and anti-Marxists. Since their discovery, the early writings have directed attention to the richness of Marx's philosophical speculation, involving in the debate groups which have not hitherto been concerned with Marx and Marxism. The study of Marx has even become academically respectable.

One of the consequences of this renaissance of the interest in young Marx has been that Marx nowadays means different things to different people. While some hold him responsible for one of the worst totalitarian régimes ever experienced by mankind, others see him as the last of the utopian socialists; while some see him as a

Introduction

narrow-minded materialist and determinist, others point to the basically humanistic vision of his early writings. Still others see him as the father of the modern social sciences, whereas others discern in him a forerunner of modern existentialist thought. If some view him as the theoretician of scientific socialism, others find resemblances between some aspects of his thought and Zen Buddhism. And if forty years ago 'surplus value' was the most popular of Marx's phrases, now the most popular is 'alienation'.[1]

This confusion arises mainly from two causes. First, the recent renaissance of interest in Marx concentrates almost exclusively on his earlier writings; his later works have hardly been reconsidered and scrutinized in the light of the new discoveries. A gap between the 'young' and the 'older' Marx is almost taken for granted. Secondly, much of what is traditionally considered orthodox Marxism is based on the more popular of Engels' later writings. If they seem to differ widely from those of the young Marx, the conclusion usually drawn from this disparity is a statement about a difference between the early and the later Marx.

This study seeks to overcome some of these difficulties. Our methodological goal is to emancipate the study of Marx's thought from the historical circumstances through which we have become acquainted with the various stages of Marx's intellectual development. Instead of considering the mature writings of Marx as a closed system with which his earlier writings must be confronted, I prefer to view Marx's life works as one corpus. Any internal differentiation, chronological or other, must follow a structural analysis of the whole of Marx's thought. If such an enquiry would suggest shifts of interest and emphasis in both Marx's analysis and his vision during his development, this would still not amount to the totally unacceptable attitude sometimes taken by those who write off—according to preference—either the 'young' or the 'old' Marx as wholly irrelevant.

Secondly, a strict differentiation between Marx and Engels will

---

[1] For the history of the interpretation of Marx, see: E. Thier, 'Etappen der Marx-interpretation', *Marxismusstudien*, I (Tübingen, 1954), pp. 1–38; G. Lichtheim, 'Western Marxist Literature', *Survey*, no. 50 (Jan. 1964), pp. 119–28; *idem*, 'The Origins of Marxism', *Journal of the History of Philosophy*, III, no. 1 (April, 1965), pp. 96–105. Cf. also A. James Gregor, *A Survey of Marxism* (New York, 1965).

2

Introduction

be observed, and the collective personality image projected by partisan propaganda will be discarded. Whatever the affinity, intimacy, life-long friendship and intellectual partnership between the two, they were still two distinct human beings, and it would be unreasonable—even monstrous—to suppose that with all their difference in family background, education and attitude to life they would be of one mind on every issue. Marx, who came from a highly sensitive family of Jewish origins, was educated at a university and his main initial intellectual interest was philosophical. Engels came from a straightforward German industrial family with strong Pietist leanings; he was educated for the commercial world and was mainly interested in economic issues. These different backgrounds can be easily traced in their writings and even in their style, and should be respected for the sake of the writers' personalities. The following is, then, a study of Marx's thought, and Engels' writings will be mentioned in passing and for reference purposes only.[1] A detailed study of the development of Engels' thought would be a natural corollary to this study, but it cannot be undertaken here. It might also be less rewarding.[2]

It is a further aim of this study to view the various aspects of Marx's thought against the background of their intellectual origins. The Hegelian background of Marx's thought will be discussed in some detail. Because Marx's first systematic work is a critique of Hegel's *Philosophy of Right*, this relationship has both systematic and biographical significance. In this critique both Marx's indebtedness to, and his struggle against, the Hegelian system become evident; moreover, it can be shown that all the main achievements, as well as dilemmas, of Marx's later thought (like the abolition of private property, of alienation and of the state) originate in this work. Marx's use of these terms is meaningless if divorced from the specific context in which he employs them, as well as from the manner and method of their application.

---

[1] This raises of course the question of Marx's and Engels' joint works, e.g. *The Holy Family, The German Ideology, The Communist Manifesto*. Since their final version was in each case set down by Marx, they can be considered Marx's writings for the purposes of this discussion.

[2] An interesting attempt in this direction has recently been undertaken by Donald C. Hodges, 'Engels' Contribution to Marxism', *Socialist Register 1965* (London), pp. 297–310.

3

Introduction

From this point of view, the main achievement of Hegel's philosophy seems to be his incorporation of the historical within a philosophically relevant system. In contrast to its place in other philosophical systems, history ceased for Hegel to be accidental and arbitrary, nor was it just the area of fulfilment of philosophical ideas. In this respect Hegel's view of history as 'the March of God on Earth' seems to be a unique synthesis between the theological traditions of the Judeo-Christian world and the intellectual achievements of the Enlightenment. Consequently, the eschatological element in Marx's thought cannot be traced to any direct influence of the Judeo-Christian tradition as such, nor did it originate in Marx's Jewish ancestral background.[1] It is a consequence of his Hegelian antecedents.

Hegel's view of history is analogous to the mainstream of Christian theology in its seeing in history an elaborate pattern of meaningful events which must be deciphered and explained in terms of a cosmic significance. Yet since theology was handicapped in its view of history by the doctrine of original sin, man's history had always been subsumed by the theologians under God's trans-historical providential guidance. Within the Augustinian tradition, the very existence of history attested to the loss of grace, and history remained ultimately the handmaid of theology. The French Enlightenment, on the other hand, despite its attempt to systematize history within a philosophical whole, turned out to be far from successful in evolving a coherent view of history. Condorcet's view of human perfectibility and historical progress could hardly fit the common eighteenth-century view of past history. More than one philosopher of the Enlightenment was unable to reconcile his belief in progress with his view of the Middle Ages as a regression, attributable to the base and dark forces of superstition; nor could the first dawn of what Adam Ferguson called 'civil society' be viewed without regarding the price society was paying for material as well as spiritual progress. The regression from the heights of the classical world into the 'Dark Ages' made nonsense of any linear view of historical pro-

[1] This has been recently suggested by A. Künzli, *Karl Marx: Eine Psychographie* (Wien, 1966). Künzli begs the question by wholly disregarding the problem of the extent of Marx's own awareness of those specific Jewish traditions held responsible for his views.

4

gression, and the ambiguities of modernization are reflected in the ambiguities of Rousseau's views on the nature of historical development.

Hegel's historiosophical system attempts to unite these varied elements into a speculative totality. By postulating the Cunning of Reason (*List der Vernunft*) as the vehicle of historical development, Hegel could divorce the subjective element in history from the objective significance of the historical process. Though this method has its own difficulties and internal tensions, Hegel could anchor history within a philosophical system without running into the difficulties of his predecessors. Such a historization of philosophy consequently caused every critical discussion of Hegelian philosophy to imply a discussion of historical reality. If the rational is the actual, if philosophy is 'its own time apprehended in thought', every philosophical critique becomes simultaneously an immanent social criticism of the historical present. Philosophical discussion becomes a social debate, and in this sense Marx's socialism can be viewed as a direct outcome of Hegel's intellectual and speculative achievements.

One can indeed show how Marx, in his first confrontation with Hegel, could construct his materialist view out of the Hegelian system itself. Marx's later writings merely articulate the conclusions at which he arrived at this early stage of his intellectual odyssey. The various economic, social and historical studies undertaken by Marx are but a corollary of the conclusions he drew from his immanent critique of Hegel's political philosophy.

What is so outstanding and intellectually stimulating in Marx's discussion when compared to the writings of the other Young Hegelians is his attempt to measure Hegel according to the criteria of his own system. By this yardstick Hegel is judged—and found wanting. In the Preface to his *Philosophy of Right* Hegel postulates the this-worldness of philosophical speculation while referring to the traditional 'Hic Rhodus, hic saltus'. In this respect Marx takes Hegel at his word, and tries to confront the Hegelian political philosophy with political historical reality, pointing out that though Hegel always emphasized that his idea of the state could never be identified with any particular historical state, it still should be the

5

underlying principle of modern political life. Hence, Marx says, if the universality postulated by Hegelian political philosophy could be proved to be negated and emasculated by the modern political state, Hegel's philosophy would disqualify itself as an adequate ideal expression of the actual world.

Hegel saw his system as the apotheosis and close of philosophy. Paradoxically it can be said that Marx tried to support this view, though he did this in a way that would have startled and disturbed Hegel considerably. For the unique and specific achievement of Hegel's philosophy makes its own subversion possible.

Once Hegel had solved the problem implicit in the tension between matter and spirit by postulating matter as one of spirit's manifestations, albeit an inferior one, the traditional dualism of Western philosophy was overcome, and Hegel was of course the first to point this out. But once the spiritual substance of matter was recognized, i.e. once matter was shown to be nothing but spirit in self-alienation, then, paradoxically, matter was also rehabilitated in a fashion more far reaching than anything hitherto known to Western philosophy. Even eighteenth-century French materialism could not have achieved anything like it. From Hegel on, matter could no longer be conceived as the absolute negation of spirit or as its total absence. Hegel's phenomenology of spirit could thus really become the culmination of philosophy—in more than one sense. Since the secret of spirit was solved, only the movement of matter, its historical manifestation, remained significant. The discussion of the physical, material world would not henceforward be a negation of spirit, as in traditional materialism, but its very affirmation. Here Engels' materialism, based on the mechanistic traditions of the eighteenth century, differed markedly from the main stream of Marx's thought.

For Marx, on the other hand, matter earns its legitimacy not through the traditional materialist school, but through a transforming contemplation of the principles of German idealist philosophy itself. Marx's materialist *Weltanschauung* can thus be called one of the dialectical consequences of Hegel's speculative philosophy. This would also imply that some of the internal tensions of Hegel's thought were carried over into Marx's theory as well, since in Hegel's

6

words: 'Philosophy too is its own time apprehended in thought. It is just as absurd to fancy that a philosophy can transcend its contemporary world as it is to fancy that an individual can overleap his own age, jump over Rhodus.'[1]

It is the aim of this study to seek to bring out this ambivalent indebtedness of Marx to the Hegelian tradition.

[1] Hegel's *Philosophy of Right*, trans. T. M. Knox (Oxford, 1942), p. 11.

HEGEL'S POLITICAL PHILOSOPHY
RECONSIDERED

THE IMPACT OF HEGEL AND FEUERBACH

Marx's programmatic letter to his father, 10 November 1837, informs us that his first encounter, at the age of nineteen, with Hegelian philosophy, occurred through his acquaintance with the *Doktorenklub* at Berlin University. In this most revealing letter Marx gives a comprehensive account of his studies at Berlin, trying to justify to his father his switch from legal studies to philosophy.

It becomes clear from this letter that even at this early stage Marx was drawn to Hegel's philosophy because he saw in it a powerful instrument for changing reality. He might have used such an argument in the attempt to anticipate his father's possible objection to the change of subject: the father, himself a lawyer, felt that his son's step was impractical and immature. Marx writes that what troubled him about German philosophy since Kant was 'the antagonism between the "is" and the "ought"'. But now, since he has become acquainted with Hegel, the young student feels he has found the idea within reality itself: 'If the Gods have dwelt till now above the earth', he tells his father, 'they have now become its centre.'[1]

This first evidence of Marx's encounter with the Hegelian tradition seems to foreshadow the way in which Hegel was absorbed by Marx from the outset. It was neither the institutional conclusions of Hegel's doctrine that attracted him, nor the philosophical premises *per se*. For Marx, Hegel's chief attraction lay in his philosophy's apparent ability to become the key to the realization of idealism in

[1] *Marx-Engels Gesamtausgabe* (*MEGA*; Berlin, 1929), I, 1/2, p. 218. It seems Marx had Hegel's words on the Enlightenment in mind: 'Immediatedness and actuality are united. Both worlds are reconciled and heaven is transplanted to the earth below' (*Phenomenology*, Baillie's edition, p. 598). This strong trend towards the actual present is also apparent in one of Marx's aphorisms of the same year: 'Kant and Fichte reach for ethereal heights, look there for a distant land, while I just try to comprehend that which I found on the street' (*MEGA*, I, 1/2, p. 42).

reality, thus eliminating the dichotomy Kant bequeathed to the German philosophical tradition. Coupled with this Marx developed an immanent critique of the Hegelian system. He felt that though Hegel's philosophy claimed to bridge the gap between the rational and the actual, it did not stand up to the test, and that this dichotomy, though philosophically abolished, remains hidden in the inner contradictions of Hegel's theory of social and political institutions. Hence the sphere of social institutions served as Marx's crucial point in his confrontation with Hegel's philosophy. Marx's correspondence of this period clearly indicates that this point of view characterized the gradual development of his appreciation of Hegel's philosophy.

At the beginning of 1842, when Arnold Ruge asked Marx to contribute an article to a literary miscellany which he was about to publish, Marx promised to send a critique of Hegel, adding that he would concentrate his attack on the *Philosophy of Right*, because 'The main thing is to fight against the constitutional monarchy as a hybrid creature, full of internal contradictions and bound to be self-destroying'. In a later letter, Marx returned to the same theme, only to excuse himself for not having written the article.[1]

Possibly Marx was prevented from writing the critique of Hegel at that time by his entry into active editorial work on the staff of the radical *Rheinische Zeitung*. But Marx's second letter to Ruge hints at reasons that transcend the mere impact of current events: in so far as a retrospective judgment can now be based on the critique as it was ultimately written, Marx lacked in 1842 a methodological device that would enable him to tackle the institutional implications of Hegel's philosophy without simultaneously destroying the whole edifice of the Hegelian system.

Marx seems to have his formula a year later: early in 1843, Ruge sent him a copy of the second volume of the literary miscellany, the *Anekdota zur neuesten deutschen Philosophie und Publizistik*. This volume included a brief anonymous article, written by Marx. It stated categorically that there is no other way for the emancipation

---

[1] Marx to Ruge, 5 and 20 March, 1842 (Marx/Engels *Werke*, Berlin, 1963, XXVII, 397, 401). For a useful contemporary account of the German idea of constitutional monarchy, see J. C. v. Aretin, *Staatsrecht der constitutionellen Monarchie*, 2. Aufl. (Leipzig, 1838).

9

of philosophy but through the purgatory of a *Feuer-bach*.[1] The main piece in this volume was indeed Feuerbach's own 'Vorläufige Thesen zur Reformation der Philosophie'. Thanking Ruge for the delivery of the volume, Marx commented on Feuerbach's 'Thesen': 'I approve of Feuerbach's aphorisms, except for one point: he directs himself too much to nature and too little to politics. But it is politics which happens to be the only link through which contemporary philosophy can become true.'[2]

Marx's interest in Feuerbach was of the same systematic nature as his initial fascination with Hegel. Feuerbach's ideas promised to 'realize' philosophy. Marx felt that this realization, postulated by Hegel, could now be brought about through an application of Feuerbach's method to the problems raised by Hegel's political philosophy.

The corollary to this is of both biographical and intellectual interest. Marx departed from the *Rheinische Zeitung* six days after he had written this letter to Ruge.[3] Sixteen years later, in 1859, Marx referred to this period of his life in his Preface to *A Contribution to the Critique of Political Economy*, calling his retirement a withdrawal 'from the public stage into the study'.[4] He withdrew indeed into a study. During the spring and summer of 1843 he shut himself up in the small town of Kreuznach, immersing himself in intensive reading and producing a long and detailed critique of Hegel's *Philosophy of Right*. This study applies Feuerbach's general critique of Hegelian philosophy to politics. Marx's distinctive application of Feuerbach's transformative criticism here requires some remarks on Feuerbach's 'Vorläufige Thesen zur Reformation der Philosophie'.[5]

Feuerbach saw in speculative philosophy from Spinoza to Hegel an attempt to liberate man from the alienation immanent in religion. This accords with his general view of religion as a projection of

[1] *Werke*, I, 27.
[2] Marx to Ruge, 13 March 1843 (*Werke*, XXVII, 417).
[3] A note to this effect, signed by Marx and dated 17 March 1853, appeared in the *Rheinische Zeitung* of the following day, 18 March.
[4] Marx/Engels, *Selected Works* (Moscow, 1962), I, 362.
[5] For a more detailed study of this problem, cf. W. Schuffenhauer, *Feuerbach und der junge Marx* (Berlin, 1965), especially pp. 36–51. Cf. also G. Lukács, 'Zur philosophischen Entwicklung des jungen Marx', *Deutsche Zeitschrift für Philosophie*, II (1954), no. 2, pp. 288 ff.

human wants on the imagined figure of God; hence the attributes of God, for Feuerbach, were those human attributes which seem to be lacking in present man. God is alienated man.[1]

Feuerbach argued that speculative philosophy did not, after all, transcend alienation. 'Just as theology splits up and alienates man in order to identify him subsequently with that alienated being, so Hegel duplicates and splits the simple essence of nature and man, which is one identity, in order to reunite later forcibly what was initially forcibly separated.'[2] To Hegel, nature and man were two distinct and separate entities. Feuerbach saw man as part of nature; hence in his view the Hegelian mediated reconciliation of man and nature was false. Similarly, Hegel's statement that absolute spirit manifests itself in art, religion and philosophy, was made possible by his prior separation of art from human feeling for art, of religion from human mood and of philosophy from the process of human thought. Hegel did concede that absolute spirit is ultimately actualized in the human subject, but to do this he had to posit absolute spirit as an essence different from the phenomenal subject. Feuerbach, on the other hand, began with the concrete individual as a subject, and saw in the Hegelian notion of absolute spirit a distorted self of subjective conscience parading about as its own spectre. According to Feuerbach, Hegel's absolute spirit was 'man's essence outside man, the essence of thinking outside the act of thinking'.

This separation of essence from existence seemed to Feuerbach to be the mainstay of Hegel's inversion of the epistemological process. Hegel, he asserted, supposed thought to be the subject, and existence to be a mere predicate. Consequently, Hegel's subject exists out of space and time, but Feuerbach most emphatically stated that 'space and time are modes of existence...Timeless feeling, timeless volition, timeless thought are no-thing, monsters (*Undinge*).'[3] This statement of materialism accompanied a recognition of Hegel's difficulties and of his achievements: Feuerbach remarked that Hegel recognized that spirit thinking about itself had to emerge from abstraction and become objectified. But when Hegel

---

[1] L. Feuerbach, *Das Wesen des Christentums*, ed. H. Schmidt (Leipzig, 1909), pp. 7–20.
[2] L. Feuerbach, 'Vorläufige Thesen zur Reformation der Philosophie', *Anekdota zur neuesten deutschen Philosophie und Publizistik* (Zürich and Winterthur, 1843), II, 65.
[3] *Ibid.* p. 71.

postulated nature as this objectification of spirit, according to Feuerbach, he reached the farthest point in abstraction: nature thus did not appear as a subject in Hegel's system, but as a mere predicate of thought. Hence the concrete in Hegel was always alienated, and consequently Hegel's process of overcoming these dichotomies had begun at the wrong end.[1]

Since Hegel's philosophical idealism seemed to Feuerbach to be based on a misleading conception, he asserted that it could not disentangle itself from its internal contradictions: it was bound to end as a mystification. At this point Feuerbach set out to develop his own materialistic philosophy as an inversion of Hegelianism. He transformed the traditional subject of idealistic philosophy, thought, into a predicate, and the traditional predicate, man, into a subject. This, Feuerbach's *transformative method*, postulated a completely new starting-point for philosophy, based on turning Hegelian philosophy upside down: if one starts with man, with the concrete, man can be liberated from the subservience imposed on him by Hegelian philosophy. 'Only the perception of objects and experiences in their objective actuality can free man from all prejudices. The transition from the ideal to the real takes place only in the philosophy of *praxis*.[2]

This reform of philosophy was suggested by Feuerbach in his 'Thesen': he proposed a re-reading of traditional philosophy which would substitute predicate for subject and vice versa, and advocated the transformation of philosophy by this method which makes man the starting-point of philosophic discussion. Thus man would be liberated from the alienated power his own mental creations had over him.

Marx effected this translation in the sphere of political philosophy, writing his *Critique of Hegel's Philosophy of Right* in this Feuerbachian language and basing it exclusively on the transformative method. Marx's materialism dates from this immanent critique of Hegel.

---

[1] Feuerbach, *Anekdota*, II, 71. Marx follows the same line of argument in the last chapter of the 'Economic-Philosophical Manuscripts'; cf. K. Marx, *Early Writings*, ed. T. B. Bottomore (London, 1963), pp. 195–219.

[2] *Anekdota*, II, 71. Cf. W. R. Beyer, 'Hegels Begriff der Praxis', *Zs. f. dt. Phil.* 6. Jg. (1958), no. 5; M. Riedel, *Theorie und Praxis im Denken Hegels* (Stuttgart, 1965).

Hegel's political philosophy reconsidered

THE PREMISES OF HEGEL'S POLITICAL PHILOSOPHY

Marx's *Critique of Hegel's Philosophy of Right* (referred to hereafter as *Critique*) has been preserved in the form of thirty-nine sheets of manuscript, setting out Marx's comments on Paragraphs 261–313 of Hegel's *Philosophy of Right*. Marx first copied from Hegel's book the paragraph under discussion and then added his own comment. There is no doubt that in its present form the manuscript was not intended for publication: it resembles an advanced student's effort to work through a difficult text. The manuscript was published for the first time by Riazanov in 1927, and even now it remains little known. It has hardly been translated, and is rarely discussed at length in the various studies of the young Marx.[1] This *Critique* can demonstrate that the distinctive patterns in Marx's later thought had already taken shape when he attacked Hegel in this work.

Marx's technique of discussion and writing suits his methodological approach: he accepts both Hegel's concepts and his system as a whole, and then subjects both to Feuerbach's transformative criticism. He thus vindicates a comment made by Engels at the same period, that the Hegelian system, comprehensive and overpowering as it was, could be overthrown only from the inside, by thinkers who were themselves Hegelians.[2] Marx accepts and uses such concepts as 'civil society' (*bürgerliche Gesellschaft*) or 'property' as they appear in the Hegelian system, but he sets them in a revolutionary relationship to the concept of the state. As a result this concept undergoes a significant change of meaning. Critical analysis of the Hegelian concepts of property, civil society, state, etc., leads Marx to a fundamental critique of Hegel's philosophical premises; but it is from Hegel's *political* philosophy that Marx works toward the roots of the Hegelian system—and not the other way round. Marx starts with the socio-political implications of Hegel's philosophy and only then proceeds to a review of the Hegelian system as a whole.

---

[1] Cf. J. Hyppolite, 'La conception hégelienne de l'état et sa critique par Karl Marx', *Cahiers internationaux de sociologie*, II (1947), 142 f.; J. Barion, *Hegel und die marxistische Staatslehre* (Bonn, 1963).

[2] F. Engels, 'The Progress of Social Reform on the Continent: II. Germany and Switzerland', *MEGA*, I, 2, p. 446.

This procedure, after all, accords with the programmatic hints in Marx's letter to Ruge, mentioned earlier in this chapter. Marx attacks the political philosophy of Hegel first, and he begins by subjecting the main institutional consequences of Hegelian political philosophy to Feuerbach's transformative method. Here, at one stroke, Marx transcends the limitations of other Young Hegelians imprisoned by the Hegelian system. Marx suggests that such a transformative criticism of Hegel's political philosophy could easily reveal that for Hegel the individual, the real subject, appeared a mere predicate of an abstraction hypostatized into an independent, all-embracing subject. Marx seeks to prove that Hegel's inverted point of departure made it impossible for him to realize his theory in practice. By ascribing existential significance to the organizing concepts of human activity and experience, Hegel, according to Marx, committed himself to the view that the phenomenal world always appears as a cloak for the idea behind it. Actuality (*Wirklichkeit*) always appears different from its phenomenal manifestation. Marx sees in the transformative method the cipher which would enable him to decode the hidden truth in Hegel's thought.[1]

Marx begins by applying this method to three themes of Hegel's political philosophy: monarchy, sovereignty and general consciousness. He argues that Hegel invested empirical reality with a philosophical halo; hence the Idea, which should have been a criterion for judging reality, turns out to be a mere rationalization. This hypostasis leads to a quietistic acceptance of the socio-political situation as it is, and elevates a contemporary phase of history arbitrarily into a philosophic criterion.

The treatment of the monarch is a case in point. In Paragraph 275 of his *Philosophy of Right*, Hegel vindicated monarchy by saying that it expresses in an ideal form the principle that subjectivity and self-determination are the underlying sources of the objective norms and institutions of the state. By saying 'le Roi le veult', the monarch expresses the individual self-determination which, according to Hegel, characterizes political institutionalization in the modern world. For Marx this is a rationalization which must be unmasked. Only *formally* does the will of the monarch stand for the expression

[1] *Kritik des Hegelschen Staatsrecht, Werke*, I, 240–1.

14

of individual self-determination; its real content is the solitary, arbitrary will of one person, cut off from the universality of the general social consciousness. It can hardly be a paradigm for rational self-determination, since its exclusive and particular position makes it wholly arbitrary, as Hegel himself had to admit. Only the universal can be rational, and the monarch's will, by definition, negates universality.

Marx saw, hidden behind Hegel's formula and the elevation of the monarch's will into general consciousness, the given historical situation which he felt should be viewed as it really was, not as an incidence of a general pattern. One should really say: 'In the historical context of the early 19th century, the will of the monarch finally decides.' Instead of this analytical statement, Hegel hypostatized this into: 'The final decision of the will is the monarch.'[1] The subject, Marx points out, has become a predicate, the predicate a subject, and an historical fact has become a metaphysical premise of universal validity. By ascribing to monarchy as a principle of government the attributes of personified sovereignty, Hegel excluded from sovereignty and political consciousness all other members of the body politic. Sovereignty thus becomes a hollow crown of unspecified arbitrariness, personified in the monarchical will. All *raison d'état*, all political consciousness, is made to depend on the arbitrary will of one empirical individual person. Reason becomes an abstraction of an arbitrary 'I will': *L'état c'est moi.*

Marx contends that this reduction of the state to one person could have been prevented had Hegel started from the real subject, the underlying principle of the state, instead of starting from an imaginary subject called 'sovereignty'. The Feuerbachian background of Marx's criticism comes through very clearly in the text:

If Hegel had started with the real subject as the basis of the state, he would not have needed this mystic subjectification of the state...Hegel makes the predicates, the objects, into independent beings, but he makes them independent divorced from their real independence, their subject. Later the real subject appears as a result of this, while one has to start from the real subject and its objectification...

So sovereignty—the essence of the state—is being conceived here first

[1] *Ibid.* pp. 200, 225–7.

15

as an independent being, objectified (*vergegenständlicht*). It goes without saying that this objective side then appears as self-embodiment of sovereignty—while sovereignty is never more than the objectified spirit of the state's subjects.[1]

The claims of the Hegelian state to direct itself towards the general and the universal, and its pretension to become an object of general consciousness, can, according to Marx, be realized only on a purely formal level. Hegel should not be blamed for adequately describing the political arrangements prevalent in his contemporary world; he erred, however, in seeing nineteenth-century political institutions as the hidden meaning of the *essence* of the state *sub specie aeternitatis*. This systematization was made possible only at the expense of a mystification which presents empirical facts as the predicate of a hidden subject lurking behind them.

Once Marx has reached this point in his philosophic argument, his discussion of Hegel gains a new dimension: it ceases to be a purely philosophical discussion and becomes social criticism. For if Hegel's *Philosophy of Right* was the theoretical justification of the modern state, then a critique of it is necessarily a critique of modern political institutions. Henceforward Marx's arguments always run on two parallel lines, and it is sometimes difficult to disentangle the arguments against the contemporary state from the general argument against Hegel's justification of it.

The object of Marx's criticism is therefore the same as the one implied in his letter to Ruge: Hegel's idea of the state merely reflected modern constitutional monarchy; as such, it failed to live up to its own theoretical standards. It contained contradictions and lacked any legitimacy except that of its own empirical existence inflated into a universal criterion of validity.

Since Hegel's political philosophy set the seal of approval upon a reality basically defective and distorted, Hegelian philosophy cannot be reformed without reforming reality itself. Marx took the same view three years later in the famous words of the eleventh thesis on Feuerbach.[2] The need to look into the con-

---

[1] *Werke*, I, 224–5. Marx's skilful usage of the double meaning of 'subject' in this context makes his remarks even more penetrating.

[2] *Selected Works*, II, 405: 'The philosophers have only *interpreted* the world in various ways; the point, however, is to *change* it.'

ditions of social life is a direct outcome of the inner contradictions of Hegelian philosophy as they come to light through transformative criticism.[1]

STATE AND CIVIL SOCIETY

The main achievement of Hegel's political philosophy was its attempt to construct the state as an entity abstracted from the social and historical forces which create and condition it in empirical reality. Hegel did this by depicting civil society as the clash of the social forces, to be transcended by the universality of the state. If this separation between civil society and the state could be shown to be fallacious, i.e. if it could be analytically proved that the objective arrangements of the state are just so many particular interests parading under the banner of the general and the universal, then the whole imposing edifice of Hegelian political philosophy would tumble down.

This is precisely what Marx sets out to do. He shows that Hegel's discussion of the state ignores the social context of human relationship at the same time as it rationalizes existing social organization. In Hegel's theory, the state is described as if it can be discussed without a simultaneous reference to the individuals whose roles it organizes. Consequently, the individual appears in Hegelian philosophy only after the construction of the state has already been accomplished and perfected, as if 'state' and 'individual' could be discussed separately. Marx points out that for this reason Hegel is forced to mediate between the state and the individual in order to close the gap between them; but this mediation, according to Marx, is as erroneous and as superfluous as the original gap. Marx asserts that the individual cannot be conceptually isolated from his social context: by definition any meaningful sentence about an individual must simultaneously refer to his environment, and an atomistic model of an individual is philosophically unsound.[2] Hegel, according to Marx, sees in the individual only his physical traits, 'his beard

---

[1] Moses Hess arrived at very similar results at about the same time, but without the philosophical *rigueur* of Marx; cf. M. Hess, *Philosophische und sozialistische Schriften*, ed. A. Cornu and W. Mönke (Berlin, 1961), pp. 201–26.

[2] Marx's criticism of the individualistic model of classical political economy is derived from the same philosophical premises; cf. K. Marx, *The Poverty of Philosophy* (Moscow, n.d.), pp. 33–46.

17

and blood', and ignores the social connotations of the individual *per se*. Hence the political state is just one of the modes of individual human existence. Marx aims at Hegel the same sort of criticism that Hegel previously directed against Natural Law.[1]

According to Marx, all the tensions revealed by Hegel's account of the structure of political life arise from this separation of man from his social essence: Marx holds that this theoretical premise gives rise to a human being divided into a sphere of privacy, mainly consisting of economic activity, and a sphere of universality where man is supposed to overcome his egoism and strive for the common good. In Marx's words, Hegel thus confronts civil society as a sphere of 'materialism' with the 'idealism' or 'spiritualism' of the state. Man's alienation, according to Marx, is a consequence of the bifurcation of life into those two spheres.[2] The nineteenth-century constitutional monarchy, as well as Hegel's theoretical apotheosis of it, was an attempt to bridge the gap between the two spheres by means of political representation, which sought to legitimize private interests within the general political structure. But Marx argues that representative assemblies of that limited nature (or Estates, *Stände*, as they were still called in Germany at that time) are self-contradictory: the delegates of civil society assembled in a representative estate enjoy their status only because they are members of a *political* organization, not because they legitimize the particular interests of civil society. It would seem that the *Stände* represent the population, but as the delegates are not bound by an imperative mandate and are not subordinate to their voters in any way whatsoever, they are totally alienated from those whom they are supposed to represent. The particular interests of the voters and the political status of the *Stände* are different and distinct. Conversely, delegates are elected in order to serve the general interest of society, but in practice they tend to be unashamed spokesmen for their particular interests, and the mediation between the particular and the general never really takes place.[3]

---

[1] *Werke*, I, 222.   [2] Cf. *On the Jewish Question, Early Writings*, pp. 15–31.
[3] *Werke*, I, 267–8, 328; for Marx's later views on parliamentarism, which are strikingly similar though couched in a different language, cf. *The Civil War in France, Selected Works*, I, 516–22. On the principle of representation in early nineteenth-century German thought, cf. W. Conze, *Staat und Gesellschaft im deutschen Vormärz* (Stuttgart, 1962), pp. 207–69.

State and civil society

The conditions of material life thus stand in an ambivalent relationship to the political sphere. Hegel's theory shows them to be completely outside the political structure; in practice, Marx points out, they penetrate every corner and crevice of the political realm. Political institutions, despite their claim to universality and generality, only mask the particularistic, egoistic interests of civil society. The very differences between the political institutions of Prussia and those of the United States, despite the nearly identical property laws in both societies, help Marx prove how many disguises can be used to hide the economic realities of political power.[1]

If the political sphere, to which Hegel allotted the task of putting the idea of the universal into practice, is nothing more than an empty shell, a 'scholasticism of material life' in Marx's language, then the differences between the various forms of government lose their importance. The differences between a monarchy and a republic may only obscure their common ground, viz. that both forms of government have failed to overcome the alienation between the general and the particular: 'Monarchy is the most perfect expression of this alienation, the republic is the negation of this alienation within its own sphere.'[2] Thus republicanism only accentuates the gap between the various economic interests and the common weal.

At this stage of his argument Marx reviews the changing relationship between state and civil society in various historical periods. His account derives its basic conceptual assumptions, as well as its criteria for periodization, from Hegel's *Philosophy of History*;[3] but Marx shifts the emphasis from conceptual development to the specific field of socio-political organization, thus substituting a study of social development for the Hegelian examination of various forms of consciousness.

As Hegel saw the Graeco-Roman world as an undifferentiated substantiality, so Marx characterizes the classical *polis*—whether monarchical, aristocratic or democratic—by its lack of a differentiation between the social and the political. Here civil society is

---

[1] *Werke*, I, 273. Cf. *The Critique of the Gotha Programme, Selected Works*, II, 32, for the suggestion of this discrepancy between the socio-economic structure and political institutionalization.　　　　　[2] *Werke*, I, 233.

[3] G. W. F. Hegel, *Vernunft in der Geschichte*, ed. J. Hoffmeister (Hamburg, 1955), pp. 242–57.

being wholly subsumed under the state; no political structure separates and differentiates itself from real, material society and from the real content of human life. When the political state is just a form of socio-economic life, of the material state, *res publica* means that public life is the real content of individual life. Therefore anyone whose private life lacks political status is a slave: political unfreedom means social servitude. The political penetrates all private spheres and there is no distinction between society and state, between the private and the public ego, between the sphere of the individual and the commonwealth.[1]

The Middle Ages, on the other hand, offer the reverse of this relationship: here the private sphere, civil society, acquires political status. Property, commerce, social relations and stratification, even the private person, become political. Marx says that in feudal times the power of property is paramount only because the distribution of private property is a political arrangement. Only in medieval times is politics an automatic reflection of socio-economic relations; all other political systems witness a tension between both spheres. This integration of the political and the social is emerging also from linguistic usage: the term *Stände* refers both to social stratification and to political organization.[2]

Marx's description of medieval Europe echoes some of the romantic notions prevalent at that period in Germany: Marx feels that the Middle Ages produced an integrated way of life, in which 'the life of the people was identical with that of the state'; but, Marx adds, this was so because medieval man was an utterly unfree individual. If the Middle Ages were a 'democracy', 'they were a democracy of unfreedom'.[3]

In modern times, Marx continues, civil society and state appear to be wholly distinct and differentiated, and hence the consciousness of alienation is formalized and institutionalized: what was only latent in earlier periods becomes manifest in modern life. Civil society is totally emancipated from political limitations; private life, including economic activity, becomes completely independent of any

[1] *Werke*, I, 234. It is of some interest to compare this view of the *polis* with Hegel's description of it in his early writings; cf. *Hegels theologische Jugendschriften*, ed. H. Nohl (Tübingen, 1907), pp. 219–29.
[2] *Werke*, I, 275–6. [3] *Ibid.* p. 233.

considerations relevant to the commonwealth; and all political restrictions on property and economic activity are abolished. Economic individualism and *laissez faire* express this dichotomy between civil society and state, with human society now fully conscious of its alienation and of the division of human life into a private and a public sphere. The transformation of economic activity into an aim in itself is both a testimony to, and a condition of, this alienation of man from the universal contents of his being.

Marx draws two conclusions from this historical account:

(1) The separation of civil society and state, formulated by Hegel as a matter of principle, is an historical phenomenon occurring at a given moment. Its causes can be easily analysed and are by necessity ephemeral.

(2) Since Hegel, however, was unaware of these historical factors, he did not realize that the ideal, integrated unity of the Middle Ages has disappeared in modern times and been superseded by the antagonism between a person's private status and the political sphere. Oblivious to this historical change, Hegel endeavoured to re-create this unity by reverting to *Stände*, but this strategy is doomed to fail. In modern society, a person's social position does not automatically affect his political standing—this, at least, is the theory of post-1789 society; an infringement of the private sphere by the state is considered a negation of the idea of the modern state. It is therefore anachronistic to look for the mediation of the *Stände* in a situation totally different from the medieval unity of state and civil society. Nineteenth-century ills cannot be cured by fifteenth-century prescriptions.[1]

Marx then shows that the shift in emphasis which turned the political estates into a-political classes occurred in the age of absolutism, when the traditional estates were stripped of their political power and meaning and became merely social classes. The process was completed by the French Revolution which utterly abolished the formal significance of social stratification in the political sphere. But the birth of the modern state coincided, according to Marx, with the polarization of alienation. Class differences have now become completely fluid and the principles that define

[1] *Ibid.* pp. 283-5.

them are decidedly arbitrary: the possession of money and education.[1]

When Marx, in his letter to Ruge, called the modern constitutional state a 'hybrid', he had not yet thoroughly worked out the theoretical problem; but the expression referred to the Hegelian solution which tried to use the device of the medieval *Stände* to overcome the internal contradictions of a society which grew out of the very decomposition of the *Stände* themselves.

CLASS STRUCTURE AND MODERN SOCIETY

Several insights into modern society can be drawn from Marx's conclusion that the modern state as conceived by Hegel is the apotheosis of the alienation of the political from the real social sphere. If the modern state represents extreme dissociation between the formal and the material, as well as between man as an individualistic abstraction and man as *zoon politikon*, then Hegel's attempt at re-association and reconciliation will only make this disparity more acute.

Thus Hegel states, for example, in Paragraph 302 of the *Philosophy of Right* that the *Stände* embody both the consciousness of the state and the consciousness of the particular social strata. They seem to achieve, in Hegel's view, a synthesis between the particularism of civil society and the universality of the state. But in no way, Marx argues, did Hegel realize this mediation, for no empirical content can overcome the antagonisms in more than an abstract sense. The difficulty lies in Hegel's wish to make modern social classes perform functions which characterized medieval estates. Moreover, Hegel wants to reverse the casual relationship: if in the Middle Ages the private nature of the estates determined their public, political status, Hegel now wishes the public, political sphere to determine a person's private standing.[2] This being so, civil society represented in the Assembly of Estates gives to particular interests the legitimacy of a political universality which is illusory and misleading. Hence Hegel's state is but a rationalization of the interests of civil society. Its institutions have only a formal reality; they cover a situation full of irreconcilable antagonisms.

[1] *Werke*, I, 276.   [2] *Ibid.* p. 295.

Class structure and modern society

Marx draws attention to the apparent paradox that the modern state is itself aware of the unresolved ambivalence in the Assembly of Estates: every attempt to invest representative assemblies with real political power creates constant tension between government and the governed. Consequently the government is always careful to divest representative assemblies of any real decision-making power. The proposed resolution of the contradictions is revealed as a sham and a hoax, and Hegel must acknowledge that subjective freedom, which he proposed as the premise of modern society, remains purely formal. What began as an experiment in conflict resolution ends with the total domination of the individual by the political state, while the political state can never detach itself from its civil society background: 'The element of the *Stände* is the political illusion of civil society.'[1]

This failure to resolve contradictions and the resulting double-talk are apparent, according to Marx, in Hegel's treatment of the bureaucracy. According to Hegel, the bureaucracy is the *universal class* (Paragraph 205 of the *Philosophy of Right*). On one hand it is one class of civil society, on the other its business is directed to, and motivated by, the general interest. It is, in a word, the paradigm of mediation between the particular and the universal, i.e. between civil society and the state. Marx, however, holds that the bureaucracy just uses the name of the common weal to further its own interests. The bureaucracy represents the practical illusion of the universality of modern political life, and on account of this Marx calls it 'theological' in a Feuerbachian sense. Modern bureaucracy, according to Marx, is an institutional licence for sectional interests.

This formulation means that according to Marx the bureaucracy exploits for its own ends the affairs of the community entrusted to it; affairs of state are made into private patrimony and presented to the outsiders as a mystique. The apparent idealism of the bureaucracy's dedication to the general well-being of society is nothing but a mask for its own coarse, materialistic ends. Marx's comment on this is certainly one of the first theoretical confrontations with the problems involved in a modern bureaucracy:

The bureaucracy has in its possession the affairs of the state, the spiritual being of society; it belongs to it as its private property. The general spirit

[1] *Ibid.* p. 265.

23

of bureaucracy is the official secret, the mystery...Conducting the affairs of state in public, even political consciousness, thus appear to the bureaucracy as high treason against its mystery. Authority is thus the principle of its knowledge, and the deification of authoritarianism is its credo. But within itself this spiritualism turns into a coarse materialism, the materialism of dumb obedience...As far as the individual bureaucrat is concerned, the goals of state become his private goals: a hunting for higher jobs and the making of a career...Bureaucracy has therefore to make life as materialistic as possible...Hence the bureaucrat must always behave towards the real state in a Jesuitical fashion, be it consciously or unconsciously...The bureaucrat sees the world as a mere object to be managed by him.[1]

By converting itself from a means to an end, bureaucracy gives rise to the fiction of an imaginary state, and side by side with the real state appears the chimera of perfect bureaucratic dedication to the body politic: 'The bureaucracy is the illusory state alongside the real state, it is the spiritualism of the state. Everything has, therefore, a double meaning: the real and the bureaucratic one.'[2] Since it institutionalizes the inverted nature of the modern state, where everything, according to Marx, looks different from its true character, bureaucracy can be abolished only when the state becomes the real, and not the apparent, general interest. Under present circumstances, 'bureaucracy identifies the interest of the state with particular private goals in such a way as to make the interests of the state into a particular private goal opposed to other private goals'.[3] The state is thus degraded to a private interest with others of the same sort, its claim to universality deprived of justification.

At this stage Marx's view of social classes takes a radical turn. Because the *Critique* as a whole remains a rough draft, it is possible to follow the various stages in the crystallization of Marx's ideas on the subject. We have seen that according to Hegel the *Stände* were

[1] *Werke*, I, 249–50.
[2] *Ibid.* p. 249; cf. K. Axelos, *Marx penseur de la technique* (Paris, 1961), pp. 97–101.
[3] *Ibid.* p. 250. It should be remembered that though Marx rejects Hegel's description of the bureaucracy as the 'universal class', he does not discard the analytical usefulness of the term itself. The first time that Marx mentions the proletariat in the *Deutsch-Französische Jahrbücher*, he suggests that the proletariat possesses the attributes of a universal class. Consequently the Hegelian terms determined Marx's initial interest in the proletariat. Cf. *Early Writings*, pp. 55–9.

24

meant to mediate between the state and civil society; in fact, Hegel made a person's private position determine his political status. Even the etymological background of the term *Stand*, with the over-lapping of the socio-economic and the political connotations, em-phasizes the determination of the political sphere by economic considerations. Class differentiation becomes for Marx the decisive factor in the formation of the body politic, although on Hegel's assumption property relations should be neutralized *vis-à-vis* the political sphere.[1]

As a person's private status is determined in modern society by his property relations, these relations are now no longer private, as they should have been according to both the French Revolution and Hegel's premises. The sphere of private property, i.e. civil society, now determines politics, and politics becomes a rationalization of property relations: 'Private status may therefore appear in the political sphere only as the class differences of civil society. The class differences of civil society become political differences.'[2]

Through these considerations Marx sought connections between property arrangements and political structure, and the Hegelian context of his ideas can be traced in Marx's later writings on the subject. For Marx never actually said that the state *as such* reflected property relations: his view was that the state's *claim* to appear as the general interest could be shown to be a cloak for class interests. Not the state as it is, but the Hegelian state as it aspires to be—oriented towards the universal and the general—is a distorted mirror of civil society. For this reason the core of Hegel's political theory is never what it seems.

From this determination of the political structure by class dif-ferences Marx arrived at the dilemma facing that social class which is marginal to civil society. Following Paragraph 243 of the *Philosophy of Right*, Marx calls this class 'the class which stands in immediate need of work', but he moves beyond what Hegel had said about it in that work. Marx clearly anticipates his dictum in the *Deutsch-Französische Jahrbücher* that the proletariat is 'a class of civil society which is not a class of civil society',[3] when he says: 'The

[1] *Werke*, I, 274.   [2] *Ibid*. p. 275.
[3] *Early Writings*, p. 58.

characteristic thing is only this: the lack of property, and the class which stands in immediate need of work, i.e. the class of concrete labour, is less a class of civil society than the basis on which the spheres of civil society rest and move.'[1]

This is of immense importance. The 'class of concrete labour' is not just a marginal phenomenon of modern society. Its existence is the condition for the functioning of civil society itself; hence an understanding of modern society presupposes an analysis of the conditions of the working class. Here, in 1843, the nucleus for Marx's life work is already clearly visible.

The circle is thus complete: since Hegel's theory ignores the human subject, it must ultimately reach an institutionalization from which a whole stratum of human subjects will be excluded. It is only natural that the modern state should be reduced accordingly to the private individual isolated from his social context. Empirical man is torn to pieces between the rival claims of real society and the pretensions of political idealism:

Civil society and the state are disassociated from one another. The citizen of the state and the member of civil society are also separated. Man has to effect an essential schism with himself. As a real member of civil society he finds himself in a double organisation: the bureaucratic (i.e. the external formal determination of the other-wordly state, the government, which does not impinge upon him and his independent reality)—and the social one, the organisation of civil society. But in the latter he is, as a private person, outside the pale of the state; as such, it does not impinge on the political state...In order to behave as a real citizen, to attain political meaning and actuality, he must get out of civil society, abstract from his self, withdraw from the whole organisation into his individuality...His existence as a citizen is an existence that lies outside his communal existence, it is hence purely individual...The gap between civil society and the political state appears of necessity as the gap between the political man, the citizen, and civil society, i.e. his real, empirical

[1] *Werke*, I, 284. It is interesting to compare this with Hegel's own language in Paragraphs 243–245 of the *Philosophy of Right*. Marx still uses the traditional *Stand* to connote the 'class of concrete labour', whereas Hegel refers to it almost twenty-five years earlier by the modern term *Klasse*. It would seem that the reason for this difference lies in Hegel's acknowledgment of the fact that it would be inconsistent within his own theory to refer by *Stand* to a class with no institutional *status* in society. Marx, seeking to undo the whole theory of Hegel's *Stände*, is only too happy to point this out.

reality; for as a political idealist (*Staatsidealist*) he is completely torn from his other, differentiated and opposed actuality.[1]

If this is so, Marx points out, modern society treats people not according to their immanent attributes but according to their external connection with social class. One is thus treated as a 'landowner', a 'worker', etc., rather than as a human being who happens to be owning land or physically working. Again, the predicate becomes the subject: 'Man is not a subject [in modern society], but is being identified with his predicate, class...This lack of critical attitude, this mystification, are the riddle of modern constitutions... as well as of Hegel's philosophy, especially his philosophy of law and religion.'[2]

Marx has thus arrived at the discussion of social class and property purely through a Feuerbachian transformative criticism of Hegel's political philosophy.

PROPERTY

Marx continues to use Feuerbach's method to show that property itself inverts the relations between the human subject and the world of objects. Property, Marx argues, is transformed under Hegel's hands from an object of the will into a master. In saying that a person is determined by his class status one really says that man becomes a predicate of his property. In other words, Marx's first discussion of property is conducted within the terms of reference of Feuerbach's method.

Since Marx arrives at this conclusion in a rather roundabout, if not tiresome and pedantic way, it may be argued that he inflates to ridiculous proportions a very minor affair. Despite this, his application of the transformative method to property is brilliant and the conceptual consequences are extremely interesting. That Marx devotes about forty pages to three paragraphs (Paragraphs 305-307) of Hegel's *Philosophy of Right* may give some indication of the nature and scope of the argument.

In these paragraphs Hegel discussed the position of the landed gentry with entailed estates. In Prussia, as in England, primogeniture

[1] *Werke*, I, 281.   [2] *Ibid.* pp. 286-7.

27

as applied to the landed property of the gentry (*majoratsherrlicher Grundbesitz*) ensured that the family estate passed *in toto* from father to first-born son; the eldest son inherited both the title and the estate in its entirety, all the other children being excluded from the inheritance as far as landed property was concerned. By making the landed estates of the nobility and gentry virtually inalienable by way of sale, this arrangement prevented the fragmentation of noble estates and preserved them intact.

Not only was Hegel very much in favour of this arrangement; but he saw in it an expression of, and a guarantee for, the gentry's higher ethical conduct. He argued that the entailed estate vests the property of the aristocracy not in the hands of arbitrary individuals but in the hands of the family. In Hegel's system the family is the repository of substantive ethical life; consequently any social group which makes its property dependent upon the family minimizes the arbitrary effects civil society has on its members. Possessing property that can neither be interfered with by the state nor affected substantially by unexpected market fluctuations, the aristocracy are unusually fitted to undertake positions in the civil service and in political leadership. Members of this group could, according to Hegel, be expected to be far freer than any other section of society from the habit of reading self-interest into their functions as servants of the commonwealth.

Marx attacks this view by pointing out that Hegel's preference for a type of property free from the pressures of civil society and the state alike contradicted Hegel's earlier definitions of property. By protecting the noble estate from dependence on the power of the state and the needs of society, Hegel suggested that the pure concept of property, as maintained in the entailed estate, is isolated from the social context. Although Hegel initially defined property as an object to be freely disposed of by its owner, now he seemed to say that property is totally severed from individual will.[1]

Furthermore, this severance of entailed property from the social texture raises an ever deeper problem. The Hegelian state was initially presented as a universality that mediates the particular interests; now it seems that the class most suited to ruling the state

[1] *Werke*, I, 303.

Property

possesses a kind of property 'whose social sinews have been cut and torn out and whose isolation from civil society has become complete'.[1] The ethical content thus claimed for the nobility is open to attack. Hegel says that the nobility's necessary reliance on family makes its life more ethical; but Marx points out that as a matter of fact the exact opposite is true for the noble estate. Ultimately entailed property makes nonsense of family solidarity, since none of the children (with the exception of the eldest son) has any share in it. In Paragraph 157 Hegel conceives the family as 'the ethical spirit in its natural and immediate phase', yet he now deprives this solidarity of any real meaning:

> That class founded [according to Hegel] on the family [the aristocracy] lacks therefore the basis for family life—love as the real, active and determining principle. It is family life without spirit, the illusion of family life. In its highest form of development, the principle of private property contradicts the principle of family...This is then the sovereign magnificence and superiority of private property, landed property, about which in modern times so many sentimentalities have been uttered and for whose sake so many multicoloured crocodile tears have been shed.[2]

By contrasting Hegel's definition of private property in Paragraphs 65–66 of the *Philosophy of Right* as alienable and freely disposable by its owner with his later remarks about entailed estates, Marx shows that the statements are incompatible. Entailed property determines self-consciousness and the essence of personality. If property is inalienable, all other properties of man (i.e. personality, self-consciousness, ethical life and religion) become alienable: 'The non-transferability of property amounts to the transferability of free will and ethics.'[3]

Marx also considers Hegel's ideas about entailed property from the point of view of the relation between private and public law. In Paragraph 71, within the context of private law, Hegel defined property by its transferability and its dependence on the social and common will. This definition implies that the state may regulate property and legislate in connection with it. Yet, coming to public

[1] *Werke*, I, 303.
[2] *Ibid.* pp. 303–4; cf. *Economic-Philosophical Manuscripts, Early Writings*, pp. 114–15.
[3] *Werke*, I, 305.

law, Hegel could not maintain this 'true idealism' of property. By becoming inalienable even by its owner, entailed property becomes absolute, and property turns into a virtual subject. It ceases actually to be property at all: *its owners are themselves transformed into the property of property.* What Marx will call in *Das Kapital* 'the fetishism of commodities' appears here for the first time, though without its later analytical economic and historical context.[1]

The entailed estate, Marx argues, ceases to be a legal proprietary institution created by man. Man himself becomes an object of property, since the absoluteness of the entailed estate has transformed it into an independent subject while degrading man to property's predicate. Again Marx reverts to the *leitmotif* of the whole *Critique*, to Feuerbach's transformative method:

We have already pointed out how the social nerves of landed property were cut because of its being inalienable. Private property (landed property) is secured against the owner's own arbitrary will by having the whole sphere of arbitrary will turned from a general human into a specific arbitrary will of private property; private property becomes the subject of the will, whereas the will becomes a mere predicate of private property. Private property is no longer a determined object of will: will is the determined predicate of private property...

Every first-born son is the inheritance, the property, of inalienable landed property, the predestined substance of its will and its activity. The subject is the thing and the predicate is the man. The will becomes the property of property...The owner of entailed landed property becomes the serf of the landed estate...The profundity of Germanic subjectivity appears everywhere as the roughness of a spiritless objectivity.[2]

Marx needs this complicated reasoning to show that property has become man's master. He has reached this conclusion through a purely philosophical argument, with no reference to social criticism or economic analysis, and this radical conclusion exposes the whole Hegelian political structure. The entailed estate should have served Hegel as an example for the possibility of divorcing politics from the claims of civil society and property; *per contra*, this citadel has proved man's subservience to property sundered from all its social relations. What Hegel wanted to present as a conditioning factor

[1] K. Marx, *Capital* (Moscow, n.d.), I, 71–83.   [2] *Werke*, I, 305, 311.

30

appears conditioned, and vice versa. The state is not even under the domination of property-owners, since they themselves are the fettered slaves of their own property. *Maxima libertas, maxima servitudo.*

The state is then an illusion of self-determination—a mystery that must be deciphered.[1] State and property are thus incontestably shown to be interlocked with one another. Far from being protected from the claims and pressures of property and civil society, the state reflects, according to Marx, property relations and class differences —but in a twisted, distorted and illusory manner. The state's claims to ignore these forces only obscure reality:

> The significance of private property in the political state is its essential, its true significance...The political state is the true mirror of the various aspects of the concrete state. At its ultimate heights the state turns to be private property...Instead of making private property into a quality of citizenship, Hegel makes citizenship into a quality of property-holding.[2]

Marx sees therefore in the Hegelian state a rationalization of material reality—an ideology, if one chooses Marx's later language; or, if one sticks to Marx's usage in the *Critique*, the state is the 'idealism', the 'spiritualism', of the 'materialism' of real life. Hegel reached the heights of this contradiction when he had the naturalistic and accidental fact of a person's birth as the oldest son of another person make him eligible for political office.[3] Hegel could not disengage himself from this contradiction, and every attempt he made to base the state on the realization of free spirit ends by reducing it to contingencies. The state is and remains an inverted reality, a mystification.

CLASSLESS SOCIETY: 'TRUE DEMOCRACY' AND COMMUNISM

Marx's verdict on Hegel's political thought also constitutes his summation of the historical experience of the modern state. It would be only natural to enquire whether Marx accompanies this with a positive alternative preferable to the existing arrangements. A critical essay like the *Critique* has little scope for a systematic un-

[1] *Ibid.* p. 304.   [2] *Ibid.* pp. 312–16.   [3] *Ibid.* p. 310.

folding of a positive solution, yet the few instances in which Marx does discuss future prospects indicate the direction his thought is taking. Marx's dialectical method of discourse also suggests that the critical apotheosis could be very easily turned into a constructive premise. Since the modern, Hegelian state has been defined as an inverted reality, reality must be inverted once more by the transformative method: man must be made again into a subject.[1]

In one of his draft summaries of the same period Marx indicates what he has in mind. While collecting material for the *Critique* during his stay at Kreuznach in July 1843, he summarized some of Leopold Ranke's studies on the French Revolution. In passing he remarks that Hegel's way of making predicates into subjects is also a general trait of Restoration historians, who must always elevate a chance historical event into a criterion for ultimate reality:

Thus Hegel turns the moments of the idea of the state into a subject and makes the old political arrangements into a predicate, while in historical reality things operate always the other way round: the idea of the state is always a predicate of these arrangements. Thus Hegel only expresses the general political climate of the period, its political teleology. The same goes for his philosophic–religious pantheism. All the forms of un–reason thus become the forms of reason... This metaphysics is the metaphysical expression of the Reaction, of the old world as the truth of the new world–view.[2]

Thus applying transformative criticism to a concrete historical phenomenon endows it with immediate actuality. Such an application can actualize Feuerbach's philosophical postulate within the bounds of history. This becomes clear when Marx says: 'It may be generally pointed out that the turning of the subject into a predicate and the predicate into a subject, the inversion of the determining and the determined, always signifies the next revolution.'[3]

The method which enables Marx to criticize Hegel is, therefore, *ipso facto* the method of revolution, and the social significance of the revolution is precisely in the fact that a shift in the modes of social consciousness causes a change in the nature of social relations and social structure. The suppressed subject, degraded to the status of a mere predicate, will again become a subject, a free person.

[1] *Werke*, 1, 287. [2] *MEGA*, 1, 1/1, pp. lxxiv–lxxv. [3] *Ibid*. p. lxxiv.

'True democracy' and communism

Hegelian logic, inverted, offers the key to changing the world. This change can be carried out by nothing less than a revolution, which will start in the realm of consciousness, i.e. the critique of traditional philosophy, but will lead directly into the social world. The social content of this transformative revolution lies in the premise that human society is not a given datum, but an outcome of human agency. As society is a predicate, it calls for the activity of the human subject; what was formerly within the realm of necessity will become the province of freedom. This revolution assumes that man and his social activity are one and the same. Man, according to Marx, is the totality of his social connections, hence emancipated society is identical with the emancipated self. This self is called by Marx 'man's communist essence' (*das kommunistische Wesen des Menschen*) or 'socialized man' (*der sozialisierte Mensch*).[1]

Here Marx's logic, anthropology and political sociology meet. For Marx 'das kommunistische Wesen' is both a criterion for measuring existing political institutions and a paradigm of future society. Modern civil society, based on individualism, violates, according to Marx, man as a social being. Individualism in this sense implies a model of man as an entity whose social relations are only a means to his own private ends; it regards individual existence as man's supreme purpose, and juxtaposes society to the individual as something external and formal: 'Contemporary civil society is the consequently realized principle of individualism; individual existence is the ultimate aim: activity, work, content etc. are mere means.'[2] Such a society cannot, by its very nature, develop a socialized model of man.

The society which will overcome this 'atomization'[3] Marx calls 'democracy', sometimes 'true democracy', and his use of this term has given rise to the view that in 1843, at the time of the writing of the *Critique*, Marx was a radical, Jacobin democrat.[4] According

---

[1] *Werke*, I, 283, 231. Both terms can be traced back to Feuerbach, but he does not place them within a given historical context. Cf. L. Feuerbach, *Kleine philosophische Schriften* (Leipzig, 1950), pp. 169, 196.

[2] *Werke*, I, 285. [3] *Ibid.* p. 283.

[4] Cf. G. Lichtheim, *Marxism* (London, 1961), part II; J. Lewis, *The Life and Teaching of Karl Marx* (London, 1965), pp. 31 f.; N. Lapine, 'La première critique approfondie de la philosophie de Hegel par Marx', *Recherches internationales à la lumière du marxisme*, Cahier no. 19.

Hegel's political philosophy reconsidered

to this version, Marx's political solution at that time was democratic, and only later did communism appear in his writings.

A close inspection of what Marx really said in the *Critique* about the nature of 'true democracy' makes it extremely difficult to sustain this notion. It can be shown clearly that what Marx terms 'democracy' is not fundamentally different from what he will later call 'communism', and that in any case this 'democracy' is based on 'man's communist essence'. It also follows that the decisive transition in Marx's intellectual development was not from radical democracy to communism, any more than it was from idealism to materialism. Marx moved from an acceptance of Hegel's system to an immanent criticism of it, since Feuerbach's method necessarily led him to social criticism. The *Critique* contains ample material to show that Marx envisages in 1843 a society based on the abolition of private property and on the disappearance of the state. Briefly, the *Communist Manifesto* is immanent in the *Critique of Hegel's Philosophy of Right*.

'True democracy' is for Marx that state of society in which the individual is no longer juxtaposed against society. He uses the term 'communist essence' for the first time in this context: 'The atomisation into which civil society is driven by its political act is necessarily caused by the fact that the commonwealth (*Gemeinwesen*), the communist essence (*das kommunistische Wesen*) within which the individual exists, civil society, is being divorced from the state, or because the political state is a mere abstraction of it.'[1]

The many connotations attached to the German word *Gemeinwesen* could not have escaped Marx when he used it in this context to indicate man's universalistic nature. Moreover, the original manuscript shows that initially Marx used the word *Kommune*, and only later did he cross it out and replace it with *Gemeinwesen*.[2] *Gemeinwesen* means both commonwealth in the dual sense of *res publica* and republic in the narrower meaning, as well as man's

[1] *Werke*, I, 283.
[2] For the textual apparatus, see *MEGA*, I, I/I, p. 496. It seems that Marx preferred using the Germanic *Gemeinwesen* to repeating the Romance *Kommune* in the same sentence. Compare this with Engels' advice to Bebel in 1875: 'We should therefore propose to replace *state* everywhere by *Gemeinwesen*, a good old German word which can very well represent the French word "*commune*"' (*Selected Works*, II, 42).

common, universal nature and 'commune'. The word can be predicated on both the body politic and the individual, and as such it
suggests forcefully Marx's idea of an integrated human being who
has overcome the dichotomy between the public and the private
self. If Marx believed that man and society should not be antago-
nistically perceived, he has chosen the right word to denote this
belief.

Marx's philosophical position on 'true democracy' becomes evident when he postulates it as the state of society where there is no
alienation between man and the political structure. Consequently
Marx characterizes 'democracy' as the paradigm of all forms of
government, in which form and content are identical. The context
makes it clear that any radical, institutional conception of democracy
will be inadequate to express the meaning Marx read into his version
of 'true democracy':

Hegel starts with the state and transforms man into a subjectified state
(*versubjektivierter Staat*); democracy begins with man and transforms the
state into objectified man (*verobjektivierter Mensch*). Just as religion does
not create man, but man creates religion, so the constitution does not
create the people, but the people the constitution. In a certain respect
democracy relates to all other constitutions as Christianity relates to all
other forms of religion. Christianity is religion *par excellence*, the
essence of religion, man who became God as a separate religion. Thus
democracy also constitutes the essence of all forms of political constitution, the essence of socialised man (*des sozialisierten Menschen*) as a
special constitution. Democracy relates to all other political constitutions
as the species relates to its varieties...In Democracy the formal principle
is also identical with the material principle. Democracy is thus the true
unity of the universal and the particular.[1]

The Feuerbachian parallel between Christianity as a paradigm of
religion and democracy as a paradigm of political constitutions is
crucial to the whole argument. If, according to Feuerbach, Christianity by its historical appearance abolished the need for religion
and was, consequently, self-destroying, so democracy as conceived
by Marx poses the question whether it is not at the same time the
apex and the transcendence (*Aufhebung*) of the political constitu-

[1] *Werke*, I, 231.

35

tion, i.e. of the state. Methodologically, this is the outcome of Marx's dialectical parallel between Christianity and democracy; he states it explicitly as well:

In monarchy, for example, [or] in a republic as a mere political constitution, political man still possesses a separate existence besides non-political man, the private individual. Property, contract, marriage, civil society appear here...as separate modes of existence beside the political state, as the *content* to which the political state relates as an *organising* form; it is really just a determining, limiting, ratiocinating being, sometimes saying 'yes' and sometimes saying 'no', without any content of its own. In democracy the political state, as it places itself next to this content and differentiates itself from it, is just a special content as well as a special mode of existence of the nation. In the monarchy this separate entity, the political constitution, has the significance of the universal which controls and determines all the other separate elements. In democracy the state as a separate element is nothing else, but as the universal it is the real universal, i.e. not a determined differentiation of the other contents. The modern French have conceived this so, that in the true democracy the political state disappears.[1]

Not only the state disappears: civil society as a differentiated sphere of private interests disappears as well. This is brought about, according to Marx, by universal suffrage, which liberates politics from its dependence on property and civil society.[2] Emptied of its political implications, civil society ceases in fact to exist:

The vote is the actual relation of actual civil society to the civil society of the legislative power, to the representative element. To put it in another way: voting is the immediate, direct, not only imagined, but also active relation of civil society to the political state. It goes without saying that the right to vote is the main political interest of actual civil society. In universal suffrage, both active and passive, civil society has really raised itself for the first time to an abstraction of itself, to political being as its real universal essential being. But the perfection of this abstraction is also at the same time the abolition (*Aufhebung*) of this abstraction. By positing its political being as its real being, civil society has also shown that its civil, non-political being is inessential...Within the abstract political state the reform of the suffrage is hence a claim for the dissolution

[1] *Werke*, I, 231–2. [2] *Ibid.* pp. 230–1.

36

(*Auflösung*) of the political state, as well as for the dissolution (*Auflösung*) of civil society.[1]

This analysis makes sense only within the specific Hegelian usage of the term *Aufhebung*. Methodologically, since *Aufhebung* means abolition, transcendence and preservation, it is the focus of the dialectical system. Civil society is *aufgehoben* in a double sense: it is abolished and transcended, but at the same time its contents are preserved (*aufgehoben*) on the higher level to which it was raised. The same holds true for the state. Its *Aufhebung* always meant for Marx that once its universal nature had been fulfilled, it became redundant as a separate organization. Hence Marx's demand for universal suffrage does not draw its arguments from a democratic or republican radicalism. As indicated above, Marx does not see any fundamental difference between a monarchy and a republic. For him the demand for universal suffrage is a dialectical weapon destined to bring about the simultaneous abolition of the state and civil society, precisely because it vindicates both of them to the extreme. The act of the state in granting universal suffrage will be its last act as a state.

Thus the universal postulate of Hegel's state is realized within a systematic transformation—one might say *Aufhebung*—of Hegel's political philosophy. According to Marx, in Hegelian society class stands between the person and the universality of the body politic; if so, man must liberate himself from class to realize himself politically as a *Gemeinwesen*. Hegel had thought that the bureaucracy, as a universal class, would bring this about; Marx rightly pointed out that universality can be meaningful only if it applies to all, and not to a particular class.[2] To Marx, a class cannot be truly universal unless it is everybody's class, or—to put it otherwise—unless class differences disappear. In both cases this is the end of civil society and the state. Since class is based on property, and property is by nature differential, the disappearance of class differences depends upon the disappearance of property as the determinant of status. That is why Marx postulated universal suffrage. He argued that

[1] *Ibid.* pp. 326–7. In 1845 Marx outlined a book on the modern state which he probably intended to write. The last chapter was to be called: 'Universal Suffrage: the fight for the abolition (*Aufhebung*) of the state and civil society' (*Werke*, III, 537).
[2] *Werke*, I, 288, 250.

37

property is meaningless and ceases to exist once it ceases to determine status. Once it becomes ineffective from this point of view, it becomes void and irrelevant. If differentiation ceases to exist, as universal suffrage implies, so do its criteria.[1]

'True democracy' means abolishing class differences and property alike; it does not mean formal, political democracy. Radical, Jacobin democracy, on the other hand, according to Marx, is a self-contradictory term. It abolishes what it claims to realize, without being aware of the dialectical relationship involved. As the very existence of the state is an institutional expression of man's alienation, this alienation cannot be overcome within the state. This crucial position of Marx makes it impossible to construe his *Critique* as a radical democratic or republican tract. The solution Marx found lies, dialectically, beyond the state. The effort to realize the state's universal postulates makes the state itself superfluous; hence it will be *aufgehoben*. Republicanism is just an imperfect, formal way of overcoming alienation. Since it abolishes alienation within the sphere of alienation, it cannot be Marx's ultimate goal.

'True democracy', as Marx conceived it in the *Critique*, is beyond the differentiated realms of both civil society and state; its realization implies man's 'communist essence'. The realization of Hegel's political philosophy has been transported to a level which eliminates the two pillars of Hegelian political philosophy itself, state and civil society. Man's 'communist essence' is decidedly incompatible with both civil society and state.[2] Appropriately, this realization of Hegel's postulates is accompanied, by way of the *List der-Vernunft*, by their very abolition.

A close inspection of the *Critique* has shown that Marx arrived very early indeed—in the summer of 1843—at his ultimate conclusion regarding the *Aufhebung des Staats*. Marx turned to economic and historical studies only after his exegesis of Hegel had proved to him that the economic sphere ultimately determines politics and makes the Hegelian postulate of the universality of political life into a mere dream. Marx arrived at this conclusion not through an economic or historical study, but by applying Feuerbach's method to Hegel. He must thus be considered a materialist at this period, and

[1] *Werke*, I, 253.   [2] *Ibid.* p. 232.

38

'True democracy' and communism

the dichotomy between a young, 'humanistic', 'idealist' Marx
vis-à-vis an older, 'determinist', 'materialist' Marx has no foundation whatsoever in the Marxian texts themselves. The humanistic
vision of the young Marx was based on a materialistic epistemology.

In an article on 'Progress of Social Reform on the Continent',
published by Engels in November 1843 in the Owenite paper
New Moral World, this connection between Hegelianism and Communism is very aptly stated. Naming 'Dr Marx' as one of the so-
called 'theoretical communists', Engels says: 'The Hegelian
system appeared quite unassailable from without and so it was: it
has been overthrown from within only by people who were Hegelians
themselves... Our party has to prove that either all the philosophical
efforts of the German nation from Kant to Hegel, have been useless
—worse than useless; or, that they must end in Communism.'[1]
That this is also the way Marx looked at the place of the *Critique* in
his own intellectual development can be shown from the two
instances where he referred to it in his later writings.

In the Preface to *A Contribution to the Critique of Political
Economy*, Marx says in 1859:

The first work which I undertook for a solution of the doubts which
assailed me was a critical review of the Hegelian *Philosophy of Right*, a
work the introduction to which appeared in 1844 in the *Deutsch-Französische Jahrbücher*, published in Paris. My investigation led to the result
that legal relations as well as forms of state are to be grasped neither from
themselves nor from the so-called general development of the human
mind, but rather have their roots in the material conditions of life, the
sum total of which Hegel, following the example of the Englishmen and
Frenchmen of the eighteenth century, combines under the name of
'civil society', that, however, the anatomy of civil society is to be sought
in political economy.[2]

In 1873 Marx alludes even more directly to the transformative
method he used in the *Critique*; in the Afterword to the second
German edition of *Das Kapital*, vol. 1, Marx says:

My dialectical method is not only different from the Hegelian, but it is its
direct opposite. To Hegel, the life-process of the human brain, i.e. the process of thinking, which, under the name of 'the idea' he even transforms

[1] *MEGA*, I, 2, pp. 446, 448. [2] *Selected Works*, I, 362.

39

into an independent subject, is the demiurgos of the real world, and the real world is only the external, phenomenal form of 'the Idea'. With me, on the contrary, the ideal is nothing else than the material world reflected by the human mind, and translated into forms of thought.

The mystifying side of Hegelian dialectics I criticised nearly thirty years ago, at the time when it was still the fashion... The mystification which dialectics suffers in Hegel's hands, by no means prevents him from being the first to present its general form of working in a comprehensive and conscious manner. With him it is standing on its head. It must be turned right side up again, if you would discover the rational kernel within the mystical shell.[1]

Marx in his later years thus vindicated the validity and significance of the *Critique* of Hegel he had written when he was twenty-five years old. Not only is there no 'caesura' between the young and the old Marx, but the guarantee of continuity has been supplied by Marx himself.

[1] *Selected Works*, I, 456. For another description of the 'mystificatory' element in Hegel's dialectics, see Marx's letter to Dietzgen, 9 May, 1868 (*Werke*, XXXII, 547).

2

THE PROLETARIAT: THE UNIVERSAL
CLASS

Despite its chaotic arrangement, Marx's *Critique of Hegel's Philo-sophy of Right* is the most systematic of his writings on political theory. Marx had always hoped to return to the subject, as can be seen from his opening sentence to the Preface to *A Contribution to the Critique of Political Economy* (1859). There he says that Part IV of his comprehensive study will be devoted to a discussion of the modern state: 'I examine the system of bourgeois economics in the following order: capital, landed property, wage labour; state, foreign trade, world market.'[1] But Marx never reached Part IV because of the disproportionate growth of what he originally in-tended to be merely Part I, *Das Kapital*.

Nevertheless, some of Marx's later remarks about the political structure re-state the conclusions he had drawn in 1843 from his early confrontation with Hegel's political theory. This relationship is particularly evident in his treatment of the dialectical relations between economics and politics. In his later writings, as in his *Critique*, the political never appears as a mere mechanistic or auto-matic reflection of the economic.

Several instances reveal the dynamic relation of the two spheres, though Marx's failure to treat this subject systematically in his later writings has caused readers to overlook its appearances. In 1862 Marx tells Kugelmann that, though the first chapter of his *Capital* contains 'the quintessence' of all the following chapters, the rela-tionships of 'different state forms to different economic structures of society' could not be deduced from this chapter with ease.[2] The *Critique of the Gotha Programme* makes the same point in language strikingly reminiscent of the *Critique* of Hegel:

'Present-day society' is capitalist society, which exists in all civilised countries, more or less free from medieval admixture, more or less modi-

[1] *Selected Works*, I, 361; cf. also Marx's letter to Lassalle, 22 February 1858 (*Selected Correspondence*, p. 125), as well as his letter to Engels, 2 April 1858 (*ibid.* p. 126).
[2] Marx to Kugelmann, 28 December 1862 (*Letters to Kugelmann* [London, 1936], p. 23.)

The proletariat: the universal class

fied by the special historical development of each country, more or less developed. On the other hand, the 'present-day state' changes with a country's frontier. It is different in the Prusso-German Empire from what it is in Switzerland, it is different in England from what it is in the United States. The 'present-day state' is, therefore, a fiction.[1]

The idea that the political structure does not necessarily and automatically reflect the socio-economic conditions, but requires instead a more sophisticated analysis, is empirically tested by Marx in considering Britain. Here he must come to grips with the baffling phenomenon of an industrial, capitalist society operating within a political framework that is still largely pre-capitalist. In an article published in the *Neue Oder Zeitung* in 1855, Marx comes very near Bagehot's later distinction between the real and the apparent British Constitution: 'But what is the British Constitution?... Actually the British Constitution is just an old-fashioned, antiquated and archaic compromise between the bourgeoisie, which rules *unofficially* but effectively over all the spheres of civil society, and the landed aristocracy which rules *officially*.'[2]

This incongruence between the socio-economic and the political spheres illustrates once more the thesis Marx developed in his earlier writings that in modern society man must lead a double life and conform to two conflicting standards of behaviour. That Marx thought these early writings still significant after 1848 can be deduced from his intention to include both of his articles from the *Deutsch-Französische Jahrbücher* in an edition of his works which should have been printed in Cologne in 1850 by the publisher Herman Becker. As Becker was a member of the *League of Communists* the whole plan collapsed, however, with the League's disappearance in the wake of the Cologne trials.

Marx's failure ever to define his political theory in a systematic way impels an effort to deduce his theory from the fragmentary evidence in his voluminous analytical and polemic writings. Such

[1] *Selected Works*, II, 32.
[2] *Werke*, XI, 95; cf. Marx/Engels, *On Britain* (Moscow, 1962), p. 423; also Marx's letter to Lassalle, 22 July 1861 (*Werke*, XXX, 614–15), and his letter to Engels, 24 April 1852 (*Briefwechsel*, I, 377–8). That Marx maintains his distinction between *bourgeoisie* and *bürgerliche Gesellschaft* is of considerable significance in determining the continuity of his thought.

The proletariat: the universal class

an enquiry will also facilitate the integration of Marx's concept of the proletariat within the general framework of his thinking.

THE STATE AS ALIENATION

Marx uses the term 'the modern state' as it developed within traditional German philosophy with its Protestant overtones. He conceives the emergence of the modern state as a corollary of secularization, expressed by 'political emancipation', i.e. the separation of politics from religious and theological considerations and the relegation of institutional religion to a separate and limited sphere. Marx sees this process starting with the Reformation and culminating in the French Revolution.[1] Using obvious Kantian associations, in 1842 he draws an analogy to the Copernician revolution, as the state has now become rooted in human consciousness and reason:

The state's Law of Gravitation was discovered around the same time as Copernicus' great discovery of the true solar system. The state's focus was found to reside within itself, and with the initial shallowness of practice, the various European governments started to apply this result to the system of the Balance of Power. In a parallel way, people like Machiavelli and Campanella, and later Hobbes, Spinoza, Hugo Grotius and finally Rousseau, Fichte and Hegel began to perceive the state through human eyes and to develop its natural laws from reason and experience rather than from theology, just as Copernicus was not impressed by Joshua's telling the sun to stand still at Gideon [*sic*] and the moon to remain at the valley of Ajalon.[2]

This parallel leads Marx to deduce the modern concept of law from man's rational faculty and to see it as an expression of human freedom and a limitation of arbitrariness.[3] Consequently he views with extreme anxiety any attempt to restore religion to the political realm. Such tendencies, as expressed by political romanticism, Friedrich Wilhelm IV or Bruno Bauer's attitude to Jewish emancipation, are to Marx infringements on the secular state as well as

[1] *On the Jewish Question, Early Writings*, pp. 27–31; *The Holy Family*, trans. R. Dixon (Moscow, 1956), pp. 149–59.
[2] *Rheinische Zeitung*, 14 July 1842 (*Werke*, I, 103).
[3] *Ibid.* 12 May 1842 (*ibid.* p. 58).

43

contradictions in Christian terms, since Christ's kingdom is not, after all, of this world. Marx goes even further: the degree to which religion is separated from the state serves him as an index to the state's modernity, and the degree of Jewish emancipation as a convenient measuring device. 'States which cannot yet politically emancipate the Jews must be rated by comparison with accomplished political states and must be considered as underdeveloped.'[1]

Marx uses this definition of the modern state as a criterion for evaluating other forms of government and as a self-referential term. He measures the modern state by its own yardstick—and finds it wanting. In a programmatic letter to Ruge dated September 1843 and published in the *Deutsch-Französische Jahrbücher* Marx says:

Reason has always existed, but not always in rational form...As far as actual life is concerned, then the political state (even where it has not yet been consciously imbued with socialist demands) includes in all its modern forms all the demands of reason. But it does not stop at this. It assumes reason as universally realised. Hence it finds out that its ideal determination is always challenging its real preconditions.[2]

Marx holds that the realization of the postulates of the modern state is frustrated in society. The Hegelian idea of mediation, which should have made political life rational, chooses just those contents, like consciousness, capable of mediation. But declaring property outside the scope of politics does not eliminate man's dependence on it. Consequently politics has not been really emancipated from property. As the political neutralization of religion has not eliminated the human need for religion, separation of politics from property has not really made human life indifferent to it.[3]

Within this context Marx contends that in modern society man is cut into two distinct persons—into the 'citizen' (*citoyen*) and the '*bourgeois*'. Within the state man is expected to live up to universal criteria; within civil society, he is supposed to behave according to his egotistical needs and interests. Thus the state, which should have incorporated the universality of social life, appears as one

[1] *The Holy Family*, p. 149. Cf. E. Weil, 'Die Säkularisierung der Politik und des politischen Denkens in der Neuzeit', *Marxismusstudien* (Tübingen, 1962), IV, 153-7.
[2] *Werke*, I, 345; cf. Marx's article on the divorce laws, *Rheinische Zeitung*, 19 December 1842 (*ibid.* pp. 149-51).
[3] *On the Jewish Question*, *Early Writings*, pp. 11-13; *The Holy Family*, pp. 128-9.

partial organization among the other powerful interests of civil society. We have already seen that this argument, worked out systematically in *On the Jewish Question*, was immanent in the *Critique* of 1843. Its first appearance can be traced to one of Marx's articles in the *Rheinische Zeitung* of 1842. Here he castigates a borough member in the Rheinish Diet for looking at freedom of the press not from the general, political point of view, but from the narrow angle of his class interests: 'What we have here is the opposition of the *bourgeois*, not the *citoyen*.'[1]

This confrontation of *bourgeois* versus *citoyen* is not confined to Marx's thought. Some of his contemporaries, drawing as he did on the Hegelian heritage, used it as well. Max Stirner, for example, made the same terminological distinction, but his conclusions diametrically opposed Marx's. In his *Der Einzige und sein Eigentum* (1845) Stirner said about the French Revolution:

Not individual man—and it is only as such that man exists as a real person—has been emancipated: it is merely the citizen, the *citoyen*, political man, that has been liberated; and he is not real man, but just an exemplar of the human species, to be more precise, of the genus *citoyen*. It is only as such, and not as man, that he has been liberated...In the French Revolution it is not the individual that is world-historically active: only the nation.[2]

Stirner maintained that the French Revolution had subsumed the real, private person under the attributes of universality. He intended to abolish this submission and maintain the individual (*der Einzige*) in his unfettered freedom. Stirner's individualistic premise is, of course, the exact opposite of Marx's. For Marx it is not the lack of individualism but its proliferation that plagues the modern state.[3] The common terminology of such disparate opinions emphasizes even more strongly the Young Hegelians' need ultimately to choose between the individualistic and the socialistic options inherent in the Hegelian tradition.

Marx uses both economics and religion to show that man is

[1] *Rheinische Zeitung*, 15 May 1842 (*Werke*, I, 65). As in his *On the Jewish Question*, Marx uses here the French term in the original.
[2] *Die Hegelsche Linke*, ed. K. Löwith (Stuttgart, 1962), p. 69.
[3] *The German Ideology* (London, 1965), pp. 259 f. Cf. Moses Hess' letter to Marx, 17 January 1840, in M. Hess, *Briefwechsel*, ed. E. Silberner (Haag, 1959), p. 455.

45

divided into a 'citizen' and a member of civil society. He points out that the separation of the state from both religion and economic life (which occurred historically at the same time) liberated the *state* from religion and economics, but did not liberate *man* from their impact. This is the distinction Marx makes between 'political' and 'human' emancipation; the modern state's greatest achievement is thus shown to be its main limitation:

The decomposition of man into Jew and citizen, Protestant and citizen, religious man and citizen, is not a deception practised against the political system nor yet an evasion of political emancipation. It is political emancipation itself, the political mode of emancipation from religion...

The contradiction in which the adherent of a particular religion finds himself in relation to his citizenship is only one aspect of the universal secular contradiction between the political state and civil society...

Thus man was not liberated from religion; he received religious liberty. He was not liberated from property; he received the liberty to own property. He was not liberated from the egoism of business, he received the liberty to engage in business.[1]

Since the modern state cannot acknowledge this internal contradiction, it creates, according to Marx, the illusion of liberty, the learned fallacy which maintains that what is actually a *bellum omnium contra omnes* is a mediation of human consciousness, and what is essentially slavery is freedom:

The contradiction between the democratic representative state and civil society is the perfection of the classic contradiction between the public commonwealth and slavedom. In the modern world each one is at the same time a member of slavedom and of the public commonwealth. Precisely the slavery of civil society is in appearance the greatest freedom because it is in appearance the perfect independence of the individual. Indeed, the individual considers as his own freedom, no longer curbed or fettered by a common tie or by man, the movement of his alienated life elements, like property, industry, religion, etc.; in reality, this is the perfection of his slavery and his inhumanity.[2]

In *The German Ideology* Marx summarizes this contradiction by saying that human behaviour always differs from what the norms seem to require. Not only does the dichotomy between the rational

---

[1] *On the Jewish Question, Early Writings*, pp. 16, 21, 29.
[2] *The Holy Family*, p. 157.

46

and the actual remain unsolved, it is constantly strengthened.[1] The state's supposed universality and emancipation from arbitrary personal rule become the arbitrariness of a system of needs basically dependent on modes of production free from conscious direction. Personal arbitrariness has been replaced by anonymous arbitrariness, the 'hidden hand' of the market.[2] The private and the egoistic, in the guise of a false universalism, make anarchy and disorder seem the essence of rationality.[3] The state as it is becomes a surrogate for the real commonwealth.[4]

Political democracy appears to Marx in this argument as the apotheosis of such double talk; and since he regards democracy as the highest possible form of political organization, he must relegate his solution to levels beyond the separate political structure.[5] The existence of the state as a *separate* sphere of universal attributes shows, according to Marx, that all other spheres have been abandoned to particularism and egoism. The corollary of this argument would be a shift in Marx's interest from the idealism of the state to the realities of civil society, and we have already seen that this was also Marx's retrospective view in 1859, in his Preface to *A Contribution to a Critique of Political Economy*.

That Marx remained faithful to this view in later years can be discovered also in a speech delivered in 1871, in which he criticizes Mazzini's views on social action. The issue of the relative predominance of the political and the social provides his criterion for judgment on Mazzini's methods: 'The fact is that Mazzini never understood anything and never achieved anything with his old-fashioned republicanism. With his cry for nationality he has just saddled the Italians with a military despotism. For him, the state which he created in his imagination is everything, whereas society, which is a reality, is nothing.'[6]

---

[1] *The German Ideology*, p. 93.
[2] *The Poverty of Philosophy* (Moscow, n.d.), pp. 116–17.
[3] Cf. Marx's articles on press censorship, *Rheinische Zeitung*, 27 October 1842 (*Werke*, I, 116); on wood-picking, *RZ*, 30 October 1842 (*ibid.* p. 130); *The Holy Family*, p. 158.
[4] *The German Ideology*, pp. 90–2.
[5] *On the Jewish Question*, *Early Writings*, p. 20.
[6] Speech at the meeting of the General Council of the International, 6 June 1871 (*Werke*, XVII, 639).

47

The proletariat: the universal class

BUREAUCRACY: THE IMAGINARY UNIVERSALITY

In his *Critique of Hegel's Philosophy of Right* Marx saw bureaucracy as the institutional incarnation of political alienation. He viewed it as the expression of the illusion that the state realizes human universality. If for Hegel the 'universal class' of civil servants proves that the state's social content is adequate to its conceptual determination, for Marx, on the other hand, the illusory universality and the practical egoism of the bureaucracy reveal the gulf that divides the Hegelian concept of state from its actual existence.

Marx's approach to bureaucracy is strikingly similar to Weber's handling of the bureaucratic 'ideal type'.[1] Like Weber, Marx characterizes bureaucracy by division of functions and hierarchy.[2] That bureaucracy is the alienation of public life implies, according to Marx, two consequences: on one hand, the abolition of the state will be achieved institutionally by the destruction of the bureaucratic apparatus; on the other, the bureaucratic dimension of political reality offers a criterion for the assessment of different political structures.

As early as 1847 Marx characterizes the political system of the various German states as bureaucratic, and thus brings out a central characteristic of German public life overlooked by later Marxists at their peril.[3] In 1868 Marx saw in the bureaucratic traditions of the German working class a main difficulty which might frustrate the emergence of a revolutionary working-class movement in Germany. This was, again, an anticipation of developments universally explained in such terms only many years later.[4]

---

[1] M. Weber, *Essays in Sociology*, Trans. H. H. Gerth and C. Wright Mills (New York, 1946), pp. 196-239.

[2] *Selected Works*, I, 332-3; First draft of *The Civil War in France*, *Werke*, XVII, 539. Lenin's view of bureaucracy differs from this and does not include hierarchy among the characteristics of bureaucracy: even in the so-called 'second stage' of socialist society Lenin never mentions the abolition of hierarchy though he refers explicitly to the other characteristics of bureaucracy that would be abolished (cf. V. I. Lenin, *State and Revolution* [Moscow, n.d.], p. 171). Lenin may have followed here the ideas developed by Engels in his essay 'On Authority' (*Selected Works*, I, 636-9).

[3] *Deutsche Brüsseler Zeitung*, 12 September 1847 (*Werke*, IV, 193). Engels arrived at similar conclusions the same year in his article 'Der Status Quo in Deutschland' (*Werke*, IV, 40-57); this article, one of the more perceptive pieces of writing Engels produced, was published only in 1929. It is a pity that it is so little known.

[4] Marx to J. B. von Schweitzer, 13 October 1868 (*Selected Correspondence*, p. 259).

48

Bureaucracy

Most studies of Marx have neglected his concern with bureaucracy, and some have even accused Marx of wholly overlooking the fact that bureaucracy is one of the central phenomena of modern political and socio-economic life. But an insistence on the importance of understanding bureaucracy both historically and functionally runs through all of Marx's writings after 1843. For Marx, bureaucracy is central to the understanding of the modern state. Because it is the political expression of the division of labour, it must be explained not only in functional but also in structural terms. Far from overlooking the growth and significance of bureaucracy, Marx even makes the degree of bureaucratization of any particular society determine the degree of violence required by the proletariat in overthrowing it. These countries which have not been bureaucratized offer, according to Marx, better chances for peaceful take-over: England, the United States, perhaps Holland. In the bureaucratic societies on the Continent, however, political power could be transferred only by a violent revolution aimed at the bureaucratic structure itself.[1]

It is none the less true that some changes occurred over the years in Marx's analysis of the historical emergence of bureaucracy. In *The German Ideology* he sees bureaucracy as typical to the retrograde conditions of the German petty states: here bureaucracy emerged as a result of the impasse in class relations, when no single class was strong enough to impose its rule on society. Within this political vacuum the bureaucratic apparatus of absolutism arrogated to itself the leading roles in society and developed its pretensions to independence from the social powers.[2]

Six years later, in his *The Eighteenth Brumaire*, Marx asserts that France, not Germany, is the classic abode of bureaucracy. He even uses allusions to Feuerbach's transformative criticism, stating that under bureaucracy the human subject becomes a mere object of manipulation. What the 'fetishism of commodities' is to economics, bureaucracy is to politics. This is how Marx described the French bureaucracy, thrice perfected under Absolutism, Jacobinism and Bonapartism:

---

[1] Marx to Kugelmann, 12 April 1871 (*Letters to Kugelmann*, p. 123); the Amsterdam Speech of 1872 (*Werke*, XVIII, 160).
[2] *The German Ideology*, p. 208.

49

The proletariat: the universal class

Every *common* interest was straightway severed from society, counter-posed to it as a higher, *general* interest, snatched from the activity of society's members themselves and made an object of government activity, from a bridge, a schoolhouse and the communal property of a village community to the railways, the national wealth and the national university of France...It was the instrument of the ruling class, however much it strove for power of its own.[1]

Marx recapitulates this same idea in *The Civil War in France*:

The State power, apparently soaring high above society, was at the same time itself the greatest scandal of that society and the very hotbed of all its corruptions...Imperialism [i.e. Bonapartism] is, at the same time, the most prostitute and the ultimate form of the State power which nascent middle-class society had commenced to elaborate as a means of its own emancipation from feudalism, and which full-grown bourgeois society had finally transformed into a means for enslaving labour by capital.[2]

In the original draft of *The Civil War in France*, far more extensive than the published version (and not printed till 1934), Marx develops this idea at some length. The similarities with his arguments in the *Critique* of 1843 are striking:

Every minor solitary interest engendered by the relations of social groups was separated from society itself, fixed and made independent of it and opposed to it in the form of state interest, administered by state priests with exactly determined hierarchical functions.

This parasitical excrescence upon civil society, pretending to be its ideal counterpart, grew to its full development under the sway of the first Bonaparte...But the state parasite received only its last development during the second Empire. The governmental power with its standing army, its all directing bureaucracy, its stultifying clergy and its servile tribunal hierarchy had grown so independent of society itself, that a grotesque mediocre adventurer with a hungry band of desperadoes behind him sufficed to wield it...Humbling under its sway even the interests of the ruling classes, whose parliamentary show work it supplanted by self-elected Corps Legislatifs and self-paid senates...the state power had received its last and supreme expression in the Second Empire. Apparently the final victory of this governmental power over society, it was

---

[1] *Selected Works*, I, 333. For an extremely interesting study of the implications of the difference between 'common' and 'general', cf. I. Mészaros, 'Collettività e alienazione', *Nuova Presenza*, no. 5 (1962).

[2] *Selected Works*, I, 518.

in fact the orgy of all the corrupt elements of that society. To the eye of the uninitiated it appeared only as the victory of the Executive over the Legislative, of the final defeat of the form of class rule pretending to be the autocracy of society by its form pretending to be a superior power to society. But in fact it was only the last degraded and the only possible form of that class ruling, as humiliating to those classes as to the working classes which they kept fettered by it.[1]

The sociological significance of Marx's analysis of bureaucracy lies in his insistence that bureaucratic structures do not automatically reflect prevailing social power relations but pervert and disfigure them. Bureaucracy is the image of prevailing social power distorted by its claim to universality. Hence Napoleon III's government cannot be readily explained in class terms. In his *Critique of the Gotha Programme* Marx remarks that:

It is by no means the aim of the workers, who have got rid of the narrow mentality of humble subjects, to set the state free. In the German Empire that 'state' is almost as 'free' as in Russia. Freedom consists in converting the state from an organ superimposed upon society into one completely subordinate to it...The German workers' party...instead of treating existing society (and this holds good for the future one) as the *basis* of the existing state (or of the future state in the case of future society) treats the state rather as an independent entity that possesses its own intellectual, ethical and libertarian bases.[2]

Marx also saw the development of independent bureaucracies within capitalist corporations. The significance of this analysis for his views on the internal changes of capitalism will be dealt with later in its specific context. Suffice it to say that these insights indicate that instead of overlooking the 'managerial revolution' or avoiding it because it undermined his theories, Marx anticipated it.[3]

This insight may perhaps serve as a clue to Marx's reluctance to

---

[1] For the original English text of this draft, see *Archiv Marksa i Engelsa* (Moscow, 1934), III (VIII), 320-2.   [2] *Selected Works*, pp. 31-2.
[3] *Capital* (Moscow, 1959), III, 426-32. Cf. Marx's remarks on the structure of the East India Company: 'Who, then, govern in fact under the name of the Direction? A large staff of irresponsible secretaries, examiners, and clerks at India House, of whom... only one individual has ever been in India, and he only by accident...The real Court of Directors and the real Home Government of India are the permanent and irresponsible *bureaucracy*, "the creatures of the desk and the creatures of favour" residing in Leadenhall Street' ('The Government of India', *New York Daily Tribune*, 20 July 1853)

systematize his views on the modern state. Though he never conceived the state, or the bureaucratic structure, as a mere reflection of socio-economic forces, he still considered it a projection, even if a distorted one, of those forces, their ideal pretension. The basic contradiction in which the modern state finds itself reveals that, to attain its expectations and standards, the state must reject its origins in the material world. It is doomed to appear different from what it really is—its alienation lies in its very essence. Like religion, which projects onto God what is lacking in this vale of tears, the state ascribes to itself (and to bureaucracy) those attributes which should have been part of every person as a subject.

If so, why waste time in studying the distorted looking glass instead of looking through it at the reality hidden behind it? Instead of discussing the imaginary arrangements of the state, why not analyse the reality of civil society and its economic form? This is the way Marx summed up his own programmatic position in 1859 in the Preface to *A Contribution to a Critique of Political Economy*. This is also at the root of Marx's polemics against the 'True Socialists' whom he considered still prisoners of the Hegelian view that the state is independent of economic and social life.[1]

THE PROLETARIAT

Only at this late stage does the proletariat appear in Marx's thinking and social criticism. Its appearance at this point has systematic significance, because it explains Marx's interest in the proletariat within the theoretical framework of this thought. As we shall see later in this chapter, the proletariat, for Marx, is not just an historical phenomenon: its suffering and dehumanization are, according to Marx, a paradigm for the human condition at large. It is not the proletarians' concrete conditions of life but their relation to an anthropological determination of man which primarily interest Marx. Consequently, though Marx is certainly not the first to discuss the proletariat and its position in industrial society, he is the first to relate it to general terms of reference which, for their part, draw very heavily on the Hegelian heritage and tradition.

[1] *On the Jewish Question, Early Writings*, pp. 14–15; *The Holy Family*, pp. 154–5.

The proletariat

Marx is fully cognizant of his debt to his predecessors, though there is a significant difference between his readily admitted indebtedness to French Restoration historians and his more ambivalent acknowledgment to Lorenz von Stein. Most of Marx's reading notes for the crucial summer of 1843, when his views on state and society took shape, deal with historical accounts of the role of social classes in the French Revolution, and most of his sources are naturally French; Marx even arranged an index to his various notebooks, according to the social background of the different constitutional instruments of the Revolution.[1] In 1852 Marx tells Weydemeyer that the 'bourgeois historians' discovered the role of the classes in determining developments in modern society.[2] Two years later, in a letter to Engels, he specifically refers to Thierry's contribution, but points out that like other Restoration historians Thierry overlooked the fact that social struggles did not end with the emergence and hegemony of the bourgeoisie. The real and final struggle, according to Marx, occurs at the moment of the bourgeoisie's victory, when it becomes a ruling class and ceases to be a *tiers état* alongside the clergy and the nobility.[3]

Marx's relation to Lorenz von Stein is more complex and remains controversial. Robert Tucker recently pointed out how much Marx's description of the proletariat draws on Stein's *Der Sozialismus und Kommunismus des heutigen Frankreichs*. In this Tucker follows several earlier writers who maintained that Marx had become acquainted with French socialist thinking through Stein's book, and that only later did he read the French authors themselves.[4] Others, however, maintain that, because of the writers' different levels of discussion and conceptualization, Stein's influence on Marx should be rather held at a minimum. It would indeed be

---

[1] *MEGA*, I, 1/2, pp. 118–36; the index pp. 122–3.
[2] Marx to Weydemeyer, 5 March 1852 (*Selected Correspondence*, p. 86).
[3] Marx to Engels, 27 July 1854 (*ibid.* p. 105).
[4] R. C. Tucker, *Philosophy and Myth in Karl Marx* (Cambridge, 1961), pp. 114–16; cf. G. Adler 'Die Anfänge der Marxschen Sozialtheorie und ihre Beeinflussung durch Hegel, Feuerbach, Stein und Proudhon', *Festgabe für Adolf Wagner* (Leipzig, 1905), pp. 16 ff.; P. Vogel, *Hegels Gesellschaftsbegriff und seine geschichtliche Fortbildung durch Lorenz Stein, Marx, Engels und Lassalle* (Berlin, 1925); B. Földes *Das Problem Karl Marx—Lorenz Stein* (Jena, 1927).

difficult to suppose that Marx could be too impressed by Stein's somewhat simplistic arguments.[1]

It is difficult to take issue with these arguments if the problem is posed as if Stein were Marx's only conceivable source. Stein's book does not appear in Marx's reading lists of 1842—but Marx's notes for that year include only books on art and mythology, and he certainly read books on history as well, so the notes as they survive cannot be considered comprehensive. Marx's remarks about Stein are none too clear. In *The Holy Family* Marx reproaches Bruno Bauer for concentrating in his discussion on French socialism and not paying any attention to the English working-class movement on the sole ground that Stein has nothing on it. Marx feels this is a serious weakness of Stein's book. In *The German Ideology*, however, Marx compares Stein's study quite favourably with Karl Grün's book on French and Belgian socialism, and points out that Grün's book is a muddled rehash of Stein's work.[2]

In contrast, Marx refers for the first time to 'a propertyless class' whose problems 'cry out to heaven in Manchester, Paris and Lyons' in an article in the *Rheinische Zeitung* in autumn 1842, a short time after the publication of Stein's book. Though this article ostensibly deals with one of Wilhelm Weitling's books, Marx mentions here writings by Leroux, Considérant, Proudhon and Fourier. They are not mentioned by Weitling at all and Marx could not have read them in the original at that time. He probably got the information about them from Stein's book. But the problem, after all, is not biographical but methodological. Concentrating on the possible—and even quite probable—influence of Stein on Marx begs the question, assuming that Stein's book could have been Marx's only link with French socialist and communist ideas or with a sociological description of the proletariat in industrial society. This is clearly not the case, though some of the evidence has not always been considered.

[1] F. Mehring, *Nachlass*, I, 186; S. Hook, *From Hegel to Marx*, new edition (Ann Arbor, 1962), p. 199. Hook, however, is mistaken in dating Stein's book at 1845, instead of 1842. For some recent valuable studies of Stein, see K. Mengelberg, 'Lorenz v. Stein and his Contribution to Historical Sociology', *Journal of the History of Ideas*, XXII, no. 2 (1961); J. Weiss, 'Dialectical Idealism and the Work of Lorenz v. Stein', *International Review of Social History*, VII, no. 1 (1963).

[2] *The Holy Family*, p. 180; *The German Ideology*, pp. 534 f. Engels refers to Stein's book in 1843 as 'dull drudgery' (*Werke*, I, 477).

The proletariat

Stein's book caused a minor sensation in Germany, mainly because of the peculiar circumstances of its composition; but Stein was evidently not the first German author to raise the question of the proletariat. Volume XIII of Rotteck's and Welcker's *Lexikon der Staatswissenschaften*, published in 1842, includes the following statement in its entry on 'Revolution':

But this is the content of history: no major historical antagonism disappears or dies out unless there emerges a new antagonism. Thus the general antagonism between the rich and the poor has been recently polarised into the tension between the capitalists and the hirers of labour on the one hand and the industrial workers of all kinds on the other; out of this tension there emerges an opposition whose dimensions become more and more menacing with the proportional growth of the industrial population.

Moreover, discussion of working-class conditions began in Germany many years before the problem existed in Germany itself and this discussion was started not by radicals or socialists, but by conservative romantics, who used it as an argument against *laissez faire* liberalism. Two of the most reactionary German romantics, Adam Müller and Franz von Baader, took up the issue years before the radicals of Rotteck's or Welcker's stamp even considered it. In an essay published shortly after 1815, Adam Müller discussed the conditions of the working class in England in a language which seems to prefigure Marx's analysis in the *Economic-Philosophical Manuscripts* of 1844. Analysing Adam Smith, Müller arrives at the conclusion that political economy breaks the productive process, which should be unitary, into capital and labour.[1] In a work of 1816 Müller maintains that the division of labour emasculates the worker's personality:

Man needs a many-sided, even an all-rounded, sphere for his activity, limited and restricted as this activity itself may be...But if the division of labour, as it is now being practised in the big cities and the manufacturing and mining areas, cuts-up free man into wheels, cogs, cylinders and shuttles, imposes on him one sphere of activity in the course of his many-sided search for one object—how can one expect this segmented segment to be adequate to the full and fulfilled life or right and law?

[1] A. Müller, *Gesammelte Schriften* (München, 1839), I, 275.

55

The proletariat: the universal class

How can partial forms, which are cut out from the full circle of activity and are being divorced from one another, how can they fit into the full circle of political life and its laws? This is the miserable outcome of the division of labour in all the branches of private industry.[1]

Franz von Baader approaches the same issue in an essay written in 1835, which includes the term *proletair* in its title. Baader says that the moneyed classes impose the burden of taxation almost exclusively on the proletariat and make it simultaneously impossible for the proletarians to participate in political life and become full-fledged *citoyens*. According to Baader, the proletarians pay for the upkeep of the state but do not belong to it. He concludes that, according to the premises of political economy, capitalist competition is doomed to end in a monopoly that would leave the worker in a position far worse than that of the medieval serf:

One can actually say that serfdom...is less terrible and more humane... than this reckless, defenceless and welfare-less freedom to which so many parts of the public are exposed in our so-called civilised and enlightened nations. Anyone who looks at this will have to admit that in what is called Christian and enlightened Europe, the civilisation of the few is generally made possible by the lack of civilisation and even barbarism of the many. We approach the state of ancient slavery and helotism far more than the Middle Ages.[2]

That both Müller and Baader sought to avoid this conclusion by a return to neo-feudal, corporative and romantic arrangements does not detract from the demonstration that Lorenz von Stein cannot be regarded as Marx's only source for his characterization of the industrial proletariat, much as Marx might have drawn from Stein's book some information about individual French writers. Marx draws on a mood and a general malaise prevalent at that time in intellectual circles in Germany among radicals and conservative romantics alike. It would be difficult—and utterly wrong—to choose one writer and make him responsible for moulding Marx's thought. Marx was responding to a *Zeitgeist*, and it was from a common stock far more

[1] A. Müller, 'Die heutige Wissenschaft der Nationalökonomie kurz und fasslich dargestellt', *Ausgewählte Abhandlungen*, ed. J. Baxa (Jena, 1921), p. 46.
[2] F. v. Baader, 'Über das dermalige Misverhältnis der Vermögenslosen, oder Proletairs, zu den Vermögen besitzenden Klassen der Sozietät', *Schriften zur Gesellschaftsphilosophie*, ed. J. Sauter (Jena, 1925), p. 325.

than from any individual writer, that he drew his ideas and inspiration.

This common background also emphasizes Marx's specific contribution to this discussion of the working class, his suggestion that the condition of the proletariat should not be considered within the narrow historical circumstances of its emergence. Marx's intellectual *tour de force* must be approached by confronting his description of the proletariat with the universal postulates of Hegel's political philosophy.

We have already seen that in the *Critique* Marx is aware that the class of 'immediate labour', though vital to the function of civil society, is not cared for by, nor integrated in, the general structure of society. Empirically Marx studied this phenomenon several months earlier when he discussed in some newspaper articles the situation of the village poor in the Rhineland. He comments that it seems inconsistent with Hegelian political philosophy for the village poor to be treated far better by the irrational countryside customs and traditions than by the rational arrangement of the institutional modern state: something must be wrong with the state if it fails to take account of this sector of the population.[1]

In the *Rheinische Zeitung* and in the *Critique* Marx is still obviously thinking in traditional terms of 'the poor'. This undifferentiated terminology shows that the issue has not yet been approached by philosophical speculation and insight. This happened only after Marx had finished his account of the Hegelian notion of the bureaucracy.

All of Marx's discussions about the bureaucracy conclude that the Hegelian postulate of a 'universal class' is an illusion of Hegel's inverted political world. The bureaucracy does not embody universality, but merely usurps it, using the pretexts of the commonwealth for its particular interests, which are no different from other class interests. But if Marx does not accept the Hegelian identification of bureaucracy with universality, he still retains the dialectical concept of a 'universal class', i.e. a partial social stratum which is, however, an ideal subject of the universal concept of the *Gemeinwesen*. If Hegel's 'universal class' hypostatizes a given historical pheno-

---

[1] *Rheinische Zeitung*, 27 October 1842 (*Werke*, I, 119).

57

menon into a self-fulfilling trans·ʰistorical norm, Marx uses it differently. For Marx the term will always be open to the dialectical dynamics of the historical process. He does not invest any one class with the attributes of universality: for him every generation, every historical situation, gives rise to a class which aspires to be the subject of society's general consciousness. Historical developments actually allow this class for a time to represent the *res publica*, society at large, but after a while, with changes in the distribution of social forces and in general conditions, this claim for universality no longer accords with the interests of society as a whole. The class which had hitherto represented society must vacate its place to a new class, which will henceforward claim that *it* represents society. 'Rising' classes are those whose claims for universality represent, at a given moment, the general will of society and realize the potential of its development. 'Declining' classes are those whose claim for universality is no longer valid and real. They cling to past glories and to present privileges derived from them. In these terms Marx sees the rise and decline of the feudal aristocracy, and applies the same analysis to the bourgeoisie. The Hegelian idea of a 'universal class', stripped of its hypostasis, becomes, for Marx, a vehicle for historical explanation.

In the *Introduction to the Critique of Hegel's Philosophy of Right* Marx formulates this for the first time:

No class in civil society can play this part unless it can arouse, in itself and in the masses, a moment of enthusiasm in which it associates and mingles with society at large, identifies itself with it, and is felt and recognised as the *general representative* of this society. Its aims and interests must genuinely be the aims and interests of society itself, of which it becomes in reality the social head and heart. It is only in the name of the general interest that a particular class can claim general supremacy...that genius which pushes material force to political power, that revolutionary daring which throws at its adversary the defiant phrase: *I am nothing and I should be everything*.[1]

And in *The German Ideology*:

For each new class which puts itself in the place of one ruling before it, is compelled, merely in order to carry through its aims, to represent

[1] *Early Writings*, pp. 55–6.

The proletariat

its interest as the common interest of all the members of society, that is, expressed in ideal form: it has to give its ideas the form of universality... The class making a revolution appears from the very start...not as a class but as the representative of the whole of society.[1]

This tension between particularism and universality—between a class's appearance as a protagonist of the general will and its search for its own interests—comes to a head, according to Marx, with the emergence of the modern proletariat. It can be overcome only by the simultaneous abolition of the proletariat as a separate class and the disappearance of class differences in general. Marx does not postulate the abolition of class antagonisms because any economic mechanism points in that direction. No economic analysis precedes his dictum about the abolition of classes; they will be abolished (*aufgehoben*) because historical development has brought the tension between the general and the particular to a point of no return. The tension, according to Marx, is now radically general. It permeates every nook of society and cannot be transformed into just another change of the ruling class. Only a dialectical *Aufhebung* will give rise to a humanity with no dichotomy between the general and the particular.

Only because he sees in the proletariat the contemporary, and final, realization of universality, does Marx endow the proletariat with a historical significance and mission. He mentions the proletariat for the first time in the last section of the *Introduction to the Critique of Hegel's Philosophy of Right*, immediately after the passage cited above about the role of 'universal classes' in history. The reference to the proletariat is heavily loaded with allusions to its function as the ultimate 'universal class':

A class must be formed which has *radical chains*, a class in civil society which is not a class of civil society, a class which is the dissolution of all classes, a sphere of society which has a universal character because its sufferings are universal, and which does not claim a *particular redress* because the wrong which is done to it is not a *particular wrong* but *wrong in general*. There must be formed a sphere of society which claims no *traditional* status but only a human status, a sphere which is not opposed to particular consequences but is totally opposed to the assumptions of

[1] *The German Ideology*, pp. 61-2.

the German political system; a sphere, finally, which cannot emancipate itself without emancipating itself from all the other spheres of society, without, therefore, emancipating all the other spheres, which is, in short, a *total loss* of humanity and which can only redeem itself by a *total redemption of humanity*. This dissolution of society, as a particular class, is the *proletariat*...

When the proletariat announces the *dissolution of the existing social order*, it only declares the *secret of its* own existence, for it *is* the *effective* dissolution of this order. When the proletariat demands the *negation of private property* it only lays down as a *principle for society* what society has already made a principle *for the proletariat*, and what the *latter* already involuntarily embodies as the negative result of society.[1]

The abolition (*Aufhebung*) of private property merely universalizes the situation the proletariat already experiences in society. Communism is not the starting-point of the discussion but its outcome as it emerges from philosophical principles. A political revolution, changing the balance of power within the social framework, will not do, because the proletariat remains in total alienation.[2] Hence the emancipation of the proletariat must be predicated on the emancipation of humanity, as the enslavement of the proletariat is paradigmatic to all forms of human unfreedom:

From the relation of alienated labour to private property it also follows that the emancipation of society from private property, from servitude, takes the political form of the *emancipation of the workers*; not in the sense that only the latters' emancipation is involved, but because this emancipation includes the emancipation of humanity as a whole. For all human servitude is involved in the relation of the worker to production, and all the types of servitude are only modifications or consequences of this relation.[3]

The victory of the proletariat would mean its disappearance as a separate class. In this the proletariat, according to Marx, would differ from other classes, which, on attaining victory, still depended on the continuing existence of their opposite and complementary classes. The feudal baron needed a villein in order to be a baron; a bourgeois needs a proletarian in order to be a bourgeois—only the

---

[1] *Early Writings*, pp. 58–9; cf. *The German Ideology*, pp. 86–7.
[2] This is the crux of Marx's argument against the narrow view of a political revolution; see his article in *Vorwärts*, 8 August 1844 (*Werke*, I, 408).
[3] *Early Writings*, pp. 132–3.

The proletariat

proletariat as a true, 'universal class' does not need its opposite to ensure its own existence. Hence the proletariat can abolish all classes by abolishing itself as a separate class and becoming co-eval with the generality of society. Even the programmatic and necessary connection between the proletariat and philosophy becomes possible, because both are universal, and because the proletariat carries out the universal postulates of philosophy: 'Just as philosophy finds its material weapons in the proletariat, so the proletariat finds its intellectual weapons in philosophy...Philosophy is the head of this emancipation and the proletariat is its heart. Philosophy can only be realised by the abolition of the proletariat, and the proletariat can only be abolished by the realisation of philosophy.'[1]

The universalistic nature of the proletariat does not disappear in Marx's later writings, when his discussion concentrates mainly on the historical causes of the emergence of the proletariat. What was at the outset a philosophical hypothesis is verified by historical experience and observation: the universalistic nature of the proletariat is a corollary of the conditions of production in a capitalist society, which must strive for universality on the geographical level as well.[2]

A careful reading of *The Communist Manifesto* brings the argument from universality to the surface. The proletariat as a 'universal', 'general', 'national' class can only be emancipated universally; its existence defies the norms of bourgeois society:

In the conditions of the proletariat, those of old society at large are already virtually swamped. The proletarian is without property; his relation to his wife and children has no longer anything in common with the bourgeois family-relations; modern industrial labour, modern subjugation to capital, the same in England as in France, in America as in Germany, has stripped him of every trace of national character...

All previous historical movements were movements of minorities or in the interests of minorities...The proletariat, the lowest stratum of our present society, cannot stir, cannot raise itself up, without the whole superincumbent strata of official society being sprung into the air...

The Communists are distinguished from other working-class parties by this only: 1. In the national struggles of the proletarians of the dif-

[1] *Ibid.* p. 59.   [2] *The German Ideology*, pp. 75–6.

61

ferent countries, they put out and bring to the front the common interests of the entire proletariat, independently of all nationality. 2. In the various stages of development which the struggle of the working class against the bourgeoisie has to pass through, they always and everywhere represent the interests of the movement as a whole...

The working men have no country. We cannot take from them what they have not got. Since the proletariat must first of all acquire political supremacy, must rise to be the leading class of the nation, must constitute itself *the* nation, it is, so far, national, though not in the bourgeois sense of the word.

National differences and antagonisms between peoples are daily more and more vanishing, owing to the development of the bourgeoisie, to freedom of commerce, to the world market, to uniformity in the mode of production and in the conditions of life corresponding thereto.

The supremacy of the proletariat will cause them to vanish still faster...[1]

This strong emphasis on the universal aspects of the proletariat recurs also in the Preamble to the General Rules of the International, drafted by Marx in 1864.[2] It is also behind Marx's opposition to Proudhonist mutualism, which he saw as an avoidance of this universalism. Appropriately enough, when Marx summarizes the deficiencies of the British labour class in 1870, he sees its inability to universalize its experience as its major weakness.[3]

This universalistic element in the proletariat can also explain the systematic nature of Marx's quarrel in the 'forties with Bruno Bauer and the 'True Socialists' about the role of the 'masses' in the struggle for emancipation. The disdain of Bauer and his disciples for the masses and their tendency to avoid complicity with the proletariat were motivated by a fear lest the general vision of liberty be replaced by advocacy of a particular class and espousal of its cause. For Marx, however, the proletariat was never a particular class, but the repository of the Hegelian 'universal class'. The debate about the place and significance of the proletariat was again conducted within the conceptual tradition of the Hegelian legacy.[4]

---

[1] *Selected Writings*, I, 44, 46, 51.   [2] *Ibid.* p. 386.   [3] *Werke*, XVI, 415.
[4] Cf. D. Hertz-Eichenrode, 'Massenpsychologie bei den Junghegelianer', *International Review of Social History*, VII, no. 2 (1962), 231–59. This excellent study does not, however, bring out the connection between Marx's view of the proletariat and his Hegelian background.

The proletariat

Nevertheless, because Marx's relation to the proletariat is not immediate but is reached through speculative considerations, he does not reveal much empathy or spiritual attachment to the members of the working class. Marx's sceptical view of the proletariat's ability to conceive its own goals and realize them without outside intellectual help has often been documented. It suits his remark that revolutions never start with the 'masses' but originate in elite groups.[1] Much as Marx always opposed those socialists who tried explicitly to dissociate themselves from the proletariat, a chief reason for the split in the League of Communists in 1850 was Marx's uncertainty about what would happen to the League if it were to be exclusively proletarian in membership. Marx's opponents within the League even went so far as to accuse him of trying to impose intellectual discipline on the proletarian movement; and Weitling was sometimes snubbed by Marx as the Tailors' King.[2]

This enquiry leads Marx to the conclusion that the conditions of the emergence of the proletariat guarantee their own overcoming. He couples this conclusion with the insight that the same forces produce poverty and wealth within society:

Private property, as private property, as wealth, is compelled to maintain itself and thereby its opposite, the proletariat, in existence. That is the positive side of the contradiction, self-satisfied private property...

The proletariat, on the other hand, is compelled as proletariat to abolish itself and thereby its opposite, the condition for its existence, what makes it the proletariat, i.e. private property. That is the negative side of the contradiction, its restlessness within its very self, dissolved and self-dissolving private property.[3]

Poverty, then, does not exist beside wealth: it is the source of wealth. Both are the consequences of human action. This reasoning

[1] See Marx's article 'The Indian Revolt' (*New York Daily Tribune*, 16 September 1857): 'The first blow dealt to the French Monarchy proceeded from the nobility, not from the·peasants. The Indian Revolt does not commence with the *ryots*, tortured, dishonoured and stripped naked by the British,·but with the sepoys, clad, fed, petted and pampered by them.'

[2] Cf. *Werke*, VIII, 598–600. In a letter to Engels (20 July 1852) Marx has this to say about a group of German working-class men: 'Asses more stupid than these German workers do not exist' (*Werke*, XXVIII, 93).

[3] *The Holy Family*, p. 51.

63

makes clear Marx's refusal to see communism in distributive terms. The problem as he sees it is not a redistribution, more just or more equal, of existing wealth. For Marx, communism is the creation of new wealth, of new needs and of the conditions for their satisfaction. Hence the key to the understanding and changing of actuality is in the economic mechanism which characterizes man as a creative being. The question whether poverty is or is not an outcome of objective circumstances ceases to be relevant: objective circumstances themselves are an outcome of human agency.

The nature of human activity thus becomes the next subject for Marx's enquiries. The enquiry into the historical conditions of the emergence of the proletariat makes it clear that the traditional problems posed by philosophy are soluble within historical development.

3

HOMO FABER

Though Marx's *Weltanschauung* is widely called materialistic, Marx himself never dealt with materialism systematically. This neglect caused some speculation about the exact content of his materialistic approach,[1] and led scholars to rely heavily on Engels' later writings on materialism. Much of what is known as 'Marxist materialism' was written not by Marx but by Engels, in most cases after Marx's own death. Students sometimes forget that Marx himself never used the terms 'historical materialism' or 'dialectical materialism' for his systematic approach.[2]

Marx's postulate about the ultimate possibility of human self-emancipation must be related to his philosophical premise about the initial creation of the world by man.[3] Philosophically such a view is a secular version of the Hegelian notion that actuality (*Wirklichkeit*) is not an external, objective datum, but is shaped by human agency.[4] For Hegel this shaping is performed by consciousness; Marx extricates the activist element of Hegel's doctrine from its metaphysical setting and combines it with a materialist epistemology.[5]

Even at this early stage of the enquiry it becomes evident that such a view of materialism differs sharply from the mechanistic materialism expounded by Engels in his *Dialectics of Nature*. By applying dialectics to nature Engels divorces it from the mediation of consciousness. Strictly speaking such a view cannot be termed dialectical at all. Although Hegel included inanimate nature in his dialectical system, for him nature is spirit in self-estrangement.

[1] H. B. Acton, *The Illusion of the Epoch* (London, 1955); G. Leff, *The Tyranny of Concepts* (London, 1961). Cf. also T. G. Masaryk, *Die philosophischen und soziologischen Grundlagen des Marxismus* (Wien, 1899).
[2] The only time when Marx approaches anything like such an expression is in his article 'Quid pro Quo', *Das Volk*, 6 August 1859 (*Werke*, XIII, 454 f.).
[3] *Selected Works*, II, 403.
[4] K. Löwith, *Die Hegelsche Linke* (Stuttgart, 1962), p. 7.
[5] For a comprehensive discussion of the impact of German idealism on Marx see N. Rotenstreich, *Basic Problems of Marx's Philosophy* (Indianapolis/New York, 1965), pp. 27–63.

Homo faber

Hence he did not eliminate consciousness but reasserted it pan-logistically. This was not the case with Engels, who saw in in-animate nature only opaque matter. Moreover, Engels says in *Dialectics of Nature* not only that matter historically preceded spirit, but also that it is the cause and the source of the evolution of consciousness. It became commonplace and fashionable to credit Marx with such a reductionist view which sees in spirit a mere biological by-product of matter.[1] Engels tried to leave an escape clause by stating that the 'ideological spheres' can re-act on their own socio-economic causes; but this formulation does not basically change the systematic role of matter as the prime mover.[2]

Lenin's *Materialism and Empirio-Criticism* intensified this identification of Marxist epistemology with a highly mechanistic view of materialism. Because Lenin viewed consciousness as a mere reflection of the objective world, some writers still ascribe such a view to Marx himself. Even after the discovery of the *Economic-Philosophical Manuscripts* Jacques Barzun wrote in 1944 that 'we have all—or nearly all—capitulated to Marx's dogma that economic facts produce ideas...Marx reduced thought and action to material facts...Consciousness to Marx is an embarrassing illusion.'[3] Ironically, many of the views of Engels, Plekhanov, Kautsky and Lenin on this subject are identical with the mechanistic materialism Marx criticized in his *Theses on Feuerbach*.

Marx's comments on eighteenth-century French materialism in his *Theses on Feuerbach* foreshadow his awareness of the social consequences of a mechanistic epistemology. They place the epistemological problem in the centre of Marx's own views. Marx here takes issue with the view that consciousness is nothing but a reflection of the material, environmental condition of man's existence. According to him the internal contradiction of a reflectionist theory of consciousness is very simple: both eighteenth-century materialists

[1] F. Engels, *Dialectics of Nature*, trans. C. Dutt (Moscow, 1954), pp. 274-5.
[2] Engels to Mehring, 14 July 1893 (*Selected Correspondence*, pp. 541-2).
[3] J. Barzun, *Darwin, Marx, Wagner* (Boston, 1946), pp. 142, 212. For a most lucid account of Lenin's view, see G. A. Paul, 'Lenin's Theory of Perception', *Analysis*, v, no. 5 (1938), 65-73. Cf. also A. Heusel, *Untersuchungen über das Erkenntnisobjekt bei Marx* (Jena, 1925), pp. 3-17; J. de Vries, *Die Erkenntnistheorie des dialektischen Materialismus* (Salzburg/München, 1958); M. Cornforth, *Dialectical Materialism* (London, 1954), II, 11-68.

Consciousness and society

and Feuerbach combine a passivist view of human existence (man determined by objective-material conditions) with a social optimism implying immanent and necessary progress of human history. These views, Marx argues, are mutually incompatible and their combination produces a social philosophy ultimately quietistic, a-political and conservative. If man is a product of material conditions, he can never emancipate himself from their impact. If the world is not of man's own making, how can he change it?[1] That such a reflectionist view of consciousness was adopted by the German SPD under Engels' influence may perhaps explain, on at least one level, the ultimate conservatism and quietism of German social democracy despite its overt radicalism.

Marx admits that 'old materialism' offers an alternative to this latent conservatism, but he points out that its creation of an ideal world rejects its materialistic premises.

The materialistic doctrine that men are products of circumstances and upbringing, and that, therefore, changed men are the products of other circumstances and changed upbringing, forgets that it is men that change circumstances and that the educator himself needs education. Hence the doctrine necessarily arrives at dividing society into two parts, of which one is superior to the other.[2]

But this escape from conservatism returns to the old dichotomy between the real and the ideal, expressed this time in terms of social classes. Feuerbach provides a case in point, as do the so-called utopian socialists. To make social change possible, Marx argues, they must postulate one section of society not determined by material economic conditions and, then entrust the role of universal emancipator to this class. But such a division of mankind into those who are materially and economically determined and those free from such a determination makes nonsense of the very foundations of a materialistic view, since 'the educator himself needs education'.

Marx's approach to this basic epistemological dilemma is imbued with the legacy of the philosophical tradition within which he was educated. Though Marx acknowledges the importance of eighteenth-century French and English materialism in the emergence of early

[1] *The German Ideology*, p. 58.
[2] Thesis III on Feuerbach, *Selected Works*, II, 403–4.

socialist and communist thought,[1] he notices that the utopian strain in that socialism is a direct outcome of its epistemological premises. The origins of Marx's epistemology, in contrast, are deeply imbedded in the German idealist tradition, and his reliance on this tradition enables him to solve the dilemma of social action and change on a more satisfactory level. Marx's deep attachment to Feuerbach never involved an uncritical acceptance of his epistemology; what fascinated Marx about Feuerbach were the potentialities of his transformative method. We have already seen how much Marx felt that Feuerbach was wrong in not extending his analysis to the social world. This methodological weakness of Feuerbachian philosophy arose from its mechanistic materialistic conception. Marx, who perceived this flaw from the very beginning, was never a Feuerbachian who later turned against his master. He had acknowledged Feuerbach's achievements as well as his limitations from the outset.

From Hegel's *Phenomenology of Mind* Marx derived his view that reality is not mere objective datum, external to man, but is shaped by him through consciousness. As will be later shown in chapter 4, Hegel and the idealists assumed that the object of human consciousness is itself illusory and created by human consciousness, whereas Marx maintains that there always exists a 'natural substratum' which is a necessary condition for the activity of human consciousness.[2] From this Marx concludes that the constructive nature of human consciousness cannot be limited to merely cognitive action. He views cognitive action as the whole process of the development and evolution of reality: getting acquainted with reality constitutes shaping and changing it. Epistemology ceases to be a merely reflective theory of cognition, and becomes the vehicle for shaping and moulding reality:

The main shortcoming of all materialism up to now (including that of Feuerbach) is that the object, the reality, sensibility, is conceived only in the form of the *object* or of *perception* [*Anschauung*], but not as sensuous

---

[1] *The Holy Family*, p. 178.

[2] *Early Writings*, pp. 122-3. This makes it impossible to accept the neo-Catholic interpretation of Marx, which is otherwise extremely interesting, that follows the early Lukács in maintaining that Marx was not basically a materialist at all. Cf. J.-Y. Calvez, *La Pensée de Karl Marx* (Paris, 1956), p. 380; J. Hommes, *Der technische Eros* (Freiburg, 1955), p. 84.

Consciousness and society

human activity, *practice* [*Praxis*], not subjectively. Hence, the *active* side was developed abstractly in opposition to materialism by idealism, which naturally does not know the real, sensuous activity as such. Feuerbach urged the real distinction between sensuous activity and thought objects; but he does not conceive of human activity itself as an *objective* [*gegenständlich*] activity.[1]

Marx's epistemology occupies a middle position between classical materialism and classical idealism. Historically it draws on both traditions; and, since it synthesizes the two traditions, it transcends the classic dichotomy between subject and object. Indirectly this synthesis solves the Kantian antinomy between the cognitive and the moral spheres. But Marx thinks that present circumstances still make it impossible to practise this new, adequate epistemology: alienation indicates the continuing existence of the dichotomy between subject and object, as a result of the still distorted process of cognition.

Marx's epistemology thus conceals an internal tension. It tries to solve the traditional epistemological problems, but it tacitly holds that human consciousness could operate according to the new epistemology only if the obstacles in its way in present society were eliminated. Hence Marx's epistemology is sometimes divided against itself: it is both a description of consciousness and a vision of the future. Consequently Marx never fully denies the validity of traditional mechanistic materialist modes of consciousness as expressions of alienated life in existing society. These imperfect modes of consciousness will exist as long as bourgeois society continues to exist. This, at least, seems to be the upshot of Thesis x on Feuerbach.

Such a conclusion of course raises the question how far Marx's views are exclusively related to the socio-historical sphere and how far they can be extended to natural sciences as well. Marx's views cannot be squared with Engel's theories as described in *Anti-Dühring* or *Dialectics of Nature*: Lukács and his disciples are perfectly right in maintaining that the dialectics of nature, in Engels' sense of the term, has very little in common with the way Marx

---

[1] Thesis I on Feuerbach; I have followed here Rotenstreich's translation (*op. cit.* p. 23) which is far superior to the standard translation of the *Selected Works*. For a later Marxian critique of mechanistic materialism, cf. *Capital*, I, 372–3.

Homo faber

understood materialism, and that the origins of Engels' views must be sought in a vulgarized version of Darwinism and biology, with the Hegelian terminology serving only as an external, and rather shallow, veneer.[1] Alfred Schmidt formulated this extremely well when he said that while Marx built his system *pari passu* with the construction of his dialectics, Engels just applies a dialectical scheme to a set of given natural science data, as if the dialectical scheme were just an external, formal method, and not an immanent content of the subject-matter. The different approach leads to different results.[2]

Lenin himself ultimately gave up the mechanistic approach initially developed in his *Materialism and Empirio-Criticism*. Lenin's *Philosophical Notebooks* of 1914–16 include extensive excerpts of Hegel's *Logic* and strongly point to the conclusion that under the impact of this confrontation with Hegel, whom he had hardly studied before, Lenin came to appreciate the non-mechanistic character of Marx's epistemology and its indebtedness to the German idealist tradition. Orthodox Leninism may find it slightly embarrassing to be confronted with the following conclusions: 'Cognition is the eternal, endless approximation of thought to the object. The *reflection* of nature in man's thought must be understood not "lifelessly", not "abstractly", not devoid of movement, *not without contradictions*, but in the eternal *process* of movement, the arising of contradictions and their solution.'[3]

According to Marx, nature cannot be discussed as if it were severed from human action, for nature as a potential object for human cognition has already been affected by previous human action or contact. Hence nature is never an opaque datum. The phrases 'humanized nature' and 'humanism equals naturalism' recur in Marx's writings, and 'naturalism' in his sense is virtually the opposite of what is generally implied by this term in traditional philosophical discussion.

[1] G. Lukács, *Geschichte und Klassenbewusstsein*, p. 17; G. Leff, *op. cit.* pp. 22–90; L. Kolakowski, 'Karl Marx and the Classical Definition of Truth', in *Revisionism*, ed. L. Labedz (London, 1962), pp. 179–88.
[2] A. Schmidt, *Der Begriff der Natur in der Lehre von Marx* (Frankfurt, 1962), p. 42.
[3] V. I. Lenin, *Collected Works* (Moscow, 1961), xxxviii, 195. These *Notebooks* were virtually unknown under Stalinism, when *Materialism and Empirio-Criticism* reigned supreme.

Consciousness and society

The identification of human consciousness with the practical process of reality as shaped by man is Marx's epistemological and historiosophical achievement. To Marx reality is always human reality not in the sense that man exists within nature, but in the sense that man shapes nature. This act also shapes man and his relations to other human beings; it is a total process, implying a constant interaction between subject and object:

The production of life, both as one's own in labour and of fresh life in procreation, now appears as a double relationship: on the one hand as a natural, and on the other as a social relationship...

My relationship to my surroundings is my consciousness...For the animal, its relation to others does not exist as a relation. Consciousness is therefore, from the very beginning a social product and remains so as long as men exist at all.[1]

Classical materialism, on the other hand, never considered that human activity had any such philosophical significance. It reduced human activity to abstract postulates like 'the essence of man', making a discussion of history as man's self-development impossible on its own premises. According to Marx, Proudhon faced the same dilemma when he started, under the influence of classical political economy, to discuss human nature *per se*, overlooking the fact that human nature itself is the ever-changing product of human activity, i.e. of history.[2] The other alternative, the view of human nature as the lowest common denominator of all human beings, may not be particularly enlightening in such a context.

This criticism of classical materialism epigrammatically summarized in the *Theses on Feuerbach*, is reiterated in more detail in *The German Ideology*:

[Feuerbach] does not see how the sensuous world around him is not a thing given direct from all eternity, remaining ever the same, but the product of industry and of the state of society; and, indeed, in the sense

---

[1] *The German Ideology*, pp. 41–2. In his school-leaving examination in 1835 Marx wrote the following in an essay on 'A boy's reflections on the choice of a profession': 'It was Nature herself that determined the circle of activity of the animal, and the animal realises it calmly and tranquilly, without rushing outside its confines, without even sensing that another circle of activity may exist. The Deity endowed man as well with a general end—humanity and the nobility of man—but it is left to man himself to look for the means of its fulfilment' (*MEGA*, I, 1/2, p. 164).

[2] *The Poverty of Philosophy*, pp. 164–5.

71

that it is an historical product, it is the result of the activity of a whole succession of generations, each standing on the shoulders of the preceding one, developing its industry and its intercourse, modifying its social system according to the changed needs. Even the objects of simplest 'sensuous certainty' are only given to him through social development, industry and the commercial intercourse. The cherry-tree, like almost all fruit-trees, was, as is well-known, only a few centuries ago transplanted by *commerce* into our zone, and therefore only *by* this action of a definite society in a definite age it has become 'sensuous certainty' for Feuerbach.[1]

What Marx in *Das Kapital* calls 'the metabolism between man and nature' here becomes the major premise for an enquiry into the nature of human history. According to Marx, the conclusion that the world is shaped by man answers the problems posed by traditional speculative philosophy, for the philosophical postulate of the unity of man and nature is carried out daily in man's real, economic activity. Furthermore, even the natural sciences become the object of human enquiry only in so far as they respond to a human need and not by virtue of their specific attributes which refer to a given pre-human world. Again, this is totally different from Engels' argument: whereas Marx tries to find the human meaning of natural sciences, Engels looked for a natural science methodology to fit the human world.

The difference between Marx and Feuerbach can be stated from yet another point of view. Where Feuerbach saw the unity of man and nature expressed by man's being a part of nature, Marx sees man as shaping nature and his being in his turn shaped by it. Where Feuerbach naturalizes man, Marx humanizes nature:

The practical construction of an *objective world*, the *manipulation* of inorganic nature, is the confirmation of man as a conscious species-being, i.e. a being who treats the species as his own being or himself as a species-being. Of course, animals also produce. They construct nests, dwellings, as in the case of bees, beavers, ants etc. But they only produce what is strictly necessary for themselves or their young. They produce only in a single direction, while man produces universally. They produce only under the compulsion of direct physical needs, while man produces when he is free from physical needs and only truly produces in freedom

[1] *The German Ideology*, p. 57.

from such need. Animals produce only themselves, while man reproduces the whole of nature. The products of animal production belong directly to their physical bodies, while man is free in face of his product. Animals construct only in accordance with the standards and needs of the species to which they belong, while man knows how to produce in accordance with the standards of every species and knows how to apply the appropriate standard to the object. Thus man constructs also in accordance with the laws of beauty.

It is just in his work upon the objective world that man really proves himself as a *species-being*. This production is his active species-life. By means of it nature appears as *his* world and his reality. The object of labour is, therefore, the *objectification of man's species-being*.[1]

This auto-genesis of man implies not only that man satisfies his needs through his contact with nature, but also that this act creates new needs as well as the possibilities for their satisfaction. Man's needs are thus historical, not naturalistic, and the never-ending dialectical pursuit of their creation and satisfaction constitutes historical development:

[Men] themselves begin to distinguish themselves from animals as soon as they begin to *produce* their means of subsistence, a step which is conditioned by their physical organisation. By producing their means of subsistence men are indirectly producing their actual material life...

This mode of production must not be considered simply as being the reproduction of the physical existence of the individuals. Rather it is a definite form of activity of these individuals, a definite form of expressing their life, a definite *mode of life* on their part. As individuals express their life, so they are. What they are, therefore, coincides with their production, both with *what* they produce and with *how* they produce. The nature of individuals thus depends on the material conditions determining their production.[2]

That Marx never changed his views on the subject can be seen in a passage in the *Grundrisse zur Kritik der Politischen Ökonomie*, the first rough draft of *Das Kapital*, written during 1857–8 and published for the first time in 1939:

But this reproduction is at the same time necessarily new production and the destruction of the old form...

The act of reproduction itself changes not only the objective con-

---

[1] *Early Writings*, pp. 127–8.　　　[2] *The German Ideology*, pp. 31–2.

ditions—e.g. transforming village into town, the wilderness into agricultural clearings, etc.—but the producers change with it, by transforming and developing themselves in production, forming new powers and new conceptions, new modes of intercourse, new needs, and new speech.[1]

In 1880, three years before his death, Marx drafted a commentary on Adolph Wagner's book *Lehrbuch der politischen Ökonomie*. Here the forcefulness of the early *Theses on Feuerbach* has given way to a more rambling style, but his view of human history remains the same:

But according to this professional schoolmaster, human relation to nature is not, in the first place, practical, i.e. caused by deed [*Tat*], but theoretical...

Man relates to the objects of the external world as means for the satisfaction of his needs. But men never start 'to be in that theoretical relationship to the objects of the external world'. They start, like any other animal, by eating, drinking, etc., i.e. not 'to be' in a relationship but to be active, by trying to ascribe to themselves certain objects of the external world through deed and thus to satisfy their wants; they start therefore with production. By the repetition of this process, the attributes of those objects as 'satisfying their wants' impregnate themselves on their mind; men, like animals, learn also to differentiate 'theoretically' those external objects that serve to satisfy their needs from all other objects. At a certain stage of development, after both their needs and the activity through which they are satisfied, have been enlarged and augmented, they will baptise with their language this category with which they have become acquainted by their experience.[2]

This restatement of Thesis II on Feuerbach underlines the foundation of Marx's philosophy of history on his epistemological views. But this relation has sometimes led to a misunderstanding of his position: the verificatory nature of human action (*praxis*) according to Marx has caused scholars uncritically to equate Marx with pragmatism.[3] As Rotenstreich recently argued, this equation overlooks the obvious difference between the two theories. Whereas pragmatism starts with the premise that man adapts himself to a given,

[1] *Pre-Capitalist Economic Formations*, ed. E. Hobsbawm (London, 1964), pp. 92–3.
[2] *Werke*, XIX, pp. 362–3.
[3] S. Hook, *From Hegel to Marx*, p. 117; V. Venable, *Human Nature: The Marxian View* (London, 1946), p. 26.

Consciousness and society

pre-existing environment, Marx views man as shaping his world. Marx's views are also quite incompatible with William James' other premise about the basic irrationality of the external world. Marx, on the contrary, always argues that the world is open to rational cognition because it is ultimately shaped by man himself and man can reach an adequate understanding of his historical activity.[1]

The attributes of the external world as determined by the active human consciousness also make possible various modes of human cognition: the link between epistemology and history leads to a historicization of epistemology itself. The attributes of objects derive from the objects' standing in the human social context, and their meaning derives from the modes of the concrete human consciousness which relates to them:

Let us next consider the subjective aspect. Man's musical sense is only awakened by music. The most beautiful music has no meaning for the non-musical ear, is not an object for it, because my object can only be the confirmation of one of my own faculties. It can only be so for me in so far as my faculty exists for itself as a subjective capacity...For a starving man the human form of food does not exist, but only its abstract character as food. It could just as well exist in the most crude form, and it is impossible to say in what way this feeding-activity would differ from that of animals. The needy man, burdened with cares, has no appreciation of the most beautiful spectacle. The dealer in minerals sees only their commercial value, and not their beauty or their particular characteristics; he has no mineralogical sense.[2]

Reality, viewed by classical materialism as if it were a merely passive object of perception, is for Marx a human reality not only because it is shaped by men, but also because it reacts on man himself. Activity is dynamic not only in relation to the object but in relation to the subject as well. Hence Marx never reduces social experience to linear causal terms, for such a formulation would overlook the specific human-historical experience. This is also the meaning of Marx's famous saying that 'it is not the consciousness of men that determines their being, but, on the contrary, their social being determines their consciousness'.[3] 'Social being' includes by

[1] Rotenstreich, op. cit. p. 52.   [2] Early Writings, pp. 161–2.
[3] Selected Works, I, 363.

75

definition man's relation to the external world, and the worst that can be said about this much-quoted and little-understood sentence is that it is tautological. If 'social being' is purposive action, the shaping of external objects, this action implies a consciousness in relation to these external objects. In any case, Marx never said that 'being determines consciousness', but that '*social* being determines consciousness': these are two entirely different statements.

This analysis may also help to clarify one of the difficulties arising out of Marx's distinction between 'productive forces' and 'productive relations',[1] as well as that between the so-called 'material basis of production' and the 'super-structure'. It has been argued that this distinction supposes that it is possible to extricate the productive forces from the context of the social relations within which they occur. Some critics rightly point out that one cannot discuss productive forces as if they were material objects like stones or metals, since the material life of society, which determines according to Marx its political and ideological forms, already includes some forms with non-material content. This point is valid, but largely irrelevant to Marx's argument. Had Marx ever viewed productive forces as objective, economic 'facts' that do not need the mediation of human consciousness for their emergence and existence, then the problem would be serious indeed. But according to Marx 'productive forces' are not objective facts external to human consciousness. They represent the organization of human consciousness and human activity: Niagara Falls does or does not constitute a 'productive force' not because of its natural, 'objective' attributes *per se*, but because surrounding society does or does not view it as a productive force and does or does not harness it to purposive human action. Consequently, the distinction between 'material base' and 'super-structure' is not a distinction between 'matter' and 'spirit' (as Engels in his later writings would have had it), but between conscious human activity, aimed at the creation and preservation of the conditions of human life, and human consciousness, which furnishes reasons, rationalizations and modes of legitimization and moral justification for the specific forms that activity takes.

The texture of social relations is thus conceived by Marx as the

[1] Cf. Acton, *op. cit.* pp. 142–65; Leff, *op. cit.* pp. 110–35.

76

quintessence of human activity, which, in recognizing its world, continually creates and changes it. Consequently the critique of social relations is the most specific human critique, and any discussion of man must deal with his activity, for 'man is not an abstract being, squatting outside the world. Man is the human world, the state, society'.[1] The constructive quality of consciousness in its social context is also apparent in Marx's terminology. He relates the adjective *wirklich* (real, actual) to the verb *wirken* (to act, to have impact upon): 'The social structure and the State are continually evolving out of the life-process of definite individuals, but of individuals, not as they may appear in their own or other people's imagination, but as they *really* are; i.e., as they operate, produce materially [*wie sie wirklich sind, d.h. wie sie wirken*].'[2]

The concrete expression of this human activity is work, the creation of tools of human activity that leaves its impact on the world. Since he calls work man's specific attribute, Marx conceives history as the continuum of modes of work over generations. The pre-eminence in Marx's discussion of economic activity does not derive from the pre-eminence of material economic values, but from Marx's view of man as *homo faber*. The conditions in which labour manifests itself provide the key to the understanding of human history and to its ultimate and immanent vindication.

LABOUR, HISTORY AND POLITICAL ECONOMY

Marx does not consider himself the first to have suggested that man creates himself by his own work. Some of his remarks attest to his indebtedness to Giambattista Vico, and in one case he refers to Vico in connection with the development of technology, which Marx sees as the most characteristic human science.[3] Marx then relates this view to a more comprehensive method: if man is characterized by his labour, then the modern capitalist age, charac-

---

[1] *Early Writings*, p. 43.   [2] *The German Ideology*, pp. 36–7.
[3] *Capital*, I, 372. We know from at least two sources that Marx has been reading Vico in 1862, i.e. when he wrote the final draft of *Capital*, I. See Marx's letter to Engels, 28 April 1862 (*Briefwechsel*, III, 77), as well as his letter to Lassalle of the same date (*Werke*, XXX, 228). For Vico's view on man creating his world and himself through his 'poetic' reason, see G. Vico, *The New Science*, trans. T. G. Bergin and M. H. Fisch (New York, 1961), Paragraphs 332, 336, 376, 520, 692.

terized by universal application of industry, brings out to the utmost man's creative capacities. Industry as revealed in its movement, i.e. capital, differs from all previous forms of wealth. Until now wealth has been considered immanent in natural objects, land, gold, etc., whereas capital, as accumulated labour, is conceived as a form of human subjectivity. For this reason Marx calls Adam Smith 'the Luther of political economy', since he was the first to conceive property not as an object external to man but as an expression of the human subject.[1]

In an interesting aside Marx points out that what the classical economists expressed in terms of economic activity Hegel had already formulated philosophically. According to Marx, Hegel stood 'on the basis of political economy', for he saw in labour man's self-fulfilling essence. But Hegel saw only labour's creative nature and did not perceive the alienating conditions accompanying it in present society. Nevertheless, Marx sees in Hegel a clear realization that man's creative attributes make him a universal being, capable of universal creation.[2]

This enables Marx to view modern industry not only as the most polarized social system which universalizes alienation, but also as the source of the new conditions that will ultimately abolish the old antagonism.[3] This parallels Marx's suggestion in the *Critique* that democracy, because it is the paradigm of human institutional activity, will pave the way for the abolition of the conditions which make the state necessary.

Marx's description of the process of labour enables him to restate his position on both classical idealism and materialism. If in the *Theses on Feuerbach* he underlines the constructive element of human consciousness, he is still critical of Hegel who saw the objects of human activity as mere projections of man's own consciousness. According to Marx this self-enclosure of man within his own consciousness never overcomes the dichotomy between object and subject. For Marx the process of labour is real and objective, occurring in the external world, not merely in man's self-consciousness. Labour becomes an historical process only when it leaves an

[1] *Early Writings*, pp. 147–8. [2] *Ibid*. pp. 125–6, 202–3.
[3] Marx to Kugelmann, 17 March 1868 (*Letters to Kugelmann*, pp. 65–6).

impression on a world external to human self-consciousness. In saying that man acquires objective reality only because his objects are external to him. Marx offers a profound insight into the dialectical nature of his materialist views:

Man is directly a natural being. As a natural being, and as a living natural being he is, on the one hand, endowed with natural powers and faculties, which exist in him as tendencies and abilities, as drives. On the other hand, as a natural, embodied, sentient, objective being he is a suffering, conditioned and limited being. The objects of his drives exist outside himself as objects independent of him, yet they are objects of his needs, essential objects which are indispensable to the exercise and confirmation of his faculties. The fact that man is an embodied, living, real, sentient, objective being with natural powers, means that he has real, sensuous objects as the objects of his being, or that he can only express his being in real, sensuous objects...

Hunger is a natural need; it requires, therefore, a nature outside itself, an object outside itself, in order to be satisfied and stilled. Hunger is the objective need of a body for an object which exists outside itself and which is essential for its integration and the expression of its nature. The sun is an object, a necessary and life-assuring object, for the plant, just as the plant is an object for the sun, an expression of the sun's life-giving power and objective essential power...

A non-objective being is a non-being...[1]

This is a crucial point for Marx's theory of history, for this process operates also in the creation of the subjective side of human activity, i.e. human needs. History is not only the story of the satisfaction of human needs but also the story of their emergence and development. Whereas animal needs are constant and determined by nature, man's needs are social and historical, i.e. determined in the last resort by man himself.[2] Marx denies that each generation's consciousness of its own needs is a mechanistic, automatic response of the human consciousness to merely material stimuli. Man's consciousness of his own needs is a product of his historical development and attests to the cultural values achieved by preceding generations. Needs will relate to material objects, but the consciousness that will see the need for these particular objects

---

[1] *Early Writings*, pp. 206–7.   [2] *The German Ideology*, p. 39.

79

as a *human* need is itself a product of a concrete historical situation and cannot be determined *a priori*.[1]

Marx takes the same view in some of his later writings as well. In a famous passage in *Wage Labour and Capital* (1849) Marx gives the example of the small house which seemed adequate to its owner's needs as long as all the other houses in the neighbourhood were of the same order. Once a palace arose alongside it 'the house shrinks from a little house to a hut...Our desires and pleasures spring from society; we measure them, therefore, by society and not by the objects which serve for their satisfaction. Because they are of a social nature, they are of a relative nature.'[2] In the *Grundrisse* Marx takes Proudhon to task for imagining a model of human behaviour based on fixed human needs; Marx points out that as the primary needs of ancient man were few and primitive, historical explanation about the development of barter cannot serve as a model for a modern, complex society. Since historical development enriched human wants, they cannot be measured without being related to the modes of production which created them. From such a point of view class war brutally demonstrates that the satisfaction of wants lags behind the expectations arising out of the social organization. Because of the universal norms of capitalist society, these frustrated expectations are now far more numerous and potent than in any previous society.[3]

This reflects itself in Marx's vision of the future. Not only do the conditions of production constitute more than mere economic 'facts', but all forms of inter-human relationship are conscious human conduct. Hence they can be consciously mastered and directed. That men's wants are not naturalistic facts implicitly guarantees a human order able to supply and satisfy the needs adequately. If human society can generate a certain level of needs, one needs only adequate social organization to satisfy them. If society had not reached that level of potential satisfaction, the level of felt needs would not reach as high. This is behind Marx's dictum that mankind sets itself only such tasks as it can solve.[4] A need can be satisfied only when it is a human need, i.e. when it is mediated

---

[1] *The German Ideology*, pp. 41–2.   [2] *Selected Works*, I, 93–4.
[3] *Grundrisse*, p. 506.   [4] *Selected Works*, I, 363.

Labour, history, political economy

through consciousness. Hence economics is the key to the riddle of man's enslavement and redemption.[1]

If human wants are mediated through human consciousness and activity, men's minds must have an intentional capacity for the satisfaction of these needs which is not by itself a product of these needs. Sometimes Marx has been criticized for failing to attend to the need for such an autonomous intentional capacity. This problem is a serious problem, but in *Das Kapital* Marx, aware of it, attributes to human mind the capacity to evolve a model of the final product prior to the physical existence of the product itself. The way in which Marx treats this problem strongly suggests that he did not lose sight of the philosophical dilemma involved, though he did not spell out the process through which the ideal model is created in man's mind prior to material production. But he does make a significant distinction between purposive human labour and any parallel animal activity:

Labour is, in the first place, a process in which both man and Nature participate, and in which man of his own accord states, regulates and controls the material reactions between himself and Nature...By thus acting on the external world and changing it, he at the same time changes his own nature. He develops his slumbering powers and compels them to act in obedience to his sway. We are not now dealing with those primitive instinctive forms of labour that remind us of the mere animal...We pre-suppose labour in a form that stamps it as exclusively human. A spider conducts operations that resemble those of a weaver, and a bee puts to shame many an architect on the construction of her cells. But what distinguishes the worst architect from the best of bees is this, that the architect raises his structure in imagination before he erects it in reality. At the end of the labour-process, we get a result that already existed in the imagination of the labourer at its commencement...[2]

[1] Cf. A. D. Lindsay, *Karl Marx's Capital* (London, 1925), where the author argues against modern industry that it lives more by creating demand than by satisfying it; Marx, on the other hand, saw in this the greatest opportunity history has ever known to satisfy demand on a hitherto unheard of level. J. K. Galbraith, in *The Affluent Society* (London, 1958) uses the same argument against modern Western capitalism. Some critics have already pointed out the residual Calvinist overtones in Galbraith's argument.

[2] *Capital*, I, 177–8. Significantly the English translation published in the Soviet Union omits the following concluding phrase of the whole passage: 'i.e., had already pre-existed ideally' (*also schon ideel vorhanden war*).

81

Homo faber

From labour's relation to the historical process Marx deduces both the social and the historical nature of property relations. If needs are historical and social and not objective facts, then the concepts and institutions which organize and regulate these needs must also be historical. Hence any particular concept of property is relative, historically determined and ephemeral. Marx is aware that no one would seriously challenge such a view, but he criticizes those economic and social theories, capitalist and socialist alike, which sometimes assume the existence of economic categories and concepts not reducible to socio-historical development. From this point of view his violent attack on Proudhon is identical with his critique of classical political economy. In his 1865 lectures on *Wages, Price and Profit* Marx emphasizes that a product becomes a commodity only within a social context and that a person who produces for his own needs does not produce a commodity. His product does not satisfy a trans-subjective human need and has, therefore, no value. Production by its very nature relates to inter-human modes of contact.[1]

This reasoning implies that Marx cannot accept on principle any economic theory that starts with an individualistic model of human existence or behaviour. Such model starts from the individual producer who produces for his own needs. Ideally his production is autarchic and Robinsonesque; exchange appears only with greater development of production. Marx's objection to this theory is not limited to refuting it as an historical explanation adequate to the process of economic development as it had occurred. Like the social contract theories, of which this theory is a variant, its main aim is not to suggest an historical explanation but to provide an analytical, explicatory model for behaviour. Marx argues that as an explicatory model the 'Robinsoniade' is fallacious and misleading, for it presupposes the existence of private property prior to the existence of any human relationship, whereas property is obviously a mode of inter-human relation.

Moreover, the individualistic model also deals with undifferentiated human entities, abstracting from the individual's concrete status and condition. Instead of discussing real individuals as they appear in real, human relations, the model divests the individual of

[1] *Selected Works*, I, 416–17.

all the attributes which make his existence real. Once a discussion concerns not abstract, attribute-less individuals, but a worker, a peasant or a capitalist, the definition of one implies the existence of the other, and the discussion no longer treats atomistic individuals but real individuals in a social context, for it presupposes the division of labour.[1] As language can exist only as a trans-subjective medium, so property cannot be discussed out of human context. Marx sees Proudhon's famous dictum 'All property is theft' as the climax of this fallacy. An action can be called 'theft' only if a system of property existed prior to its occurrence. Hence Proudhon's aphorism either implies infinite regression or is a *petitio principi*. Proudhon seems to invalidate the legitimacy of property by an assumption of the legitimate existence of property. Socialism could hardly have sought a more unsatisfactory theoretical basis.[2]

Classical political economy and its socialist disciples have been trapped according to Marx in this vicious circle because they have elevated one particular historical form of property into an absolute criterion. One result is an inability to think of a situation which must still evolve existing property relations. Some of Marx's less generous outbursts against Proudhon may perhaps be explained, though certainly not pardoned, by his dismay at Proudhon's utter inability to grasp such basic issues of logic. In the same way Proudhon sees bourgeois property, which after all is but one historical form of property, as a paradigm for property *par excellence*. Any discussion of bourgeois property which does not take its historical context into account cannot offer suggestions for its abolition.[3] Thirty years after writing this in *The Poverty of Philosophy* Marx aims the same criticism at the German social democrats who abstract themselves from the historical forms of property and society, thus making it impossible for themselves to shape the historical tools for abolishing the bourgeois forms of property.[4]

Because what applies to property applies to social categories in general, Marx's polemic against traditional political economy gains a wider significance. Marx feels that these categories, product of a

---

[1] *The Poverty of Philosophy*, p. 113.
[2] Marx to Schweitzer, 24 January 1865 (*Selected Works*, I, 391).
[3] Marx to Annenkov, 28 December 1846 (*Selected Correspondence*, pp. 39 f.).
[4] 'Critique of the Gotha Programme', *Selected Works*, II, 19.

given historical-social context, are necessarily conditioned by what they aim to explain: their explicatory adequacy is thus immanently ambivalent. Such a historicist attitude does not, however, lead Marx to mere relativism. Precisely because the categories reflect a historical reality, the more developed and more complex the reflected reality, the more truthful and adequate the categories relating to it. The Hegelian view of history is very much in evidence here: each historical category incorporates the accumulated experience of past generations; each generation sits on the shoulders of its predecessors. The dialectics of *Aufhebung* ensures a progressive and expanding continuum of human capacity to experience and explain the world, not because the world is a given objective datum, but, on the contrary, because it is consciously created by man. The explicatory categories themselves contribute to man's shaping of his world. In a most revealing passage in the *Grundrisse* the traces of the Hegelian notion of philosophy as after-thought (*Nachdenken*) are clearly visible:

This example of labour clearly shows how the abstract categories themselves, in spite of their applicability to all periods (because of their abstractedness) are themselves in the determination of their abstraction a product of historical conditions and their full applicability is therefore relevant only for and within these conditions.

Civil society [*bürgerliche Gesellschaft*] is the most developed and many-sided historical organisation of production. The categories which explain its conditions, the relations of its structure, thus give us an insight also into the structure of all those forms of society which have already disappeared and on whose ruins civil society has been built...The anatomy of man holds the key to the anatomy of the monkey...and thus bourgeois economy gives us a key to ancient economy etc. But not in the manner of the economists, who blur the historical differences and see in all forms of society just the bourgeois form.[1]

This statement may pose the question whether, by reducing man to his historical conditions, Marx makes it impossible to discuss any model of man that transcends his concrete phenomenal form. Yet in criticizing the present existence of man as a violation of man as *Gattungswesen*, species-being, he uses criteria which seem to be

[1] *Grundrisse*, pp. 25–6.

84

normative. That this does not represent a dichotomy between Marx's earlier and later writings further perplexes the problem: both the reduction of man to his historical conditions and the postulate of man's ultimate emergence as *Gattungswesen* occur in the same writings of the 1843–6 period.

The solution to this dilemma may be found in the manner in which the question is posed. Marx's view of history as shaping man who simultaneously impresses himself on the world makes it quite impossible to ascribe to man any *a priori* essence. On the other hand, man's world-shaping function itself becomes the empirical content of human existence. This process makes man into man, differentiates him from animals and lies at the bottom of his ability to create and change the conditions of his life. The contents of this continual creation, dynamic and changing, furnish the contents of the historical process. What is not changing and not modified is historical creation as constant anthropogenesis, deriving from man's ability to create objects in which he realizes his subjectivity.

This view of Marx's is unique to the extent that his image of man transcends man's concrete historical situation, yet it derives not from any metaphysical premises but from an analysis of human history as a projection of human activity. This analysis sets Marx apart from both positivism and classical idealism. Man's creative ability causes the historical emergence of labour. For this reason Marx feels that the 'True Socialists' miss their point when they postulate labour as the end of human life. To Marx, labour is the source of human historical life and its daily content. What the 'True Socialists' look for in the distant future happens, though in distorted and alienated form, before their eyes in every human society.[1]

Such a non-normative criterion for human activity causes Marx to perceive that the conditions under which man's self-creation takes place in present society are self-defeating. Labour is supposed to be man's process of self-becoming because it is man's specific attribute. In present-day society it does not develop man but emasculates him. Instead of adding dimensions of creativity to man and widening his

---

[1] *The German Ideology*, pp. 501 f.; 'General Rules of the IWMA', *Selected Works*, 1, 386.

85

Homo faber

humanity, the process of labour in present-day society degrades man into a commodity, and the product of his labour, by nature the phenomenal realization of man's active consciousness impressing itself on the external world, becomes man's master.[1] In the words of Paul Tillich, the conditions of man's existence divorce him from his essential function.[2] The idea of alienation is thus inseparably bound up with the activist, constructive and non-reflective character of consciousness which Marx shows to be man's unique attribute.

The transformative method thus helps Marx in the critique of political economy as well as in his purely philosophical argument. From the analysis of alienation emerges the possibility of a radical revolution in man's conditions that will enable man to achieve the full potential of his self-creativity. Man as creator of himself and of his world also provides a criterion for the analysis of the conditions of his contemporary historical existence. Had Marx lacked such a criterion, he could not have liberated himself from a relativist positivism which invades some of Engels', Plekhanov's, Kautsky's and Lenin's writings. Such a positivist view would of course have created an unbridgeable gulf between history and philosophy, between the proletariat and the revolution as the realization of man's potentialities as *homo faber*.

SOCIAL MAN

Since production cannot be carried out single-handedly, Marx deduces man's social, trans-subjective nature from his quality as an object-creating being. Man's relation to members of his species thus determines not only the means of his existence but its contents as well. Man's objective being and his other-directedness and sociability serve therefore as criteria for the evaluation of economic theories and social structures.

The origins of this idea can be traced back to the *Critique* of 1843, where Marx postulates 'man's communist being' against an individualism that ultimately reduces man to self-defeating hedonism.

[1] *Early Writings*, p. 138.
[2] P. Tillich, *Der Mensch im Christentum und im Marxismus* (Stuttgart, 1952), pp. 3–7.

86

Social man

In the *Economic-Philosophical Manuscripts* Marx calls this image of man *Gattungswesen*, man as a species-being. This mode of human existence cannot be derived from man's existence as an atomistic or individualistic creature, but presupposes his reciprocal trans-subjective activity and orientation.

The wider significance of Marx's view of the individualistic model is obvious. Individualism, be it based on Natural Law or on Smith's *homo economicus*, holds that one can conceive of a sphere of human activity which belongs wholly and exclusively to the individual. The main difficulty encountered by such an hypothesis is that the only possible contacts between individuals behaving according to this model are antagonistic. No human action aimed at solidarity can ultimately be immanently derived from it. Even if relations deriving from this model will not be explicitly antagonistic, man will still regard other men as means. This attitude, according to Marx, precludes their behaving like species-beings, i.e. according to their basic human determination. In this anthropological way Marx restates Kant's categorical imperative, implying that only when man sees other human beings as end and not as means does he behave like a *Gattungswesen*.[1] The only way to overcome this lack of solidarity which is the natural consequence of the application of the individualistic model is to add to it a regulatory element. But as the Kantian antinomy shows, such an element must be external and heteronomous. It will only accentuate the inner contradictions of the initial model.

Marx tries to overcome this obstacle by seeing all human activity as social and other-oriented; it is either depending on or affecting others' experience. This is a direct outcome of the objectification which is the *differentia specifica* of human action, and is true even of the sciences: though science may not necessarily relate directly to any human being except the scientist himself, at least the medium of his activity—language—is a social product. The scientific discovery will ultimately be utilized by other human beings, escaping from the exclusive grips of the discoverer. Moreover, Marx feels that 'society' and the 'individual' are not two mutually exclusive entities: for him, each concept includes within itself certain moments of the

[1] *Early Writings*, p. 52.

87

other. The dichotomy between being and consciousness can be bridged by a radical view of the unity of individual and society:

It is above all necessary to avoid postulating 'society' once again as an abstraction confronting the individual. The individual *is* the *social being*. The manifestation of his life—even when it does not appear directly in the form of a communal manifestation, accomplished in association of other men—is, therefore, a manifestation and affirmation of *social life*. Individual life and species-life are not different things, even though the mode of existence of individual life is necessarily either a more specific or a more general mode of species-life...

In his *species-consciousness* man confirms his real *social life*, and reproduces his real existence in thought...Though man is a unique individual—and it is just his particularity which makes him an individual, a really *individual* communal being—he is equally the *whole*, the ideal whole, the subjective existence of society as thought and experience. He exists in reality as the representation and the real mind of social existence, and as the sum of human manifestations of life.

Thought and being are indeed distinct but they also form a unity.[1]

If thought and being are two modes of the same essence, the traditional difficulty in this sphere can, according to Marx, be resolved. On the other hand, the view of civil society that sees men as self-sufficient atoms presupposes that the trans-subjective sphere is devoid of any content that is not instrumental. It also presupposes a hiatus between the individual's self-consciousness and the external system of social phenomena that relates to it.[2]

Marx concluded that the individual can meaningfully enter into a relation only in a context that acknowledges the sociability and other-directedness of man, i.e. in a socialist or communist society, defined as the only society commensurate with man's being a *Gattungswesen*. In such a society the need for the other human being, which is at the root of human existence, rises to consciousness. According to Marx, only in such a society does man perceive that his needs cannot be reduced to the means of physical existence. Such a society must recognize that man's need for his fellow beings is basic to his humanity. The validation of such a view of man is provided by the economic structure of modern society, which un-

[1] *Early Writings*, p. 158.   [2] *The Holy Family*, pp. 162–3.

Social man

mistakably proves the universal dependence of man upon man. This dependence derives from the immanent unfolding of human nature, and Marx's way to socialism is not a collectivism which subsumes the individual under an abstract whole; it is rather an attempt to break down the barriers between the individual and society and to try to find the key to the reunion of these two aspects of human existence.[1]

Within this context Marx sees communism as the ultimate trend of human life, the identity of man with the circumstances of life. He defines communism as 'the positive abolition of private property, of human self-alienation...[and] therefore as the return of man to himself as a *social*, i.e. really human, being, a complete and conscious return which assimilates all the wealth of previous development'.[2] Marx finds the methodological proof for this proposition in the existence in society as presently organized of segments of life that behave according to this principle.

Surprisingly, Marx discovers this paradigm of the future in the family, or, to be more exact, in the relationship between the sexes. According to Marx, the unique pattern of these relations has a systematic significance which makes it possible to project them as a general model for the structure of human relations in socialist society. Sexual relations are at once necessary and spontaneous; they are also other-oriented *par excellence*. Man's need for a partner in the sexual relationship makes his own satisfaction depend upon another person's satisfaction. By definition, sexual relations are reciprocal. If they are unilateral they cease to be a relationship, degrading the other person to the status of a mere object, rather than a co-equal subject. The chapter in the *Economic-Philosophical Manuscripts* that deals with communist society has a long digression on sexual relationships, where Marx says:

The immediate, natural and necessary relation of human being to human being is also the *relation* of *man* to *woman*. In this *natural* species-

---

[1] *Early Writings*, p. 164: 'It will be seen from this how, in place of the wealth and poverty of political economy, we have the wealthy man and the plenitude of human need. The wealthy man is at the same time one who needs a complex of human manifestations of life, and whose own self-realisation exists as an inner necessity, a need.' How wide off the mark is Barzun when he claims (*op. cit.* p. 14): 'In Marx again the individual counts for nothing and has no original purpose of his own.'
[2] *Early Writings*, p. 155.

89

relationship man's relation to nature is directly his relation to his own *natural* function. Thus, in this relation it is *sensuously revealed*, reduced to an observable *fact*, the extent to which human nature has become nature for man and to which nature has become human nature for him. From this relationship man's whole level of development can be assessed. It follows from the character of this relationship how far *man* has become, and has understood himself as, a *species-being*, a *human being*. The relation of man to woman is the *most natural* relation of human being to human being. It indicates, therefore, how far man's *natural* behaviour has become *human*, and how far his *human* essence has become a *natural* essence for him, how far his *human nature* has become *nature* for him. It also shows how far man's needs have become *human* needs, and consequently how far the other person, as a person, has become one of his needs, and to what extent he is in his individual existence at the same time a social being.[1]

These considerations may also help to explain Marx's vicious, if not vulgar, attack on the bourgeois family in *The Communist Manifesto*. The text of the *Manuscripts* reveals the depths of Marx's feelings about what he conceived to be the utmost travesty of sexual relations. According to him, the nineteenth-century bourgeois world made even the limited reciprocity of family life impossible, and turned the woman into a mere object:

The bourgeois sees in his wife a mere instrument of production...On what foundation is the present family, the bourgeois family, based? On capital, on private gain...The bourgeois clap-trap about the family and education, about hallowed co-relation of parent and child, becomes all the more disgusting the more, by the action of modern industry, all family ties among the proletarians are torn asunder, and their children transformed into simple articles of commerce and instruments of labour.[2]

There are clear Hegelian overtones in this discussion, though Marx's construction of them is highly original. In Paragraph 158 of his *Philosophy of Right* Hegel regarded the family as 'ethical by nature', because it is based on reciprocity. To Hegel, the egoism of civil society abolishes this reciprocity, leaving it intact only in the restricted area of inner family relations. Marx argues that civil society makes even family life in this 'ethical' sense impossible. As

[1] *Early Writings*, p. 154.   [2] *Selected Works*, I, 50–1.

90

Social man

long as civil society will exists, it will frustrate the reciprocal content of family life. The solution is not a society constructed on the model of the family: this is the romantic *pars pro toto* fallacy. For Marx the family and sexual relations can be a paradigm only so far as they point to the possibility of other-oriented relations. The whole problem is to avoid romanticizing the family (or sex) and to reach at the same time a solution that will make the basic structural principle of sexual relations into a universal principle of social organization. A possible answer is a transformation of the whole social structure to bring out the universal dependence of man on man and to make it into the conscious principle of human conduct. Such a possibility is based, according to Marx, on a correct understanding and transformation of the system of production.

A view of private property as the specific sphere of privacy cannot come to terms with an other-directed social image of man. Marx admits that property is a social attribute, but modern theories of property have adopted the Roman notion of *plenum dominium*, making the individual's *ius utendi et abutendi* into an absolute concept of mutual exclusiveness. Such theories have no place for mutuality or solidarity. Logically, the individualistic view of property is a fallacy.[1] It is based on consensus and social solidarity ('social contract'), but it denies them. If they are denied outright, they cannot serve as the basis for property.

The only paragraph in *The Communist Manifesto* that deals directly with future society reiterates this juxtaposition of the other-directed nature of communism with the divisive individualism of bourgeois society: 'In place of the old bourgeois society, with its classes and class antagonisms, we shall have an association, in which the free development of each is the condition for the free development of all.'[2] This may, of course, seem a hollow cliché, unless the reader realizes that it is a direct consequence of Marx's theoretical premises. This 'association' is not merely organizational or economic;

---

[1] *Grundrisse*, p. 74: 'The economists express this by saying that every one cares for his own private interest and his private interest only; in this way he serves unconsciously the common good...But the point of the matter is that the private interest is already a defined social interest and it can be achieved only within conditions which have been set down by society and through means that have been supplied by it.'
[2] *Selected Works*, I, 54.

Homo faber

it relates to the social nature of man as expressed in the modes of human production and existence. Marx sees the growing intensification of the need for co-operation, socialization and solidarity, conditioned by the more and more complex forms of modern industrial production as internal evidence of capitalist society's transformation into a structure with man's social nature at its centre. Complex production requires other-directedness despite the individualistic model of capitalist economic theory. As capitalist principles will therefore be unable to cope with this situation, development will evolve toward the implication of a more intensive need for sociability and other-directedness.

This view, which bases ultimate freedom on a universal recognition of men's dependence upon each other ('association'), is a secular version of Hegel's idea that freedom lies in the recognition of necessity. But following the *Critique* of 1843 Marx gives this idea a novel meaning. Unlike Hegel's, Marx's view does not reduce man to a passive acceptance of, and acquiescence in, unchangeable and unchallengeable circumstances. On the contrary, the very alteration of the circumstances (accomplished through co-operation with other human beings) gives an activist and revolutionary meaning to what in Hegel is still a secularized version of Lutheran internal freedom, impotent to change external reality and impress itself upon it.

This also makes quite irrelevant the question whether change in individuals will precede change in circumstances or vice versa. As 'society' does not exist, according to Marx, as an entity distinct from the 'individuals', change in individuals is *ipso facto* also change in society, and change in social circumstances is also change in individuals. For Marx, socialism is about to overcome the traditional gap between individualism and collectivism. For him, the capitalist 'individualists' were as wrong as the socialist 'collectivists'.[1]

The model of future society implies solidarity also as a condition for the success of socialist activity. Marx holds that an end cannot be divorced from the historical means of its realization. It cannot be consciously realized by means that negate it—not on moralistic grounds, but on simple empirical grounds. The aim achieved by

[1] *The German Ideology*, pp. 525–6.

92

means that negate it will necessarily be different from the one initially envisioned, since every historical occurrence is the sum of its own history. Thus when Marx explains in 1864 the weakness of the proletariat, he says in the *General Rules of the International Working-Men's Association* that the absence of solidarity and of a feeling of mutual inter-dependence among workers has been a main cause of working-class failure.[1] Taking Marx's theoretical premises into account, this is no mere sermonizing. Similarly in 1870 Marx explains in a special report to the General Council of the International that the English worker, whose country objectively enjoys most advanced conditions conducive to a new society, still lacks the consciousness that will enable him to draw universal and general social conclusions from his own favoured position.[2]

Man's social nature as developed within the process of production Marx mentions in *Das Kapital* in language which draws heavily on some passages of the 1844 *Manuscripts*:

The religious reflex of the real world can, in any case, only then finally vanish, when the practical relations of every-day life offer to man none but perfectly intelligible and reasonable relations with regard to his fellowmen and to Nature.

The life-process of society, which is based on the process of material production, does not strip off its mystical veil until it is treated as production by freely associated men, and is consciously regulated by them in accordance with a settled plan.[3]

In 1880 Marx uses similar language in his commentary on Wagner's book on political economy. He maintains that one cannot deal with man in the abstract, but must point out in each case which context is meant. Concrete context prevents an assertion about a person without some information about his society—again, not because man is a 'product' of society (such an undialectical train of thought is alien to Marx, though not to Engels) but because man and society are the same thing, two moments of the same phenomenon.[4] Marx remarked

---

[1] *Selected Works*, I, 387.   [2] *Recueil*, II, 135.
[3] *Capital*, I, 79–80. Marx uses here, as well in the passage from the *Manifesto* cited above on p. 91, n. 2, the word 'free' in connection with 'association'. Freedom, hence, has a concrete meaning to Marx in his later as well as in his earlier writings. It is not a mere 'bourgeois prejudice' as dogmatic Communists and naive anti-Communists alike would have liked to have it.
[4] *Werke*, XIX, 363.

at the same period in the second draft of his letter to Vera Zasulitch that primitive communal production does not signal conscious socialization of the means of production but rather testifies to the weakness of the isolated individuals. As Marx says in the *Grundrisse*, the individual differentiates himself from naturalistic generality only through the historical process—a view, incidentally, not far removed from Hegel's.[1]

Much of this argument is already postulated in Marx's critique of Feuerbach in Thesis IX: 'The highest point attained by contemplative materialism, that is, materialism which does not understand sensuousness as practical activity, is the contemplation of single individuals in civil society.'[2] Hence Feuerbach is reduced to using an abstraction of man, since he cannot understand him through history.

From these points of view Marx's verdict that Proudhon never transcended the limits of bourgeois economy may be harsh, but it remains valid. Marx's main argument in his *The Poverty of Philosophy* is that Proudhon's individualistic economic model overlooks man's other-directedness, and presupposes the division of labour while missing its historical significance. Consequently Proudhon must propose his antinomies, which juxtapose private good and common good as though they were mutually exclusive entities. Marx also points out how Proudhon then destroys his whole model, for he concludes, on purely individualistic premises, that the 'common', the 'general' and the 'social' should become dominant, an ending utterly inconsistent with his initial premises. On top of it all, Proudhon sees humanity or society in general as 'the final subject': to Marx this means the degradation of real individuals to the status of mere objects. Proudhon's individualism leads him to a brutal collectivism; Marx endeavours to avoid such a polarization from either side.[3]

Marx is aware that in the last resort he himself gives or seems to give preponderance to society over the individual. But to him such a gloss on his theory is itself still engrossed in the imaginary antinomy

[1] *Marx-Engels Archiv*, I, 321; *Grundrisse*, pp. 395–6.
[2] *Selected Works*, II, 405.
[3] *The Poverty of Philosophy*, pp. 35–42, 100–10, 129–35.

of individualism versus collectivism, or individual versus society. For Marx there never is and never was, under any society, a preponderance of 'society' over 'individuals'. The phenomenon so described is the domination of some individuals by other individuals, with the latter aided and abetted by ideologies of the 'common good'. 'Theoretical communism', as Marx calls his theory in *The German Ideology*, sees history as a dialogue between collectivism and individualism. The concepts are interlocked, for their dialectical relationship enables them to exist only in such a relation:

The theoretical communists, the only ones who have time to devote to the study of history, are distinguished precisely because they alone have discovered that throughout history the 'general interest' is created by individuals who are defined as 'private persons'. They know that this contradiction is only a seeming one because one side of it, the so called 'general', is constantly being produced by the other side, private interest, and by no means opposes the latter as an independent force with an independent history—so that this contradiction is in practice always being destroyed and reproduced. Hence it is not a question of the Hegelian 'negative unity' of two sides of a contradiction, but of the materially determined destruction of the preceding materially determined mode of life of the individuals, with the disappearance of which this contradiction together with its unity also disappears.[1]

[1] *The German Ideology*, p. 267. The Soviet English translation has 'communist theoreticians' for *theoretische Kommunisten*. This is, of course, wilfully misleading.

4

ALIENATION AND PROPERTY

THE MATERIALIST PREMISE

Marx formed his ideas on alienation through confrontation with Hegel's views on *Entfremdung* in the *Phenomenology*. Marx's discussion is thus related to issues of general philosophical significance, and the more limited idea of alienated labour is meaningful only within this wider context. Marx's critique of the way in which Hegel handled the question of alienation restates Marx's general critique of philosophical idealism, and the Marxian version of materialism emerges from this discussion of alienation. Marx's views on alienation and his materialism are thus inseparable.

The theme of alienation in Marx's writings was taken up for the first time by Georg Lukács in his monumental *Geschichte und Klassenbewusstsein* (1923). Unaware of the existence of the *Economic-Philosophical Manuscripts*, Lukács none the less succeeded in reading the Hegelian issue of alienation back into Marx's later writings, and thus established the importance of alienation in Marx's theory. This was an outstanding intellectual feat, and the subsequent discovery of the *Manuscripts* confirmed most of Lukács' insights. Lukács was, however, wrong on some crucial issues, and his epoch-making book of 1923 must still be read with some reservations.[1]

Since alienation appears in Hegel's work in an epistemological context, Marx confronts it on the same level of discussion. He does this in the last and most neglected of the 1844 *Manuscripts*, entitled 'Critique of Hegel's Dialectic and Philosophy in general'. Alienation, for Hegel, is the state of consciousness as it acquaints itself with the external, objective, phenomenal world. At this stage objects appear to man external and alien, and consciousness feels

[1] This is especially true in Lukács' identification of *Vergegenständlichung* ('objectification') with *Entfremdung* ('alienation'). Not only is this misleading but it also entirely blurs Marx's criticism of Hegel. In his later works, e.g. *Der junge Hegel* (Zürich and Wien, 1948), Lukács took the textual evidence of the *Manuscripts* into consideration. For Lukács' personal vicissitudes, largely a consequence of the publication of *Geschichte und Klassenbewusstsein*, cf. M. Watnik, 'Relativism and Class-Consciousness: Georg Lukács', in *Revisionism*, ed. L. Labedz, pp. 142–65.

itself estranged and alienated in this otherness (*Anderssein*). According to Hegel, consciousness emancipates itself from this alienation by recognizing that what appears as an external object and thus negates the sovereignty of consciousness is a projection of consciousness itself, i.e. that consciousness remains basically 'self-consciousness' in that it perceives only itself. Objects that appear to exist outside consciousness are in the last resort only a phenomenal expression of consciousness. The final goal of consciousness is to arrive at this recognition: in Hegel's language, consciousness thus returns to itself. This famous 'negation of the negation'—the negation of the existence of objects that negate consciousness—recognizes that the objects are merely alienated, reified consciousness. When consciousness takes cognizance of this relationship, it recognizes itself in this objectified, alienated otherness. As a result, there are no cognizable objects outside consciousness itself, and this is of course the quintessence of philosophical idealism.

Marx attacks this theory on one crucial point: it identifies the very existence of objects ('Objectification', *Vergegenständlichung*) with alienation (*Entfremdung*). With the objective world reduced to a mere phantasy, a predicate of consciousness, Marx applies again the transformative method. Since such a negation of the existence of the objective world as external to consciousness is unacceptable to Marx, he reconsiders the resulting identification between objectification and alienation. He distinguishes between objectification, the premise of material existence, and alienation, a state of consciousness resulting from a specific method of relationship between men and objects.[1]

Marx maintains that by overcoming alienation through overcoming objects and negating their autonomous existence, Hegel actually reduces man to his inner self, since he considers all objects mere projections of consciousness. Such a reduction is, according to Marx, tantamount to reducing man to an internal self-sufficiency that is not an outcome of man's self-development and self-creation. Thus Hegel postulates that man is what he makes himself, yet he bestows on man a given substantiality that is not a consequence of

---

[1] Cf. the short fragment entitled 'Hegel's Construction of the *Phenomenology*', printed as an appendix to *The German Ideology*, p. 654.

his self-creation and self-becoming. Moreover, such a reduction of man to his inner self accepts an image of man as isolated from his fellow-men. While opposing classical individualism on what seem to Marx to be sound grounds, Hegel re-introduces this individualism through the back door. Hegel thus stands, despite himself, 'on the ground of political economy,' but not before he hypostasizes the real predicates of man into an abstract subject.[1]

There is another aspect to Hegel's view: if objectification is an illusory projection of consciousness that will ultimately return to itself, then the whole effort of man's shaping himself and his world is pure phantasy. Hence alienation itself is illusory. Since Marx sees alienation as residing in a concrete relationship between man and his products, such a relationship cannot be illusory provided the products are, as Marx maintains, real. For Marx human labour always presupposes a material basis, a 'natural substratum' distinct from consciousness and from human effort. This, of course, is the difference between idealism and materialism, yet the sophisticated level on which Marx confronts Hegel reveals the extent to which he built his system out of the internal difficulties of Hegel's thought. Since Marx recognizes the autonomous existence of objects, he cannot be satisfied with the merely cognitive overcoming of alienation but must seek his solutions in object-creating *praxis*. For Hegel alienation is a state of consciousness subject to elimination by another state of consciousness; for Marx, alienation is related to real, existing objects subject to elimination only in the real sphere of object-related activity. This position gives particular significance to Marx's jibe that since Hegel reduces everything to phenomenal images with no real existence, Hegel calls his theory most justifiably *Phenomenology*: there is nothing more to it than that.[2] As always in Hegel, the subject becomes here an object. Hegel's man is thus an object-less being, and, following Feuerbach, Marx says that an object-less being is a non-being.[3]

The connection between Marx's critique of Hegel's views on alienation and his general disagreement with what he considers the mystificatory element in Hegel's philosophy is most forcefully

---

[1] *Early Writings*, pp. 204–5, 209.
[2] *Ibid.* p. 204. [3] *Ibid.* p. 207.

The materialist premise

expressed in the following passage taken from the last section of the *Manuscripts*:

This process must have a bearer, a subject; but the subject first emerges as a result. This result, the subject knowing itself as absolute self-consciousness, is therefore *God, absolute spirit, the self-knowing and self-manifesting idea.* Real man and real nature become mere predicates, symbols of this concealed unreal man and unreal nature. Subject and predicate have, therefore, an inverted relation to each other; a *mystical subject-object*, or a *subjectivity reaching beyond the object*, the *absolute subject* as a process of self-alienation and of return from alienation into itself, and at the same time of reabsorption of this alienation, the *subject* of this process; pure, *unceasing* revolving within itself.[1]

Marx goes on to show that Hegel's train of thought leads inescapably to some far-reaching consequences. First, history is reduced to the act of thinking; it ceases to deal with concrete events and limits itself to speculations whose relation to concrete events is ambivalent. It abstracts from concrete events, yet sees concrete events only as manifestations of spirit.[2] Secondly, such a view leads to quietism and conservatism, and Marx brings out the ambivalence of Hegel's political conservatism very clearly. Hegel does not derive his conservatism from his reaction to contemporary events: on this level he sometimes expresses suprisingly radical views. His conservatism stems from the ambivalence of his epistemology which ultimately makes thought dependent on existing, historical reality though it denies doing this.

Pursuing this connection between Hegel's epistemology and its political consequences, Marx says that the abolition of alienation on the level of mere consciousness recognizes the immanent impossibility of abolishing real alienation.[3] Thus consciousness only approves a reality that it cannot change. Such a merely spiritual emancipation forces man to legitimize his chains. Marx argues that in Hegel every sphere of alienated life reappears on a higher level: *Aufhebung* only preserves alienation, and does not abolish it, for Hegel uses the term in such a way that alienation is never really

---

[1] *Ibid.* p. 214.
[2] *The Poverty of Philosophy*, pp. 122–3; *The Holy Family*, pp. 114–15.
[3] *Early Writings*, pp. 210–16.

99

overcome. Hence Hegel's philosophy, despite its intellectual force, docilely legitimizes alienation:

The act of supersession [*Aufhebung*] plays a strange part in which *denial* and preservation, denial and affirmation, are linked together. Thus, for example, in Hegel's *Philosophy of Right*, *private right* superseded equals *morality*, morality superseded equals *the family*, the family superseded equals *civil society*, civil society superseded equals the *state*, and the state superseded equals *world history*. But in *actuality* private right, morality, the family, civil society, the state etc. remain; only they have become 'moments', modes of existence of man, which have no validity in isolation but which mutually dissolve and engender one another.[1]

Consequently Marx criticizes the Young Hegelians for the same reason: their social criticism becomes irrelevant on their own premises once they accept their master's views on the unreality of objects. Once they have accepted the Hegelian notion of consciousness as 'self-consciousness' they are utterly unable to come to grips with social reality. Marx's opening sentence of *The Holy Family* goes straight to the point: 'Real Humanism has no more dangerous enemy in Germany than spiritualism or speculative idealism which substitutes "self-consciousness" or the "spirit" for the real individual man.'[2] For the Young Hegelians the problem of emancipation is reduced to a purely spiritual question, while the real problem is how to create objective conditions for consciousness:

But to rise it is not enough to do so *in thought* and to leave hanging over our *real sensual* head the *real palpable* yoke that cannot be subtilized away with ideas. Yet *Absolute Criticism* has learnt from Hegel's *Phenomenology* at least the art of changing *real objective* chains that exist *outside me* into *mere ideal*, mere *subjective* chains existing *in me*, and thus to change all *exterior* palpable struggles into pure struggles of thought.[3]

Bauer's Critical School thus limits itself to emancipating consciousness, as if consciousness were the real subject and man its mere predicate. Socially, this position also limits the relevance of the Critical School by definition to a small élite of *literati*, and prevents

[1] *Early Writings*, p. 211.
[2] *The Holy Family*, p. 15.
[3] *Ibid.* Cf. the Preface to *The German Ideology*, pp. 23–4.

The materialist premise

its identification with any universal postulate of mankind as such. Again, the Critical School falls short of the Hegelian universality. This criticism of Bauer is summed up by Marx in a letter to Feuerbach written in the summer of 1844:

One can thus reduce the character of this *Allgemeine Literatur-Zeitung* [Bauer's literary review] to a metamorphosis of 'Criticism' into a transcendental being. Those Berliners do not think that they are human beings that happen to criticise, but 'Critics' who beside that are unlucky enough to be human beings as well. They therefore recognise only one real need, the need for theoretical criticism. They thus look down on people like Proudhon because their point of departure is the 'practical need'. This Criticism thus runs into a sad and pompous spiritualism. Consciousness, or self-consciousness, is perceived as the only human quality. Even love is being denied, since in it the beloved one is just 'an object'. Down with the object! This Criticism thus sees itself as the only active element in history. Confronted with it, all humanity is just a mass, a lazy mass, whose only value lies in its being contradistinct from spirit. Therefore it seems to be the worst criminal act on the part of the critic to show any feeling and passion. He must be an ice-cold, ironical *sophos*...I am going to publish a short pamphlet against this madness of Criticism.[1]

For this reason Marx feels that the Critical School cannot grasp the concrete problems of real, historical people and is limited to abstractions incapable of facing reality. Two years later Marx directs the same criticism at the 'True Socialists', who because of their epistemological position fail to see alienation as rooted in the historical situation and its consequences.[2] Indirectly Marx used this conceptual language in his argument against Proudhon as well: Proudhon's use of categories, by following classical economy, sees the problems as if they resided within the concepts and not within reality. Consequently Proudhon devotes himself almost exclusively to trying to overcome conceptual dichotomies.[3]

[1] Marx to Feuerbach, 11 August 1844 (*Werke*, XXVII, 427). The 'short pamphlet' turned out in the end to become the bulky *The Holy Family*.
[2] *The German Ideology*, p. 514: 'Here then, the cause of the "cleavage of life" is shown to be theory. It is difficult to see why these true socialists mention society at all if they believe with the philosophers that all real cleavages are evoked by the *cleavage of concepts*.'
[3] *The Poverty of Philosophy*, p. 112; cf. also *Early Writings*, p. 156; Thesis IV on Feuerbach, *Selected Works*, II, 404.

This differentiation between his own position and traditional Hegelian idealism leads Marx to suggest that it may also differentiate between existing and future society. Accordingly, he says that in present society the creations of objects (objectification, i.e. production), instead of helping man to realize himself causes alienation, whereas in future society, objectification will lead to the unfolding of all human potentialities. Alienation and objectification, which overlap phenomenologically in present society though they differ ontologically, will be radically distinguished in the future, when alienation will disappear.[1]

This distinction between objectification and alienation is discussed in much detail in at least two of Marx's major writings. Significantly they cover both the period of his early development and his later, mature period as well. The first instance occurs in the 1844 *Manuscripts*, and the second in the 1857–8 draft of *Das Kapital*, known as *Grundrisse*. This again shows the continuity of Marx's thought and proves that his preoccupation with the theme of alienation continued during the period of his intensive economic studies.

In the *Economic–Philosophical Manuscripts* Marx begins by saying that under the conditions of capitalist economy production is conducted in alienating circumstances which thus make man's creative activity, i.e. objectification, into a process of de-humanisation:

The object produced by labour, its product, now stands opposed to it as an alien being, as a power independent of the producer. The product of labour is labour which has been embodied in an object and turned into a physical thing; this product is an objectification of labour. The performance of work is at the same time its objectification. The performance of work appears in the sphere of political economy as a vitiation of the worker, objectification as a loss and as servitude to the object, and appropriation as alienation...

So much does objectification appear as loss of object that the worker is deprived of the most essential things not only of life but also of work. Labour itself becomes an object which he can acquire only by the greatest

---

[1] Some of the recent research into problems of alienation seems to have overlooked the distinction drawn by Marx between objectification and alienation, e.g. D. Bell, 'The Debate on Alienation', in *Revisionism*, p. 195. For an extremely interesting account of some of the philosophical issues involved, cf. Rotenstreich, *Basic Problems of Marx's Philosophy*, pp. 144 ff.

effort and with unpredictable interruptions...The worker puts his life into the object, and his life then belongs no longer to himself but to the object. The greater his activity, therefore, the less he possesses. What is embodied in the product of his labour is no longer his own. The greater this product is, therefore, the more he is diminished. The alienation of the worker in his product means not only that his labour becomes an object, assumes an external existence, but that it exists independently, outside himself, and alien to him, and that it stands opposed to him as an autonomous power. The life which he has given to the object sets itself against him as an alien and hostile force.[1]

The specific conditions of objectification 'in the sphere of political economy' and not the nature of objectification itself make this activity alienating. As a result, the objects become man's master, since alienation inverts the subject-object relationship.

In the *Grundrisse* Marx discusses this problem in three different contexts. First, Marx says that property and wealth are attributes of man as an object-creating being, since human activity needs real objects for its realization. Consequently the bourgeois form of wealth must be emancipated from its alienated forms to give back to the object-producing activity its true character.[2] Marx goes on to say that in former periods, when wealth was still conceived as residing in natural objects and not in commodities that are products of human labour, no alienation existed at all, since alienation can be only related to an inverted form of human activity. But the non-existence of alienation also implied the non-existence of human objectification. Therefore this period of pristine innocence was incapable of unfolding the fullness and richness of human potentialities. Consequently primitive communism cannot serve in any way as a model for fully developed communism that presupposes alienation as well as its abolition.[3]

The second instance occurs in a discussion of a different aspect of the same issue. Here Marx takes up Adam Smith's contention that the time man devotes to work should be considered a price to be deducted from his normal state of being, leisure. Leisure, according to Smith, must be considered as man's ideal state. Political economy consequently divides human activity into coercive activity (labour)

[1] *Early Writings*, p. 122.   [2] *Grundrisse*, p. 391.   [3] *Ibid.* p. 375.

and spontaneous and free activity (leisure). To Marx this argument demonstrates once more political economy's basic misunderstanding of the nature of human activity. Political economy thus becomes a mere theoretical expression of human alienation. Marx denies that labour is naturally coercive. On the contrary, he asserts, it realizes human spontaneity. What makes it coercive is not its nature *per se*, but the historical conditions under which it is performed. Adam Smith's classification thus involuntarily criticizes civil society which condemns man to this dualism of coercion and spontaneity. A society that will abolish alienation, will abolish not labour, but its alienating conditions. Marx is well aware that even non-alienated labour can be difficult. He expressly refers to artistic creation, which serves him as a paradigm for non-alienated labour, although it can be very hard work indeed. The physical ease or difficulty of any particular kind of work is not the issue. The question is whether the work serves man as a mere means for existence or becomes the very contents of his life.[1]

The third and last instance of detailed discussion of alienation in the *Grundrisse* is undoubtedly the most intriguing. Though the passage is written in graceless language, and English words and expressions appear most surprisingly in the German text, it is of immense importance in perceiving the intense continuity of the considerations underlying the 1844 *Manuscripts* and *Das Kapital*:

The fact that in the development of the forces of production of labour the objective conditions of labour, objectified labour, must grow in proportion to live labour (this is nothing else than a tautological statement, since what is the meaning of growing productive forces of labour if not that one uses less immediate labour in order to produce more, that consequently social wealth expresses itself more and more in the conditions of labour created by labour)—this fact, then, appears from the point of view of capital not in such a way that the one moment of social activity (objectified labour) becomes the ever growing body of the other moment, subjective, live labour, but that (and this is important for wage-labour) the objective conditions of labour achieve an ever-increasing colossal independence, that expresses itself in their very extent, vis-à-vis live labour. Consequently social wealth appears in enormous portions as

[1] *Grundrisse*, pp. 505–6.

The materialist premise

an alien and overpowering force as against labour. What is being underlined is not *objectification* but the process of *alienation*, externalisation,
estrangement, the fact that the immense objective power belongs not to
the worker but to the objectified conditions of production, i.e. to capital...
Insofar as this production of the objective body of activity occurs from
the point of view of capital and wage labour as opposed to the immense
faculty of labour (i.e. insofar as this process of objectification appears in
fact from the point of view of labour as alienation and from the point of
view of capital as appropriation)—this inversion and perversion is then a
real one, not a mere *notion* that only exists in the imagination of the
workers and the capitalists. Yet there is no doubt that this inversion is a
mere *historical* necessity, a mere necessity for the development of the
productive forces from a certain historical point of view as a basis; but it
is not an *absolute* necessity of production as such; it is far more a dis-
appearing necessity, and the result and the (immanent) end of that
process is to abolish [*aufzuheben*] this basis as well as the form of this
process. The bourgeois economists are so much stuck in the image of a
certain historical stage of development of society that the necessary
objectification of the social powers of labour appears to them inseperable
from the necessity of *alienation* of these powers as against live labour.
But with the abolition [*Aufhebung*] of the immediate character of live
labour as mere particular, or merely internal, or merely externally universal, with the positing of the activity of the individuals as immediatedly
universal or *social*, this form of alienation will disappear from the objective
moments of production; they will be set as property, as the organic social
body within which the individuals reproduce themselves as individuals,
but as social individuals.[1]

ALIENATION AND THE FORMS OF PROPERTY

Alienation, according to Marx, has three aspects: in modern society,
man is alienated from nature, from himself and from humanity.
These aspects are interconnected, since in man's alienation from
nature Marx sees his alienation from his faculty of shaping his world.
This aspect of alienation, in its turn, is expressed in the appearance
of the man-shaped world as man's master, determining his con-

[1] *Ibid.* pp. 715–17. Though this text has been available since 1939, Sidney Hook still
writes in 1962 that 'aside from the specific sociological doctrine of "the fetishism of
commodities"...the central notion of "self-alienation" is foreign to the historical,
naturalistic humanism of Marx' (New Introduction to the Ann Arbor Paperback
edition of *From Hegel to Marx*, p. 5).

ditions of life. Man's creative activity also appears to be merely a means of preservation of physical existence. The concept of alienation thus presupposes an essential image of man as object-creator and it is the attainment of this image that is being frustrated in existing society. This image of man is not created by material conditions *per se*. Rather it is the faculty which enables man to master his material conditions. Much as material conditions are the prerequisite for the realization of man's creative and productive potentialities, they can also limit these potentialities.[1] The Hegelian distinction between existence (*Dasein*) and actuality (*Wirklichkeit*) thus re-emerges in Marx's writings and shows that the Hegelian effort to bridge the gap between them is unsatisfactory.[2]

The most obvious phenomenal expression of alienation is the worker's inability in capitalist society to own the product of his work. When Marx says that existing conditions of production dehumanize the worker, he implies that, once the products of the worker's creative, self-realizing activity have been taken away from him, he retains only his biological, animal-like functions:

What constitutes the alienation of labour? First, that the work is *external* to the worker, that it is not part of his nature; and that, consequently, he does not fulfil himself in his work but denies himself, has a feeling of misery rather than well-being, does not develop freely his mental and physical energies but is physically exhausted and mentally debased. The worker, therefore, feels himself at home only during his leisure time, whereas at work he feels homeless. His work is not voluntary but imposed, *forced labour*. It is not satisfaction of a need, but only a *means* for satisfying other needs. Its alien character is clearly shown by the fact that as soon as there is no physical or other compulsion it is avoided like the plague...

We arrive at the result that man (the worker) feels himself to be freely active only in his animal function—eating, drinking and procreating, or at most also in his dwelling and in personal adornment—while in his human functions he is reduced to an animal. The animal becomes human and the human animal.[3]

[1] *Selected Works*, I, 363.
[2] *Philosophy of Right*, p. 10; *Enzyklopädie der philosophischen Wissenschaften*, ed. Nicolin-Pöggeler (Hamburg, 1959), pp. 38–9. For Marx's retention of this distinction even in his later writings, see *Capital*, III, 205, 797–8.
[3] *Early Writings*, pp. 124–5. It should be borne in mind that alienation is here specifically related by Marx to the worker, and not to an undifferentiated condition of man.

Alienation and forms of property

In *Wage Labour and Capital*, published in 1849, Marx comes back to these aspects of labour, and though the purely economic considerations are much more in the foreground, the philosophical elements are no less explicit:

But the exercise of labour power, labour, is the worker's own life-activity, the manifestation of his own life. And this *life-activity* he sells to another person in order to secure the necessary *means of subsistence*. Thus his life-activity is for him only a means to enable him to exist. He works in order to live. He does not even reckon labour as part of his life, it is rather a sacrifice of his life. It is a commodity which he has made over to another. Hence, also, the product of his activity is not the object of his activity. What he produces for himself is not the silk that he weaves, not the gold that he draws from the mine, not the palace that he builds. What he produces for himself is *wages*, and silk, gold, palace resolve themselves for him into a definite quantity of the means of subsistence, perhaps into a cotton jacket, some copper coins and a lodging in a cellar. And the worker, who for twelve hours weaves, spins, drills, turns, builds, shovels, breaks stones, carries loads, etc.—does he consider this twelve hours' weaving, spinning, drilling, turning, building, shovelling, stone breaking as a manifestation of his life, as life? On the contrary, life begins for him where this activity ceases, at table, in the public house, in bed. The twelve hours' labour on the other hand, has no meaning for him as weaving, spinning, drilling, etc., but as *earnings*, which bring him to the table, to the public house, into bed. If the silk worm were to spin in order to continue its existence as a caterpillar, it would be a complete wage-worker.[1]

This alienation in real life is also reflected, Marx argues, in the consciousness of society, in its ideology. The conceptual system adequate to this society itself expresses alienation. Political economy thus, according to Marx, ideologically reflects alienated life, as indicated by its insistence that its concepts have objective, ontological reality and attain a validity external to the specific human relations whose organizational principles it tries to express and systematize. Alienation is created in capitalist society not by the production of commodities but by the transformation of this production, according to political economy, from objectified human activity into 'objective' laws which independently regulate human activity. The human subject becomes the object of his own products, and the laws of

[1] *Selected Works*, I, 82–3.

political economy are only an ultimate and radical expression of this inverted consciousness that makes man into a predicate of his own products and thus mystifies human reality.[1]

Marx uses Ricardo's labour theory of value to prove this point in connection with the distinction between the 'use value' and the 'exchange value' of commodities. Marx agrees that it is comparatively easy to discover the use value of a commodity, since it is directly related to the utility drawn from its material content. An effort to discover the exchange value makes the issue more complex. The exchange value of commodities is, according to classical economy, the ratio at which commodities exchange for each other, i.e. it is a mutual measurement of use values. The problem, however, concerns the criterion for measurement. Classical political economy answers that this criterion is the socially necessary time for the production of the commodity,[2] maintaining that whereas use value is connected with the natural, material substratum of the commodity (the use value of salt is determined by our need for the mineral), exchange value is a function of human labour. But measuring the amount of socially necessary labour required for the production of a given commodity demands an accepted standard. Here Marx argues that the amount of labour is determined by what is paid for it. The existence of exchange value, and of commodities themselves, is made possible because labour is treated as a commodity. Political economy considers labour the source of value of all commodities, but it also presupposes the value and the existence of commodities. The mystery of labour in capitalist society, Marx argues, is that it again appears to be something other than what it really is.[3]

That commodities have exchange value dependent on labour expresses alienation. This radical analysis of the concepts of political economy leads Marx to the conclusion that alienation cannot be overcome while productive relations alienate human relations into relationships between objects and while economists forget that the

---

[1] These issues, treated in the first section of *Das Kapital* ('Commodities'), were always neglected by Engels. In Engels' own résumé of *Das Kapital* he characteristically devoted two pages to them, although he felt that Marx's equally long section on the circulation of commodities merited six pages. Nor did Kautsky pay much attention to these issues. [2] *Werke*, XIII, 15–21, 29–31; *Capital*, I, 35–46.
[3] *The Communist Manifesto, Selected Works*, I, 40; *Wage Labour and Capital, ibid.* I, 79–84.

essence of commodities is human objectified labour: 'And, lastly, what characterises labour as determining exchange value is the fact that the social relationship of man simultaneously appears also in inverted form, as social relationship of things...Thus if it is true that exchange value is a relation between persons, one should add: a relation hidden under a reified mask.'[1]

This view of capital as man's alienated self goes back to the 1844 *Manuscripts*. though there Marx sometimes refers to 'capital' and 'money' interchangeably. There is little doubt that Marx was influenced in this description by some of Moses Hess' writings of the same period, though Marx differentiates capital very clearly in the *Manuscripts*, a distinction not made by Hess.[2] Moreover, whatever Marx's indebtedness to Hess, he adds to this a confrontation with Hegel's views on property, and thus attains a highly original formulation.

Hegel held that property realizes human personality in determining itself through objectification in the external, phenomenal world. For Hegel this externalization constituted realization and assertion precisely because all objects are ultimately imaginary and the only actuality is the human spirit at the root of creativity and production. Consequently property was to Hegel human freedom realizing itself in the world of phenomena, and the lack of property prevents man from participating in this universality.[3]

Marx's discussion of property and alienation attempts to subvert the Hegelian identification of property and personality. For Marx property is not the realization of personality but its negation: not only are the property-less alienated, but so are those who have property. The possession of property by one person necessarily entails its non-possession by another—a dialectical relation totally absent from Hegel. Consequently the problem is not the assurance of property to all—to Marx an inherent impossibility and immanent contradiction—but the abolition of all property relations as such.

---

[1] *Werke*, XIII, 21; cf. *Capital*, I, 36–7.
[2] For the extent of Marx's indebtedness to Hess, cf. E. Silberner, 'Beiträge zur literarischen und politischen Tätigkeit von Moses Hess, 1841–1843', *Annali dell'Istituto Giangiacomo Feltrinelli*, VI (1963), 387–437.
[3] *Philosophy of Right*, Paras. 243–246. Cf. J. Ritter, 'Person und Eigentum', *Marxismus-studien*, IV, 196–228.

Alienation and property

Marx arrives at this radical separation of property and personality through another application of the transformative method. In the 1844 *Manuscripts* he argues that money is man's alienated self, since it reduces all human qualities to quantitative, interchangeable values devoid of any specific value. Moreover, accumulation of money diminishes man's real capacity for externalization and self-expression. Since money saved is deferred consumption, the values inherent in money have been preserved in it because they have not been realized by man:

The less you eat, drink, buy books, go to the theatre or to balls, or to the public house, and the less you think, love, theorize, sing, paint, fence, etc. the more you will be able to save and the greater will become your treasure which neither moth nor rust will corrupt—your capital. The less you are, the less you express your life, the more you have, the greater is your alienated life and the greater is the saving of your alienated being. Everything which the economist takes from you in the way of life and humanity, he restores to you in the form of money and wealth. And everything which you are unable to do, your money can do for you; it can eat, drink, go to the ball and to the theatre. It can acquire art, learning, historical treasures, political power; and it can travel. It can appropriate all these things for you, can purchase everything; it is the true opulence [*Vermögen*].[1]

It comes consequently as no surprise that Marx characterizes capitalism as 'practical' asceticism. This characterization, typical of Max Weber's later enquiries into the spirit of capitalism, implies that capitalism views with suspicion the very values created by capitalist activity itself. Yet only a wide social acceptance of such an ethos creates the pre-conditions necessary for the emergence of capitalism. Thus Marx says in the passage just quoted that political economy, 'despite its worldly and pleasure-seeking appearance, is a truly moral science, and the most moral of all sciences. Its principal thesis is the renunciation of life and human needs.' This asceticism is the ultimate ideological expression of alienation, and its apex is the Malthusian theory, which sees human procreation itself as waste.[2]

---

[1] *Early Writings*, p. 171.
[2] The ascetic nature of capitalist ethics is mentioned by Marx several times, e.g.: 'Political economy, the science of wealth, is, therefore, at the same time, the science of renunciation, of privation and of saving...This science of a marvellous industry is

Alienation and forms of property

Money's power of inversion derives, according to Marx, from its capacity to invest its possessors with qualities missing in them. They can now acquire these qualities through the power of capital. In this inverted world man's faculties are determined by his money. His personal attributes become a function of his purchasing power and not of his immanent self. After quoting Shakespeare's Timon and Goethe's Faust, Marx says:

That which exists for me through the medium of money, that which I can pay for (i.e. which money can buy), that *I am*, the possessor of the money. My own power is as great as the power of the money. The properties of money are my own (the possessor's) properties and faculties. What I am and can do is, therefore, not at all determined by my individuality. I am ugly, but I can buy the most beautiful woman for myself. Consequently, I am not ugly, for the effect of ugliness, its power to repel, is annulled by money. As an individual I am lame, but money provides me with twenty-four legs. Therefore I am not lame...I who can have, through the power of money, everything for which the human heart longs, do I not possess all human abilities? Does not my money, therefore, transform all my incapacities into their opposites?[1]

Since only the possession of money creates effective demand, only he who possesses money and can realize his demand has effective needs. He who has no money has no effective needs and no objective reality. Property is, again, not the realization of personality but its negation.[2]

Marx's later writings do not treat property as such or money as such. A more differentiated approach emerges, and though Marx's earlier remarks in the *Manuscripts* do contain an historical analysis, he deals with it more carefully in *The Holy Family* and *The Poverty of Philosophy*.[3] The a-historical approach of Proudhon also prompts Marx to his remark in 1865 in a letter to Schweitzer that Proudhon's famous question 'What is property?' cannot be answered at all on these terms.[4]

Consequently Marx must embark on a systematic enquiry into the

at the same time the science of asceticism. Its true ideal is the ascetic but usurious miser and the ascetic but productive slave. Its moral ideal is the worker who takes a part of his wages to the savings bank' (*ibid.* p. 171). Cf. K. Löwith, 'Max Weber und Karl Marx', *Archiv für Sozialwissenschaft und Sozialpolitik*, LXVII (1932).

1 *Early Writings*, p. 191.
2 *The Holy Family*, pp. 59–69; *The Poverty of Philosophy*, pp. 173 ff.
3 *Ibid.*   4 *Selected Works*, I, 390 f.

development of the historical forms of property. Such a discussion occurs in *The German Ideology* and the *Grundrisse*. According to Marx the first form of property is tribal property, conditioned by productive relations which precede permanent settlement and agriculture.[1] Once agriculture starts to develop, this type of primitive common ownership gradually disappears. In the classical *polis*, based on agriculture, two kinds of property exist side by side. Theoretically, property is still vested in the *res publica*, and individuals only enjoy possession and usufruct.

In the *Grundrisse* Marx adds a speculative element to his discussion of ancient tribal property.[2] The appearance of such an element at this stage of his intellectual development (1857-8) is again highly significant for the continuity of his theoretical pursuits, especially as it draws strongly on the insights gained by Marx in 1843 in his *Critique of Hegel's Philosophy of Right*. Marx shows that the initial emergence of property must by necessity be tribal, since it originates in the capacity of a human group to gain possession of land. Such an act depends on a prior existence of group cohesion, i.e. some kind of social, tribal organization. Even if the immediate outcome of this gaining of common possession should be the division of this land into individual, private holdings, the prior existence of tribal property makes such a division possible. Thus the roots of individual property are found in common property, and property does not pre-date society but results from it. Marx speculates that an individual's tribal existence is the first historical property, and reiterates his belief that one cannot separate an historical individual from his social context. Terminology in this discussion points in the same direction, and Marx uses the term *Gemeinwesen* to denote both common, tribal property and membership in a tribal organization.[3] Since within this social structure the relation to property is mediated through membership in the group, property appears as a relationship signifying social identification, a form of property without alienating elements. Property realizes man's positive relation to his fellow-tribesmen. Consequently tribal property, because

[1] *The German Ideology*, p. 33.
[2] These chapters of the *Grundrisse* are now available in English under the title K. Marx, *Pre-Capitalist Economic Formations*, trans. J. Cohen, ed. E. Hobsbawm (London, 1964). [3] *Ibid.* p. 90.

of its communal and co-operative form, is a socially limiting factor. It arrests the individual's power to disengage himself from the generality of society and establish a self-interest distinct from the general interest of society. No distinction between the state and civil society occurs, of course, at this stage. Marx had, however, never thought that all humanity once experienced a uniform or common form of tribal property; he goes into some detail to show that the numerous existing forms of tribal property cannot be reduced to the one variable of the mode of production. According to Marx a wide range of pluralistic causes determines this diversification: climate, the quality of the soil, the nature of the neighbouring tribes and peoples, the history of the tribe itself, etc.[1]

This pristine yet unsophisticated and undifferentiated unity of individual and society, mediated through the relation to common property, is preserved in more complex societies according to Marx by two devices mainly: oriental despotism and the classical *polis*. In oriental despotism property belongs to one being who symbolizes the totality of society. The despot personifies society, and all property ultimately belongs to him.[2] In the *polis*, on the other hand, the form of settlement is the form of society. Private property does develop, but, as Marx points out in another work, it develops out of the intercourse of the community with the external world, through commerce or warfare. At least in the consciousness of society it is marginal and inferior to the original common property.[3] The basic form of property is still public; political rights depend on participation in the common ownership of land, which, in its turn, depends upon possession of private property. A dialectical relationship thus develops between public and private property. Economic activity depends upon community-oriented considerations. Marx points out that, at least in the public consciousness of the *polis*, different forms of agriculture were discussed, as in Rome, on their *political* merits. That form of agricultural policy was recommended which seemed to produce better, more patriotic citizens. Since economic considerations were secondary, agriculture was considered morally and thus publicly superior to commerce.[4]

[1] *Ibid.* pp. 80–4. [2] *Ibid.* pp. 69–70.
[3] *Werke*, XIII, pp. 35–6. [4] *Pre-Capitalist Economic Formations*, p. 84.

Alienation and property

Since economic activity in the *polis* is judged on political considerations, no alienation exists between the public and the private sphere, between the state and civil society. Moreover, the *res publica* enables man to realize his social, community-oriented nature through economic activity and political participation assessed by the same criteria. *Homo economicus* and *homo politicus* are thus one and the same thing.[1]

If this identity does not lead Marx to a romantic idealization of the *polis* and to wishful thinking about a possible restoration of ancient republicanism, he avoids both because his criteria imply historical change and transformation. Like all other historical phenomena, the classical *polis* contains the seeds of its own decomposition. This quasi-idyllic form of society cannot become a model for the ultimate form of human society despite its freedom from alienation. The naïve, undifferentiated structure of this social form limits its ability to survive. Every attempt to perpetuate this form contributes to its ultimate disintegration. Thus the attempt to preserve something of the public nature of the *ager publicus* only facilitated the emergence of the *equites* as a commercial class, and the reforms of Agis and Cleomenes only aggravated the crisis of the Spartan *Gemeinwesen*. The reason for this lies in the foundation of these classical forms, as well as the feudal form Marx deals with in passing, on particularistic principles due to the dependence of the ancient form of property on naturalistic matter only (land). The foundation of ancient property on naturalistic matter is always specific and limited; it is not a general abstract product of human labour. In this sense only capital is universal.[2]

The way in which Marx describes the historical emergence of capital emphasizes its ambivalence. Its universality as objectified human labour points towards hidden potentialities that will ultimately give rise, according to Marx, to a form of production in which the process of production will enhance the fulfilment of man's capacity as *homo faber*. On the other hand, the human origin of capital causes its historical appearance to be accompanied by the moment of alienation.

[1] *Pre-Capitalist Economic Formations*, pp. 72–3.
[2] *Early Writings*, p. 138; *The Communist Manifesto, Selected Works*, I, 34–42.

Alienation and forms of property

The alienating aspects of capitalism are revealed by the fact that capital in its historical emergence develops a kind of property free from all social limitations and considerations. Conversely, since capital divorces the producer from his means and tools of production, capitalism also paradoxically ends individual private property as traditionally conceived with the producer owning his means of production. We have seen in chapter 1 that Marx criticized a specific form of landed property, the entailed estate, as a property whose 'social nerves have been cut off': now capitalist property becomes for Marx the form of property divorced from any community-oriented considerations. The end-product of this development from community-oriented property to property emancipated from all social attachment to the community is, of course, *plenum dominum*, at the exclusive disposition of its owner. But Marx points to the paradox that the more capitalist society develops, the rarer such a form of property becomes, since complex production now requires combined efforts which cannot be satisfied by individual property. The cycle now seems closed.

Moreover, whereas all former forms of property have fostered the integration between the individual and society, economic life in capitalist society becomes, under the impact of the emancipation of civil society from the universal postulates of the state, based entirely on naturalistic necessity and unlimited arbitrariness.[1] In *The German Ideology* Marx sees capital as giving the death blow to the residual idea of social cohesion and solidarity, and in *The Communist Manifesto* he implies the same, saying that bourgeois society has stripped property from its former pretensions and illusions.[2]

That under capitalism individual private property is abolished serves Marx as a starting-point in his argument about the nature of property in future society. In *The Communist Manifesto* he says that 'the distinguishing feature of Communism is not the abolition of property generally, but the abolition of bourgeois property'.[3] In *Das Kapital* he alludes to the new form of unalienated property, which would imply that property again links the individual and the

[1] *Early Writings*, pp. 29–30.
[2] *The German Ideology*, p. 77; *Selected Works*, I, 36.
[3] *Selected Works*, I, 47.

115

Alienation and property

community. In capitalist society, however, the individual by being denied his private property is denied his existence as an individual:

What does the primitive accumulation of capital, i.e. its historical genesis, resolve itself into ? In so far as it is not immediate transformation of slaves and serfs into wage-labourers, and therefore a mere change of form, it only means the expropriation of the immediate producers, i.e. the dissolution of private property based on the labour of its owner. Private property, as the antithesis to social, collective property, exists only where the means of labour, and the external conditions of labour belong to private individuals ...The private property of the labourer in his means of production is the foundation of petty industry, whether agricultural, manufacturing, or both; petty industry, again, is an essential condition for the development of social production and of the free individuality of the labourer himself.[1]

This is not merely a polemic against capitalism, trying to prove that capitalism contradicts its own methodological major premise, i.e. private property. It is precisely because of the social, collective nature of capitalism that Marx discovers the potentialities inherent in its immanent development. In any case, the uniqueness of capitalism consists of its movement beyond private property, though it does not always recognize this. In *The Civil War in France* Marx again maintains that:

Yes, gentlemen, the Commune intended to abolish that class-property which makes the labour of the many the wealth of the few. It aimed at the expropriation of the expropriators. It wanted to make individual property a truth by transforming the means of enslaving and exploiting labour, into mere instruments of free and associated labour.—But this is Communism, 'impossible' Communism.[2]

This does not imply, of course, reversion to small-scale artisan production, since Marx has always been critical of those socialist schools which tried to overlook industrial development and its potentialities. Marx never really details the organization of such a new individual, i.e. social, property.[3] But what he probably had in mind could be sensed in his earlier description of property: that only in modern society has property become a merely economic relation-

[1] *Capital*, I, 761.   [2] *Selected Works*, I, 523.
[3] In *Das Kapital* Marx says that post-capitalist property will preserve the social content of capitalist property, but without its alienating aspects (*Capital*, III, 427–8).

116

ship, erecting a barrier between *Eigentum* and *Gemeinwesen*. Marx had tried to overcome this dichotomy and strip property of its possessive nature:

In fact, however, when the narrow bourgeois form has been peeled away, what is wealth, if not the universality of needs, capacities, enjoyments, productive powers, etc., of individuals, produced in universal exchange? What, if not the full development of human control over the forces of nature—those of his own nature as well as those of so-called 'nature'? What, if not the absolute elaboration of his creative dispositions, without any preconditions other than antecedent historical evolution which makes the totality of this evolution—i.e. the evolution of all human powers as such, unmeasured by any *previously established* yardstick—an end in itself? In bourgeois political economy—and in the epoch of production to which it corresponds—this complete elaboration of what lies within man, appears as the total alienation.[1]

FETISHISM OF COMMODITIES AND DIVISION OF LABOUR

Marx views the relationship between man and his products in capitalist society under two aspects: while commodities, the products of man, become his master, man, as a worker, becomes an object-less being. These two aspects are not self-contradictory, since their interdependence is established by the transformative method. Once the objects cease to be objects of human activity and become independent beings, subjects unto themselves, man himself remains devoid of objects and realization.

It has already been pointed out that Marx sees the exchange value of commodities as ultimately based on objectified labour. Exchange value is thus a socially related concept, drawing on man's other-directedness and sociability. Marx hints at this at the outset of the chapter on commodities in *Das Kapital*, when he says that 'A commodity is, in the first place, an object outside us'.[2] 'In the first place' implies that *ultimately* a commodity may be something else: ultimately a commodity is an objectified expression of an inter-subjective relationship. Once this relationship is grasped, the laws

[1] *Pre-Capitalist Economic Formations*, pp. 84–5.
[2] *Capital*, I, 35.

117

governing economic processes can never again be discussed as if their regularity existed outside man.

That this subjective element in the commodity is reified turns the human relationship implied in it into a relation between objects. This inversion Marx calls the 'fetishism of commodities': an expression of human creativity appears to be a natural object.[1] The inversion also emerges in the failure of the capitalist to appear as a person in social relations rather than a predicate of capital; not only the workers, but the capitalists as well, are stripped of their personality.[2] Men are degraded to the status of objects, and objects receive human attributes. Society ceases to be a texture of inter-human relations and appears to be a system dependent upon objects and objective laws. To drive his argument home Marx sometimes refers to the outcome of this process by the phrase *Monsieur le Capital*.[3]

From this point of view, *Das Kapital* is a detailed study of the economic aspects of the process annunciated by Marx in his *Economic-Philosophical Manuscripts*: what was philosophically postulated in 1844 is now verified and vindicated by an analysis of capitalist economic activity undertaken with the tools of classical political economy. Thus the considerations underlying Marx's use of the transformative method reappear in *Das Kapital* when he discusses the fetishism of commodities in the following *locus classicus*:

A commodity is therefore a mysterious thing, simply because in it the social character of men's labour appears to them as an objective character stamped upon the product of the labour; because the relation of the producers to the sum total of their own labour is presented to them as a social relation, existing not between them, but between the products of their labour. This is the reason why the products of labour become commodities, social things whose qualities are at the same time perceptible and imperceptible by the senses. In the same way the light from an object is perceived by us not as the subjective excitation of our optic

---

[1] *The German Ideology*, p. 91; *Werke*, XIII, 21; *Theorien über den Mehrwert* (Berlin, 1962), III, 265.

[2] 'Except as personified capital, the capitalist has no historical value' (*Capital*, I, 592). 'Every individual capital forms, however, but an individual fraction, a fraction endowed with individual life, as it were, of the aggregate social capital, just as every individual capitalist is but an individual element of the capitalist class' (*Capital*, II, 351).　　　　　　[3] *Capital*, III, 809.

nerve, but as the objective form of something outside the eye itself. . .
There is a definite social relation between men that assumes, in their
eyes, the fantastic form of a relation between things. In order, therefore,
to find an analogy, we must have recourse to the mist-enveloped regions
of the religious world. In that world the productions of the human brain
appear as independent beings endowed with life and entering into relation
both with one another and the human race. So it is in the world of commodities with the products of men's hands. This I call the Fetishism
which attaches itself to the products of labour, so soon as they are produced as commodities, and which is therefore inseparable from the
production of commodities. . .

Value, therefore, does not stalk about with a label describing what it is.
It is value, rather, that converts every product into a social hieroglyphic.
Later on, we try to decipher the hieroglyphic, to get behind the secret of
our own social products.[1]

Marx tried for the first time to explain the economic content of
this argument in *Wage Labour and Capital* (1849): since the commodities as exchange values are objective, objectified human labour,
he said that any profit drawn by the capitalist from the commodity
originates in the labour that produced the commodity. Capital thus
crystallizes labour already performed. The statement 'in present
society capital dominates labour' is a telescoped version of 'in
present society crystallized and objectified labour, past labour, as it
is expressed in capital, dominates live and still active labour'.
This, according to Marx, is the paradox of labour in capitalist
society:

In bourgeois society, living labour is but a means to increase accumulated
labour. In Communist society, accumulated labour is but a means to
widen, to enrich, to promote the existence of the labourer.

In bourgeois society, therefore, the past dominates the present; in
Communist society, the present dominates the past. In bourgeois society
capital is independent and has individuality, while the living person is
dependent and has no individuality.

And the abolition of this state of things is called by the bourgeois
abolition of individuality and freedom![2]

---

[1] *Ibid.* I, 72–4.
[2] *The Communist Manifesto, Selected Works,* I, 48. Cf. *Wage Labour and Capital,*
ibid. p. 91: 'It is only the domination of accumulated, past, materialised labour over
direct, living labour that turns accumulated labour into capital. Capital does not consist

Alienation and property

This is also the significance of the historical antagonism between capital and labour: all previous antagonisms between property and propertylessness were devoid of any systematic issue of principle. Only in the antagonism between labour and capital, Marx argues, is the mystery of property revealed: that it is nothing other than human labour. Consequently the antagonism between property and propertylessness is itself a tension between two modes of human activity. For this reason all previous class antagonisms could not have provided the solution to the class antagonism *per se*. Only now that the antagonism has been lucidly understood does the possibility of resolving the tension emerge. In this context Marx cites the extreme class conflicts of ancient Rome (and modern Turkey) to illustrate his thesis that one must grasp the systematic issue before suggesting any solution.[1]

For Marx another consequence follows these considerations: technological change constantly increases the gap between living labour and 'dead' labour. We have already seen, in the long passage from the *Grundrisse* quoted at the beginning of this chapter, that the process of production develops constantly at the expense of immediate labour. This is the theoretical background to the statement that the machine replaces the worker: the development of machinery increases the contribution of the machine to surplus value, whereas the increment derived from the worker's direct labour constantly decreases.[2] Marx points out that this does not mean, as some over-optimistic social reformers argued, that the development of machinery diminishes and gradually abolishes 'exploitation'. On the

in accumulated labour serving living labour as a means for new production. It consists in living labour serving accumulated labour as a means for maintaining and multiplying the exchange value of the latter.'

[1] *Early Writings*, p. 152.

[2] *Capital*, I, 645: 'All means for the development of production transform themselves into means of domination over, and exploitation of, the producers; they mutilate the labourer into a fragment of a man, degrade him to the level of an appendage of a machine, destroy every remnant of charm in his work and turn it into a hated toil; they estrange him from the intellectual potentialities of the labour-process in the same proportion as science is incorporated in it as an independent power; they distort the conditions under which he works, subject him during the labour-process to a despotism the more hateful for its meanness... It follows therefore that in proportion as capital accumulates, the lot of the labourer, be his payment high or low, must grow worse.' Cf. also *Wage Labour and Capital, Selected Works*, I, 93 f.; *Critique of the Gotha Programme, ibid.* II, 28 f.

contrary, since machinery and its further proliferation depend on capital investment, and capital in its turn depends on its production by the worker, the growing sophistication of technology again depends in the last resort on human labour, though machinery multiplies the usefulness and durability of this surplus value for the capitalist. If capital could previously be used to hire more workers, now it is used to purchase new machinery. The domination of 'dead' objectified labour over living labour steadily increases. Machinery thus magnifies alienation: human faculties become objectified as constantly producing machines dominate human life to an unheard of extent. In this process the worker becomes, according to Marx, an 'appendage of the machine'.[1] His products become his real masters.[2]

On these premises the abolition of capital is a necessary prerequisite for the abolition of alienation. Since to Marx capital by definition engenders alienation, no amelioration in the conditions of labour can basically change the position of the worker so long as capital survives. Though Marx always concedes the possibility that psychologically as well as economically the position of the worker in capitalist society may improve, he fails to see a solution to the basic anthropological situation of the worker so long as the relation between capital and labour remains in its present state. Since Marx's concern is not the standard of living of the worker *per se* but the quality of life of the human being epitomized in the worker, the quantitative elements are of secondary importance. Hence Marx's attitude to trade union activity has always had two aspects: Marx urges trade union activity because it creates the nuclei for social, other-directed behaviour in the worker, encouraging class consciousness, and because he holds that strikes, etc., can help the worker achieve better economic conditions. On the other hand, he never believed that trade union activity as such could remake the world, since it could not change the structure of society or the quality of human labour under the conditions of capital.[3] Consequently he opposes the idea of the 'iron law of wages' propagated by Lassalle and

[1] *The Communist Manifesto, Selected Works*, I, 40.
[2] *The German Ideology*, p. 81.
[3] *Inaugural Address, Selected Works*, I, 382–5.

others, not only because of its quietistic and passivist implications, but also because it substituted a mechanistic interpretation of capital for a dialectical understanding of its working. But he never believed that trade union activity can do more than eliminate some of the more glaring atrocities of capitalist society.[1]

Marx further argues that the inversion of human relations in capitalist society dislocates the function of production. Basically production widens and enlarges human opportunities and personal faculties. In capitalist society, with the universal orientation of human activity totally absent from economic production, individuals do not develop each other's potentialities through the act of production but become competitors interested in minimizing the potentialities of everyone except themselves. Economic activity and property are thus not a bond of reciprocity, but forces that separate individuals, since one achieves at another's expense. Individuals become self-enclosed atoms, and mutuality exists only in competition.[2]

The division of labour receives its historical significance from these considerations. In the 1844 *Manuscripts* Marx points to the division of labour as the source of the historical emergence of classes and class antagonisms.[3] He also maintains that the division of labour creates different capacities in different human individuals. In no way should the division of labour be considered a result of pre-existing differences in human faculties.[4] Not only does the division of labour separate spiritual from physical labour and thus create the two main archetypal modes of human existence: it also destroys man's capacity to develop towards universal production. According to Marx man is a universal producer. The division of labour reduces him to a one-sided being since it makes his occupation (e.g. farming, working for a wage) into his main characteristic (peasant, labourer). The emergence of this particularism sets one man against another, making the basic interhuman relationship one of antagonism instead of mutuality. This means that the division of labour negates man as a universal being, shuts him up within his own partial self. Instead

---

[1] *Wages, Price and Profit, Selected Works*, I, 436–8; *Critique of the Gotha Programme*, ibid. II, 19 f.   [2] *Early Writings*, pp. 31, 168.
[3] *Ibid.* p. 120.   [4] *Ibid.* pp. 181–8.

Commodities and labour

of a universal humanity different characteristic types of men emerge, strongly antagonistic to one another, drawing their *raison d'être* from the perpetuation of this distinctiveness. Man's universe is reduced to his endeavour to secure for himself the physical means of his subsistence. This function becomes the whole end of human life. Each human being is thus trapped within a shell from which he can only emerge at the risk of his whole existence.[1] When Marx envisages the abolition of the division of labour, therefore, he has in mind not only technological considerations. The abolition of the division of labour also entails the abolition of the distinctions that frustrate the effort to arrive at a universal humanity.[2]

It has sometimes been pointed out that Marx's harsh remarks in *The Communist Manifesto* about the 'True Socialists' and their usage of the term alienation constitute a critique of his own earlier stages of intellectual development. The preceding discussion should have supplied enough evidence to refute the view that the 'later', 'older' Marx disregarded the issue of alienation and that the analytical argument of *Das Kapital* is meaningless if not understood within the context of the debate about alienation. Why, then, the fulminating language against the 'True Socialists'? Mainly, one feels, because both Marx and the 'True Socialists' have used the same term, but with different meanings. Since the 'True Socialists' have been using it *ad nauseam* in an undifferentiated manner, signifying a rather general *Weltschmerz*, Marx must have thought that their uncritical use of the term might overshadow the analytical insights into the connection between philosophical issues and economic phenomena supplied by his own work. *Das Kapital* shows that alienation is empirically verifiable. In *The Communist Manifesto* Marx criticizes not the term alienation but its heavy handed use by the 'True Socialists': he never abandoned the term, and his own system is unintelligible without it.

[1] *The German Ideology*, pp. 44-5.   [2] *Selected Works*, II, 24.

5

PRAXIS AND REVOLUTION

THE FORERUNNERS

In the Preface to his *Philosophy of Right* Hegel coined the phrase that was later to divide the Hegelian school: 'What is rational is actual, and what is actual is rational.'[1]

The different glosses supplied for this sentence are at the root of the schism in the Hegelian school during the 1830s. Those who underlined the second half of the Master's dictum saw in it a philosophical justification for existing reality and drew politically conservative conclusions from it. Those who emphasized the first half of the sentence maintained that the whole phrase suggests that whatever can be shown to be rationally valid will ultimately be realized. For them Hegel's statement meant a far-reaching philosophical vindication of the radical and revolutionary postulate requiring them to shape the world according to Reason.[2]

The debate about the open-endedness of the Hegelian system towards the future as an historical dimension was opened for the first time as early as 1838 in a book called *Prolegomena zur Historiosophie*. The author, Count August von Cieszkowski, a Polish aristocrat from the Posen area educated at Berlin University, is one of the more original—and somewhat bizarre—thinkers on the margin of the Hegelian school. After having been neglected for almost a century, he is only recently being slowly rescued from obscurity and oblivion. Since research has not yet caught up with Cieszkowski, an adequate study about the links between the *Prolegomena* and the later mystic Catholicism of his Polish book *Ojcze Nasz*,[3] is entirely lacking.[4] Moses Hess admits that he was deeply influenced by

---

[1] Hegel's *Philosophy of Right*, trans. T. M. Knox (Oxford, 1942), p. 10. Engels misquoted this sentence from memory in his 'Ludwig Feuerbach and the End of the Classical German Philosophy', and sometimes this misquotation is known far more than the Hegelian original (*Selected Works*, II, 361).

[2] Cf. Rotenstreich, *Basic Problems of Marx's Philosophy*, pp. 5 ff.; J. Gebhardt, *Politik und Eschatologie* (München, 1963); H. Stuke, *Philosophie der Tat* (Stuttgart, 1963).

[3] *Notre Père*, French edition (Paris, 1904).

[4] The most important studies of Cieszkowski are as follows: A. Żółtowski, *Graf A. Cieszkowskis Philosophie der Tat* (Posen, 1904); N. O. Lossky, *Three Polish Mes-*

The forerunners

Cieszkowski,[1] and his treatment of *praxis* is so reminiscent of Marx that a claim has recently been made that one cannot fully grasp Marx without recourse to Cieszkowski.[2] The following does not pretend to be a full presentation of Cieszkowski's ideas, but is rather intended to point out those aspects which seem relevant to an understanding of Marx.

The few studies that have tried to trace similarities between Marx and Cieszkowski have justly pointed out that to a certain degree both Cieszkowski and Hess reverted from Hegel back to Fichte. Lukács says that Cieszkowski tried to overcome Hegel's absolutization of the present by confronting it with an abstract 'ought'. This, according to Lukács, clearly repudiates Hegel's realism, which, despite its politically conservative implications, always points toward Marx's materialism.[3] Nevertheless, as will be shown later, this inclination toward Fichte, quite characteristic of the Young Hegelians in general, is perhaps stronger in Hess than in Cieszkowski, though the latter refers explicitly to his indebtedness to Fichte in a programmatic letter to his Hegelian teacher Karl Ludwig Michelet.[4]

Marx himself does not mention the *Prolegomena* in his writings, yet we know that he and Cieszkowski knew each other personally and met in Paris during 1843/4, probably in connection with Marx's activity as editor of the *Deutsch-Französische Jahrbücher*. Marx refers to this meeting in a letter to Engels written about forty years later, and it is difficult to know how much of Marx's comment reflects the atmosphere of the meeting itself and how much the effect of Cieszkowski's later Polish messianic Catholicism. For Marx's recollection is extremely uncomplimentary: 'this Count (Marx writes) actually visited me in Paris during the period of the

sianists: *Sigmund Krasinski, August Cieszkowski, W. Lutoslawski* (Prague, 1937); W. Kühne, *Graf August Cieszkowski, ein Schüler Hegels und des deutschen Geistes* (Leipzig, 1938); B. P. Hepner, 'History and the Future: The Vision of August Cieszkowski', *Review of Politics*, xv, no. 3 (July 1953). J. Gebhardt, *op. cit.* pp. 130–4; H. Stuke, *op. cit.* pp. 83–122.

[1] Cf. M. Hess, *Philosophische und sozialistische Schriften*, ed. Cornu and Mönke (Berlin, 1961), pp. 77, 79.
[2] N. Lobkowicz, 'Eschatology and the Young Hegelians', *Review of Politics*, no. 3 (July, 1965), p. 437.
[3] Lukács, *Moses Hess, etc.*, pp. 3–8.
[4] The letter to Michelet, dated 18 March 1837, is cited by Kühne, *op. cit.* pp. 364–6. Michelet reviewed the *Prolegomena* favourably in the *Jahrbücher für wissenschaftliche Kritik*, November, 1838.

Praxis and revolution

Deutsch-Französische Jahrbücher and made my life so miserable that I wouldn't and couldn't read all what he had sinned [i.e. written]'.[1]

The initial stages of Cieszkowski's intellectual development are of some interest. His doctoral dissertation, presented to Heidelberg University in 1838, was entitled *De philosophiae ionicae ingenio, vi, loco*. Both the subject and the treatment are reminiscent of Marx's own dissertation on Democritus and Epicurus. Cieszkowski sees Thales as the father of materialism, Anaximander as the father of idealism and Anaximenes as the creator of speculative-concrete spiritualism. Such a heavily loaded dialectical treatment of the subject clearly suggests that Cieszkowski's own interest lies in what he calls 'speculative-concrete spiritualism', whose highest and most mature expression he finds in Hegel.

Characteristically, Cieszkowski opens his *Prolegomena* exactly where Hegel closed his *Philosophy of History*: the future. According to Cieszkowski, Hegel's system must now be projected into the future. Hegel was mistaken in neglecting to spell out the possibilities inherent in future developments. The present task of philosophy is to find out the connections between the future and historical actuality. Only then will man's self-consciousness be realized not only formally but also in historical action.[2]

Hegel very emphatically denied any possibility of recognizing the future prior to its becoming the present, or rather the past. Cieszkowski is aware that this denial is central to the whole Hegelian argument and that there are intrinsic difficulties in suiting the Hegelian system to a future-directed view. His way out of the dilemma may not be altogether satisfactory, but it would be less than just to accept Lukács' thesis that Cieszkowski projected a Fichtean abstract 'ought' as the criterion for the future. In a way Cieszkowski remained a Hegelian in his approach even where he differed so radically from his master's initial position.

Cieszkowski's formally proves the possibility of envisaging the future by analogy with the concept of organism. He argues, that as one can deduce from the form of a tooth of an ancient fossil the

[1] Marx to Engels, 12 January 1882 (*Briefwechsel*, IV, 620).
[2] A. v. Cieszkowski, *Prolegomena zur Historiosophie* (Berlin, 1838), pp. 8–9.

126

whole structure of that animal's organism, the same can be done with history: that part of history already known to us, the past, gives us information about the whole, and the totality of the whole includes the future. No doubt Cieszkowski overlooks the difficulties inherent in all organic analogies, namely, that even if human history is an organism in any sensible meaning of the word, there is still all the difference in the world between an organism whose members exist simultaneously and an organism whose members are chronologically consecutive, and may stand in some causal relation to each other. Yet in spite of this, fallacious as Cieszkowski's argument may be, he still does not deduce the future *a priori*, from an abstract 'ought' but rather *a posteriori*, through a dialectical analysis of the historical past: 'Why then do we not acknowlege this organism in history as well? Why do we not construe, out of the already occurred parts of the whole historical process, its ideal totality and especially its still lacking future part, which has to be related to the already-occurred one and may form the only true idea of history in integration with it?'[1]

This leads Cieszkowski to the synthetic creation of the future out of the antitheses and contradictions of the historical past as described by Hegel: the processes of the past are the keys to the solutions of the future, and the antitheses of the present anticipate the syntheses of the future and their ultimate 'synthesis of syntheses'. Historiosophy, according to Cieszkowski, is that interpretation of history which includes a vision of the future as part of its historical perspective. As a synthesis, this vision is not divorced from history but rather deduced from it. This strong 'historicist' element has escaped Lukács' attention.

Again in accordance with Hegel, who perceived three main periods in history, each characterized by a different mode of consciousness, Cieszkowski sees three possible modes of future-cognition, each typical of one of the three periods of history. The future, according to Cieszkowski, can be recognized through emotion, thought or will. The first mode, that of feeling, is arbitrary and subjective by nature: historically it is expressed by ancient prophecy; the second, theoretical mode, is characterized by the objec-

[1] *Ibid.* p. 13.

tive treatment of the subject through the philosophy of history: this is the Age of Reason. The third, volitional mode, synthesizes both earlier modes and embraces both the subjective urge and the relation to the objective world: this is *praxis*. According to Cieszkowski, *praxis* simultaneously recognizes and creates historical reality; it is the unity of existence and essence mediated through conscious becoming: 'The third determination [of the future] is the active-practical, applied, worked-out, spontaneous, willed, free one— and therefore it comprises the whole sphere of the deed [*Tat*], the facts and their meaning, theory and practice, the concept and its reality—and brings about the vindication of history.'[1]

The three historical periods are: (*a*) the subjective period, characterized by an arbitrariness unlimited by institutions; (*b*) the objective period, mediated through the institutional evolution of political life; and (*c*) the absolute period, the unity of existence and thinking. Cieszkowski historicizes Hegel's Absolute Spirit, eternal and trans-temporal, by projecting it on to the future. The whole Preface of Hegel's *Philosophy of Right* is aimed against such an eschatological breakthrough; yet Cieszkowski tries in his *tour de force* subtly to preserve the Hegelian edifice, while he subverts it.

This new idea of the future leads Cieszkowski to hint that the traditional view of matter must be rejected. In Cieszkowski's system matter can no longer remain, as in Hegel, the opaque expression of spirit in self-alienation, its opposite negation. Cieszkowski's vision of an historical realization of idealism clearly prefigures Feuerbach and Marx, though he himself may not always be fully aware of all the radical implications of his thought. His later, mystic development certainly points in a completely different direction.

This 'rehabilitation of matter' will, according to Cieszkowski, end the dualism left by Hegel: 'And this, then, will be the true *rehabilitation of matter* as well as the absolute, both justified and substantive reconciliation of the Real and the Ideal. In this respect the philosophy of the future will be a transcendence of philosophy beyond itself.[2]

The striking resemblance to Marx's Thesis XI on Feuerbach is

---

[1] *Prolegomena zur Historiosophie*, p. 16. Cf. p. 120, where Cieszkowski says 'Nihil est in voluntare et actu, quod prius non fuerit in intellectu'.   [2] *Ibid.* p. 127.

obvious. Nevertheless, Cieszkowski does not explain what this rehabilitation of matter is meant to be, but he does supply some indications of its possible meaning. In another passage he points out that
the Self can become a concrete Self only through action related to
external objects. In thought, man's relation to the universe remains
abstract; he can express his actuality only through an active relation
that causes objective results. This, surprising as it may sound,
accounts also for Cieszkowski's critique of both political liberalism
and Protestantism. Both, according to him, can give man only ideal
freedom, not a freedom entrenched within realized actuality. The
future's concrete freedom will be objectively realized, not like
Hegelian freedom which never really shook off its Lutheran, inner
implications.[1]

The fascination of this 'rehabilitation of matter', despite its
obscurity, lies in Cieszkowski's relating it to the social problem. In
this he is the first among the Young Hegelians to do so explicitly
and consciously. According to him, the philosophy of the future must
orient itself toward society. The translation of philosophy into
praxis will be brought about by a confrontation with the social
problem:

Philosophy has therefore to resign itself to becoming mainly *applied* philosophy; and just as the poetry of art becomes transformed into the prose of
thought, so philosophy must descend from the heights of theory into
praxis. Practical philosophy, or, more correctly, the philosophy of *praxis*
(whose concrete impact on life and social conditions amounts to the
employment of both within concrete activity)—this is the future fate of
philosophy in general...Just as thought and reflection overcame the
belles arts, so the deed and social activity will now overcome philosophy.[2]

Again, Cieszkowski is not explicit about the implications of social
activity. In another context he says that the writers of socialist
utopias always miss their point because they try to penetrate reality
from the outside and to impose on it external 'ought's' instead of
attempting to shape the new reality from within existing conditions.[3]
Again, this point is remarkably reminiscent of Marx's critique of

---

[1] *Ibid.* p. 142. In one of his later works Cieszkowski says the same when he claims that
the French Revolution has given man only formal and abstract, but not real, freedom
(A. Cieszkowski, *De la pairie et de l'aristocratie moderne* [Paris, 1844], p. 154).
[2] *Prolegomena*, pp. 129–30.   [3] *Ibid.* p. 147.

utopianism, though it does not necessarily lead to the same results, as Cieszkowski's later Social Catholicism shows.

Besides this general critique of socialist utopias Cieszkowski also takes issue directly with Fourier. He argues that Fourier considers the future the regulative dimension of history, yet he discusses future society without a prior analysis of the present. Cieszkowski admits that no vision of the future will be able to predict its details precisely. It will have to satisfy itself with a general outline of the main stream of future development. The Hegelian reserve is evident here just as in Marx's work.[1]

If the historical content of the social problem is barely mentioned, its speculative aspect is elaborated in some detail. The major end of future society, Cieszkowski says, is to return to man his social essence, to emancipate him from his abstractedness and to eliminate the separate character of the political structure:

[In future society] man will be brought back from his abstraction and will again become a social individuum *par excellence*. The naked Self will leave its generality and determine itself as a concrete person, abounding in a wealth of social relations... The state will also leave its abstract separation and become itself a member of humanity and the concrete family of nations. The state of nature among nations will be substituted by a state of society.[2]

These remarks about some of the major aspects in Cieszkowski's thought may point out that, despite all that separates him from Marx, intensive similarities between them remain, transcending the use of the term *praxis*. Cieszkowski, however, does not envisage an historical subject that can carry out his postulate of radical change, and hence he cannot, in the last resort, develop a theory of social action. Nevertheless, he voices the opinion that the future stands under the aegis of the social problem. The historicity of the change, so evident in Marx, is already anticipated in Cieszkowski's writings.

[1] *Prolegomena*, p. 148; cf. *De la pairie*, etc., pp. 152–6.
[2] *Prolegomena*, p. 17. Cieszkowski preserves his concept of alienation also in his later writings, but it acquires a strong Christian connotation: the separation of the ideal and the real is conceived as an indication of man's eternal peregrination towards God (*Notre Père*, French edition, Paris, 1904, p. 96). In his later days Cieszkowski saw social Catholicism as the redemption of the lower classes and became a strong adherent of the social doctrine of Leo XIII's *Rerum Novarum*.

The forerunners

If Cieszkowski shares with Marx an interest in developing *praxis* he owes it to the fascination of all Young Hegelians with this term. The roots of the philosophy of *praxis* cut deep into the Hegelian system itself, though Hegel himself could hardly have foreseen all its implications.

The traditional confrontation of theory and practice goes back to Aristotle's *Metaphysics*. According to Aristotle, *theoria*, the general view, seeks to know the world and understand it with the sole aim of knowledge itself. The opposite of *theoria* in this sense is *praxis*, or practical knowledge, which does not strive for the ultimate, universal truth, but contents itself with instrumental, applicable knowledge. Theoretical knowledge is thus more comprehensive and more true: the more any particular knowledge is related to principles and general rules, the more it is theoretical, i.e. aiming at a general truth and having knowledge itself as its sole aim. Practical knowledge, on the other hand, because of its applicability, is by definition less universal and more particular. While theoretical knowledge is permanent and eternal, practical knowledge is momentary and ephemeral. The main point is that both *theoria* and *praxis* are different modes of knowledge.

Karl Löwith justly pointed out that if the Young Hegelians, including Marx, tried to transform theory in this traditional sense into a critique of existence aimed at its (practical) change, then the resulting shift in the meaning of the concepts is already implied in Hegel's work.[1] Even if the 'unity of theory and practice' goes against the grain of Hegel's own philosophy, Hegel made it possible philosophically.

In the strict Aristotelian sense a 'unity of theory and practice' is quite meaningless. Since the two concepts are so defined as to be mutually exclusive, no kind of knowledge can be simultaneously both particular and universal, both applicable and inapplicable. But Hegel twists the traditional meaning of the terms: the eternal, the object of theory, for Aristotle Nature as a totality of potentials, in Hegel is shaped by human consciousness. Once the *cosmos* becomes *Weltgeschichte*, the theoretical becomes a general view of

[1] K. Löwith, *Die Hegelsche Linke*, pp. 33–7. Cf. M. Riedel, *Theorie und Praxis im Denken Hegels*.

what is practical, or applicable. If the universal and the eternal can be consciously created by thought, then the theoretical can exist only in relation to the practical. Consequently, Hegel's enigmatic final passage in the Preface to the *Philosophy of Right* ('The owl of Minerva spreads its wings only with the falling of dusk') may be, despite its obvious quietism, the key to an attempt to shape the world according to theory.

One of the first Young Hegelians to grasp this possibility was Arnold Ruge. In 1840 he suggested in an article that Hegelian dialectics can become a method of critique of contemporary affairs. He also postulated a transition within Hegelian philosophy from absolute-theoretical idealism to what he called 'practical idealism'. The immediate expression of this practical idealism would be, according to Ruge, the emergence of a political opposition in Germany which would criticize the existing political structure according to the theoretical criteria of Hegelian political philosophy. The transition from philosophy to politics he thus conceived as immanent within the Hegelian system itself.[1] A year later Ruge reiterated this, saying that the Hegelian connection between philosophy and historical actuality lies at the root of the link between philosophy and politics.[2]

This tendency to legitimize political opposition in terms of Hegelian philosophy can be found at the same time in some of Bruno Bauer's letters to Marx, where the practical, instrumental nature of philosophy *vis-à-vis* politics is strongly underlined.[3] Less than a year later a certain disillusionment can already be noticed in Bauer when he tries to dissuade Marx from political activity and talk him into trying an academic career. But even this political denial is couched in terms taken from the debate about *praxis*: 'It would be folly if you would devote yourself to a practical career. Theory is nowadays the strongest *praxis*, and we still cannot forsee how much it can turn out to be practical in the long run.'[4] If this implies a retreat from politics, it does not imply a retreat from the view that theory and praxis can, ultimately, be unified.

---

[1] *Hallische Jahrbücher* (1840), pp. 1930 f.
[2] *Deutsche Jahrbücher* (1841), p. 594.
[3] Bauer to Marx, 1 March 1840 (*MEGA*, I, 1/2, p. 237).
[4] *Idem*, 31 March 1841 (*ibid.* p. 250).

The forerunners

Perhaps this quick retreat from politics on the part of some of the Young Hegelians was not accidental, for basically they conceived their *praxis* in purely political terms, ignoring social action. In a way, this neglect may have been the ultimate nemesis of Hegelian political philosophy. Because the Young Hegelians could not, after all, divorce themselves from the primacy of political institutions, they had to admit that their political activity could never reach more than those few who must belong to a limited philosophical school, condemned to political impotence. Their *praxis*, to use Marx's language, is still too theoretical. Moses Hess was the first to grasp this. As early as 1841, in *Die europäische Triarchie*, he says that by calling philosophy *praxis* Bauer and his disciples do not guarantee its emancipation from theory. According to Hess, the revolution cannot be an outcome of mere theoretical criticism; it has to manifest itself in social action. In this Hess, as Cieszkowski's disciple, is ahead of the mainstream of the Young Hegelians.[1] In a language already drawing on Marx's essays in the *Deutsch-Französische Jahrbücher*, Hess returns to the subject four years later: all the attempts of the Young Hegelians to solve the problem of alienation theoretically have failed, he says, because the problem—and its solution—involve social practice.[2]

This connection between the new meaning of *praxis* and the social sphere is most clearly brought out at approximately the same time by Ruge and Feuerbach. Marx's own formulation in the *Deutsch-Französische Jahrbücher* seem to draw on at least those two sources. In an essay of 1843 Ruge says about Hegelian philosophy:

Nowhere has theoretical emancipation been so thoroughly carried out as in Germany...The birth of real, practical freedom is in the transition of its demands to the masses. This demand is only a symptom of the fact that theory has been well digested and has been successful in its breakthrough into existence...The ultimate end of theoretical emancipation is practical emancipation. But *praxis*, on the other hand, is nothing else than the movement of the mass in the spirit of theory.[3]

[1] M. Hess, *Die europäische Triarchie* (Leipzig, 1841), p. 12.
[2] M. Hess, 'Die letzten Philosophen', *Philosophische und Sozialistische Schriften*, pp. 381–2.
[3] A. Ruge, *Werke* (Mannheim, 1847), IV, 254.

Cieszkowski's 'rehabilitation of matter', lacking a social subject, here finds its social content, though still undifferentiated. It was Feuerbach who brought out the connection between *mass* and *masses* (in German, both are *Masse*), i.e. between matter and the social context of a political movement: he thus identifies *praxis* with the material forces inherent in the masses In a letter to Ruge, dated 1843 and published in the *Deutsch-Französische Jahrbücher*, Feuerbach writes:

What is theory, what is practice? Wherein lies their difference? Theoretical is that which is hidden in my head only, practical is that which is spooking in many heads. What unites many heads, creates a mass, extends itself and thus finds its place in the world. If it is possible to create a new organ for the new principle, then this is a *praxis* which should never be missed.[1]

It was the Young Hegelian school that shaped the new and revolutionary relationship between theory and practice. Marx endowed this new relationship with a concrete historical content. While he articulated his own *Zeitgeist*, he carried it one significant step further.

THE UNITY OF THEORY AND PRAXIS: FROM INTERPRETING THE WORLD TO CHANGING IT

Marx's complex attitude towards the Hegelian view of the nature and scope of philosophy emerges from his very earliest writings, where he seems to combine the view that philosophy is 'its own time apprehended in thought' with a notion that ascribes to philosophy a constructive role in the shaping of human development. In his doctoral dissertation, completed in 1841, Marx remarks that a theory emancipated from the limitations of a philosophical system becomes a practical energy turning against existing actuality. But, he adds, 'The *praxis* of philosophy is still theoretical. Criticism judges every single existence according to essence, every separate actuality according to the idea. But this immediate realisation of philosophy is by its nature deeply involved in contradictions.'[2]

Recognizing these difficulties leads Marx to a somewhat less radical approach when he returns to this problem a few years later

[1] L. Feuerbach, *Briefwechsel*, ed. W. Schuffenhauer (Leipzig, 1963), p. 177.
[2] *MEGA*, I, 1/1, p. 64.

in a newspaper article on press censorship. Hegel's Preface to the *Philosophy of Right* is evident in the background:

But philosophers do not grow like mushrooms, out of the earth; they are the outgrowth of their period, their nation, whose most subtle, delicate and invisible juices abound in the philosophical ideas. The same spirit that constructs the philosophical system in the mind of the philosopher builds the railways with the hands of the trade. Philosophy does not reside outside this world just as the mind does not reside outside man just because it is not located in his belly.[1]

This acceptance of the Hegelian view of the role of philosophy also, by implication, criticizes it. Philosophy is always related to historical actuality, but the philosophical medium itself sometimes severs the link between reality and its philosophical reflection. This, according to Marx, may cause the illusion that the object of philosophy is philosophy itself. A merely contemplative attitude, according to Marx, contains its objects in its contemplation and is thus object-less. This attitude endangers all philosophical speculation that does not translate its contemplation into an objective language, i.e. a language relating to objects—*praxis*. The unity of theory and practice transfers man from an object-less world into the sphere of objective activity.

This transition is also immanent within the Hegelian view of philosophy as the reflection of historical actuality. Since Hegel, idea and reality are no longer conceived on two separate planes. There is always a distance between the two, but the distance becomes a question of historical development and not a matter of principle. A radical transformation can hence seek to make reality adequate to the philosophical idea. In the already quoted article of 1842, Marx summarizes:

As every true philosophy is the spiritual quintessence of its age, the time must come about when philosophy will get in touch with the real world of its time and establish a reciprocal relationship with it not only internally, through its content, but also externally, through its phenomenal manifestation as well. Then philosophy will cease to be just a system among systems, but will turn to be a philosophy in general, confronting the world. It will turn into the philosophy of the world.[2]

[1] *Rheinische Zeitung*, 14 July 1842 (*Werke*, I, 97).   [2] *Ibid.* pp. 97–8.

What Marx will later epitomize in the epigrammatic style of Thesis XI on Feuerbach is clearly discernible here as early as 1842, prior to Marx's extensive acquaintance with Feuerbach's philosophy. The breakthrough from philosophy to reality need not be done through Feuerbach, though he is extremely helpful in showing the method by which such a breakthrough could be achieved. The urge itself is immanent in Hegel. This breakthrough becomes possible by confronting the Hegelian system with its own premises. According to Marx, the crucial criterion for any philosophical idealism is its capacity to realize itself, and we have already observed in chapter 1 how this idea was at the root of Marx's initial inclination towards Hegelian philosophy.[1]

This determines the dialectical relationship between philosophy's comprehension of the world and its ability to change it. In Marx's opinion, theory must evolve an adequate interpretation of the world before it will be able to change it. The history of philosophy is the continuous search for such an adequate picture of the world. Once such a picture has been formed, it dialectically abolishes itself as a reflection of reality and begins to determine the shaping of a new reality.

As Marx's epistemology holds that the process of recognizing reality changes both the observed object and the observing subject, so philosophy, once it has reached its culmination in providing us with a true picture of the world, ceases to be philosophy in the traditional sense of the word. Traditional philosophy presupposes a permanent, though varying, distance between reality and its philosophical interpretation. Once this distance is overcome by philosophy's own achievement, philosophy ceases to be a theoretical reflection and turns into practical energy acting upon reality. This is the meaning of Marx's remark that philosophy cannot realize itself without abolishing itself (*sich aufheben*) and that it cannot abolish itself unless it be realized. A philosophy that has reached adequate self-consciousness abolishes itself and turns into reality. The dialectical crux of the matter is that the abolition of philosophy

[1] Cf. also the epistle dedicatory of Marx's doctorate, addressed to his future father-in-law Ludwig von Westphalen: 'You, my fatherly friend, have always been a living example for me that idealism is not a mirage but a reality' (*MEGA*, I, 1/1, p. 1).

presupposes a prior development of a philosophy that will be sophisticated enough to comprehend reality adequately. This philosophy is, according to Marx, the Hegelian system, and therefore before Marx could move into *praxis* he had to perfect philosophy—only in order to transcend it.[1]

That an adequate knowledge of reality is a philosophical prerequisite for its change is also Marx's main argument against Feuerbach. In *The German Ideology* Marx says that Feuerbach still erroneously thinks that the task of philosophy is to supply an adequate consciousness about the world, thus overlooking the real issue, that the ultimate task of philosophy is not merely to comprehend reality, but to change it. This lack of an activist, practical element, according to Marx, characterizes all traditional materialism.[2] But paradoxically, only because the philosophers have hitherto interpreted the world is it now possible to revolutionize it. Revolutionizing the world depends on an adequate understanding of it. This was, after all, also the *raison d'être* for spending a lifetime on *Das Kapital*.

From this vantage point Marx criticizes German idealism. Though it had the necessary conceptual tools, it stopped short of penetrating reality in order to change it. He couples this argument with a critique of German liberalism, which sounds now, perhaps, more profound and just than it might have sounded in pre-1848 (and pre-1933) Germany. Commenting on the Kantian legacy to German liberalism, Marx says:

We have to register a definite protest against this endless, nebulous and unclear ratiocination of those German liberals who think they honour liberty by relegating it to the starry heaven of imagination instead of basing it on the firm foundation of reality. It is to these masters of imaginary ratiocination, to these masters of sentimental enthusiasm, who are afraid lest their ideal be desecrated by its coming in touch with profane reality—it is to them, then, that we Germans owe our situation in which liberty is still a matter of imagination and sentimentality. Out of too much reverence for the ideas they are not being realised.[3]

[1] *Early Writings*, pp. 50–1.
[2] *The German Ideology*, pp. 55–6.
[3] *Rheinische Zeitung*, 19 May 1842 (*Werke*, I, 68). Cf. Marx's letter to Dagobert Oppenheimer of 25 August 1842: 'True theory has to be clarified and developed within the setting of concrete conditions and existing relationships' (*Werke*, XXVII, 409).

This need to translate philosophy into social action, which also implies that social action is guided by philosophical considerations, reappears in a letter Marx wrote to Ruge in September 1843 and later printed in the *Deutsch-Französische Jahrbücher*. Here Marx clearly says that the goals of social action are not new; only the opportunity to realize them is novel and unique:

The reform of consciousness means nothing else than that we acquaint the world with its consciousness, that we wake the world up from the dream it is dreaming about itself, that we explain to the world the nature of its own actions.

Our slogan must be: a reform of consciousness not through dogmas, but through an analysis of mystic consciousness which is unclear to itself, be it religious or political. Only then will it be discovered that the world had long been in the possession of the dream about something which can be realised once the world will be conscious of it...It will then be ultimately discovered that mankind does not set out about a new task, but realises consciously its old one.[1]

The same kind of argument is voiced by Marx against Hegel in *The Holy Family*.[2]

In this context *praxis* means for Marx both a tool for changing the course of history and a criterion for historical evaluation. *Praxis* means man's conscious shaping of the changing historical conditions. Here Marx's revolutionary *praxis* differs from Young Hegelian criticism, which is, in a way, a ghost of Hegel's self-consciousness lacking real objects in an objective world. Against German criticism, whose objects are enclosed and entombed within its own consciousness, Marx praises French and English social criticism:

The criticism of the French and the English is not an abstract, preternatural personality outside mankind; it is the *real human activity* of

---

[1] *Werke*, I, 346.

[2] *The Holy Family*, p. 115. There is also another aspect in Hegel, which sees theory as a force shaping future development: 'I am becoming daily more and more convinced that theoretical endeavour attains much more in this world than practical work. Once the realm of imagination has been revolutionised, reality can no longer hold out' (*Ist das Reich der Vorstellung revolutioniert, so hält die Wirklichkeit nicht aus*; Hegel to Niethammer, 28 October 1808; *Briefe von und an Hegel*, ed. J. Hoffmeister [Hamburg, 1952], I, 253). Such a view does not limit theory to mere 'Nach-denken', and the existence of such a strain in Hegel's thought seems generally to have been overlooked. Cf. however, W. Kaufmann, *Hegel* (New York, 1965), especially ch. VI.

Unity of theory and praxis

individuals who are active members of society and who suffer, feel, think and act as human beings. That is why their criticism is at the same time practical, their communism a socialism which gives practical, concrete measures and in which they do not think but act; even more, it is the living real criticism of existing society, the discovery of the causes of 'the decay'.[1]

This comment again has a paradoxical edge. The criterion for Marx's preference of English and French socialism to German criticism derives from the German idealist philosophical tradition: the superiority of the *practical* aspects of the French and English thinkers results from Marx's *speculative* considerations about the revolutionary character of *praxis*. Thus the theoretical grounds for Marx's preference for English and French socialism do not imply his adopting their outlook. Basically Marx always remains sceptical about the speculative shallowness of these socialist views. What he seeks is the combination of the theoretical insights of German philosophy with the practical bent of French and English socialism, but the combination is defended on theoretical grounds drawn from German speculative philosophy.

The social context of *praxis* becomes self-evident if this line of argument is consistently followed: *praxis* revolutionizes existing reality through human action. This can be achieved by man's sociability and other-directedness. In a passage strongly reminiscent of Feuerbach's letter to Ruge quoted earlier in this chapter, Marx says in his *Introduction to a Contribution to the Critique of Hegel's Philosophy of Right*: 'Can Germany attain a practical activity *à la hauteur des principes?*...It is clear that the arm of criticism cannot replace the criticism of arms. Material force can only be overthrown by material force; but theory itself becomes a material force when it has seized the masses.'[2]

Another implication of this is that revolutionary *praxis* can realize theory only through the mediation of a passive element. This passive element is supplied by human needs that give rise to the possibility of realization. By themselves, needs do not cause revolutions—they make them possible: 'Revolutions need a *passive* element, a *material* basis. Theory is only realised in a people in so far as it fulfills the need of the people...Will theoretical needs be

---

[1] *The Holy Family*, p. 205.　　　[2] *Early Writings*, p. 52.

directly practical needs? It is not enough that thought should seek to realise itself; reality must also strive towards thought.'[1]

The historical role of the proletariat is a corollary of this argument which preserves the Hegelian categories precisely when the whole character of Hegelian philosophy is radically transformed. The specific significance of the proletariat lies in its material needs, capable of starting a universal process that will change reality totally. They are also the most radical and universal needs, because they are related to a mode of production universal by its very definition. This enables Marx to state that the head of this emancipation is philosophy while its heart is the proletariat.[2] When the situation of the proletariat becomes a paradigm for the human condition it gains theoretical significance and meaning. From this point of view it is immaterial whether the proletariat in 1843 Germany comprised a small fraction of the population or hardly existed. As Mehring once pointed out, Marx sometimes considers future projections as if they were present realities.[3]

Marx pursues this line of argument by stating that the proletariat knows no theoretical questions, only practical ones.[4] This seemingly philistine statement must be retranslated from Marx's specific use of the term 'practical' in order to elucidate its meaning in daily human parlance. Marx suggests here that the proletariat knows only problems related to external objects in the real world, and that the solution to these problems depends on this reality. Thus the circle is closed: after deducing the proletariat's significance from highly theoretical considerations, Marx can conclude that the proletariat faces only practical problems.

The significance of this practical orientation of the proletariat is discussed by Marx as early as 1844. In a recently discovered letter to Feuerbach, Marx advises his correspondent:

You should be present at one of the meetings of French workers so that you could believe the youthful freshness and nobility prevailing among

---

[1] *Early Writings*, pp. 53–4. The origins of the distinction between the activity of thought and the passivity of matter are to be found in Hegel's *Vernunft in der Geschichte*, ed. J. Hoffmeister (Hamburg, 1955), p. 55.
[2] *Early Writings*, p. 59; cf. *The German Ideology*, pp. 55 ff.
[3] F. Mehring, *Karl Marx* (London, 1936), pp. 118–19. Cf. G. Sorel, *Les polémiques sur l'interprétation du marxisme* (Paris, 1900), p. 22. [4] *The German Ideology*, p. 52.

these toil-worn people. The English proletarian also makes enormous progress, but he lacks the cultural character of the French. I should not forget the theoretical achievements of the German labourer in Switzerland, London and Paris. But the German labourer is still too much a hand-worker [sc. he does not use his head].

Anyway, it is among these 'barbarians' of our civilised society that history is preparing the practical element for the emancipation of man.[1]

To Marx, that workers associate means that they create new bonds and links among themselves, that they come out of the isolation and loneliness imposed on them by capitalist society. This association implies the development of a social nexus, practical in the sense that it has a real object in actuality, outside mere consciousness: it is not merely an abstract 'critical critique'. The association of workers in their meetings and groups is by itself a most revolutionary act, for it changes both reality and the workers themselves. This association creates other-directedness and mutuality, it enables the worker to become again a *Gemeinwesen*. The act and process of association, by changing the worker and his world, offer a glimpse into future society. This 'practical communism', says Marx in the 1844 *Manuscripts*, means that activity creates the conditions for the realization of its own aims:

When communist artisans [*Handwerker*] form associations, teaching and propaganda are their first aims. But their association itself creates a new need—the need for society—and what appeared to be a means has become an end. The most striking results of this practical development are to be seen when French socialist workers meet together. Smoking, eating and drinking are no longer simply means of bringing people together. Society, association, entertainment which also has society as its aim, is sufficient for them; the brotherhood of man is no empty phrase but a reality, and the nobility of man shines forth upon us from their toil-worn bodies.[2]

In another passage, also written in the same year, Marx underlines the objective nature of the practical activity of the proletariat. He points out that association of workers overcomes the gap between being and consciousness. The relevant passage in *The Holy Family* shows clearly how the traditional concepts of being and con-

[1] Marx to Feuerbach, 11 August 1844 (*Werke*, XXVII, 426).
[2] *Early Writings*, p. 176.

sciousness, *praxis* and theory, activity and change, etc., absorb
Marx's attention when he discusses the seemingly pedestrian and
prosaic problem of workers' association:

But these *massy* communist workers, employed, for instance, in the
Manchester or Lyons workshops, do not believe that '*pure thinking*' will
be able to argue away their industrial masters and their own practical
debasement. They are most painfully aware of the *difference* between
being and *thinking*, between *consciousness* and *life*. They know that property,
capital, money, wage-labour and the like are no ideal figments of the
brain but very practical, very objective sources of their self-alienation and
that they must be abolished in a practical, objective way for man to
become man not only in *thinking*, in *consciousness*, but in massy *being*, in
life.[1]

Here life activity and life aims are one, and these proletarian
associations are *in potentia* what future society will be in practice.
A new type of a human being who *needs* his fellow-men emerges;
sociability becomes an end in itself. Seeing in communism both the
form and the principle of human life enables Marx to postulate the
closing of the gap between being and consciousness. This also
explains Marx's persistent insistence on workers' association. It
does not have a narrowly political, nor a trade unionist significance:
it is the real constructive effort to create the social texture of future
human relations. Paradoxically, a similar insight into the nature
of socio-human development has appeared within the socialist
movement only in the Israeli *kibbutzim*, whose political climate and
ideological background have been totally different. But they too
have perceived that the modes and forms of present social organization will determine the structure of future society.

The same idea can be found in the *Communist Manifesto*, though
the language employed is somewhat different. Marx points out the
obvious weakness of existing proletarian associations, but at the
same time discusses their importance in uniting the subjective
aspect of consciousness with the objective aspect of social conditions and organization. This combination gives rise to the practical
power inherent in proletarian consciousness as a practical energy
directed against the external objective world.[2]

[1] *The Holy Family*, p. 73.   [2] *Selected Works*, I, 41–4.

Unity of theory and praxis

We have already noted that Marx praised English and French socialism for their practical bent. But Marx is aware that this by itself will not suffice. The Silesian weavers' revolt of 1844, however, signified to Marx (at least at its outbreak) a new phase in the consciousness and organization of the working class. Marx arrived at this conclusion not becuase he thought that revolts of this kind have any chance to succeed, nor because he mistook the declining home industries of Silesia for a paradigm of modern industrial conditions, but because here the workers' explicit consciousness of their own living conditions was transformed into the language of social action: 'The Silesian revolt *starts* with what the French and English workers' revolt end: with the consciousness about the essence of the proletariat.'[1]

Revolutionary *praxis* has thus a dialectical aspect. Objectively, it is the organization of the conditions leading towards ultimate human emancipation. Subjectively it is the self-change the proletariat achieves by its self-discovery through organization. Through its organization the proletariat prepares the conditions for its self-emancipation. Organization and association, even considered apart from their immediate aims, constitute a crucial phase in the liberation of the workers. They change the worker, his way of life, his consciousness of himself and his society. They force him into contact with his fellow-workers, suggest to him that his fate is not a subjective, particular and contingent affair but part of a universal scheme of reality. They make him see in his fellow-proletarians not competitors for work and bread but brothers in suffering and ultimate victory, not means but co-equal ends. The end-results of the revolution are thus historically formed and determined during and by its occurence. Within this context the seemingly all-important question about the inevitability of the revolution loses its meaning. The mechanistic and determinist view, which characterized orthodox Marxism under the impact of Engels' later writings, suggested the

[1] *Vorwärts*, 10 August 1844 (*Werke*, I, 404). Marx goes on to say: 'One has to admit that the German proletariat is the theoretician of the European proletariat, just as the English proletariat is its political economist and the French proletariat is its politician. One has also to admit that Germany has a classical calling for the social revolution, just as it is incapable of a political one...Only in socialism can a philosophical nation find its adequate *praxis*, just as it can find only in the proletariat its active element of liberation' (p. 405).

143

necessary breaking out of the revolution because of the internal contradictions of capitalist economy. Such a view, considering only the objective side of historical development and not its subjective elements, is open to all of Marx's criticism in his *Theses on Feuerbach*. Such a view ultimately sees in man and in human will only an object of external circumstances and, *mutatis mutandis*, of political manipulation. Both the cruelty and harshness of Bolshevism and the intellectual wastelands of Social Democracy grow directly from this mechanistic twist Engels gave to Marxism, emasculating its specific intellectual achievement.

For Marx the question of the inevitability of the revolution is a tautology. Since the revolution needs a conscious urge and motor in the form of revolutionary *praxis* (a self-change in the proletarian *pari passu* with his striving for the revolutionary goal) the dilemma of determinism versus voluntarism is transcended by the dialectical nature of this revolutionary consciousness. Never does Marx guarantee the success of the revolution in advance or take it for granted. He only indicates its possibilities historically. If a revolutionary consciousness exists, then the revolution is bound to happen. The activist and practical elements of this consciousness imply that circumstances will change with the self-change of the proletariat. In other words, under these conditions the revolution is already taking place. If, on the other hand, such a consciousness is lacking, then the revolution lacks its main impulse and is stillborn. If the proletariat has self-consciousness, it will sustain the revolution. Its self-consciousness is already a major component of the revolutionary situation. If, however, the proletariat is still unaware of its own historical position, if it does not possess an adequate world view, then the objective conditions by themselves will not create the revolution until and unless the proletariat grasps that by shaping its own view of the world it also changes it.[1]

That objective conditions alone are not enough is evident from one of Marx's remarks in his polemic against the Bakuninists.[2] It is

---

[1] This dialectical aspect has not been grasped even by the Austro-Marxists; v. Max Adler, 'Was ist Notwendigkeit der Entwicklung', *Der Kampf* (Vienna, 1915), p. 175. Cf. A. G. Meyer, *Marxism—The Unity of Theory and Practice* (Cambridge, Mass., 1954), pp. 91–100.
[2] *Recueil*, II, 135.

Unity of theory and praxis

also Marx's justification for the existence of the International. The International, he says, should seek to organize the workers in order to change them and bring out their class-consciousness through their own activities. These theoretical considerations are expressed very forcefully, though polemically, in Marx's detailed letter of 1871 to Friedrich Bolte, Secretary of the American Federal Council of the International. The confrontation between secterianism and universalism, so one-sidedly elaborated here by Marx, should none the less be understood within the indicated general theoretical context of this argument:

The *International* was founded in order to replace the socialist or semi-socialist sects by a real organisation of the working class for struggle. The original Statutes and the Inaugural Address show this at a glance. On the other hand, the International could not have maintained itself if the course of history had not already smashed sectarianism. The development of socialist sectarianism and that of the real labour movement always stand in reverse ratio to each other. So long as the sects are justified (historically), the working class is not yet ripe for an independent historical movement. As soon as it has attained this maturity all sects are essentially reactionary...

The political movement of the working class has, of course, as its final object the conquest of political power for this class, and this requires, of course, a previous organisation of the working class developed up to a certain point, which itself arises from its economic struggles.

But on the other hand, every movement in which the working class comes out as a *class* against the ruling classes and tries to coerce them by pressure from without is a political movement. For instance, the attempt in a particular factory, or even in a particular trade, to force a shorter working day out of the individual capitalists by strikes, etc., is a purely economic movement. The movement to force through an eight-hour *law*, etc., however, is a *political* movement. And in this way, out of the separate economic movements of the workers there grows up everywhere a *political* movement, that is to say a movement of the *class*, with the object of achieving its interests in a general form, in a form possessing generally, socially coercive force. Though these movements presuppose a certain degree of previous organisation, they are in turn equally a means of developing this organisation.[1]

[1] Marx to Bolte, 23 November 1871 (Marx/Engels, *Letters to Americans* [New York, 1953], pp. 90, 93-4).

145

Praxis and revolution

That the economic struggles, i.e. trade union activities, strikes, etc., create out of their own dialectics the political emergence of the proletariat is also at the centre of the resolution accepted in September 1871 by the London Conference of the International. The resolution, drafted by Marx, says under Title 9:

The proletariat cannot act against the collective force of the property-holding classes unless it constitutes itself as a distinct political party, opposed to all political parties formed by the propertied classes.

This constitution of the proletariat as a political party is indispensable for ensuring the victory of the social revolution and its final aim: *the abolition of classes.*

The association of labour forces already achieved through economic struggle should also serve to help this class in its fight against the political power of its exploiters.

The Conference reminds members of the International that in the militant stage of the working class, its economic movement and its political actions are indispensibly united.[1]

A remarkable continuity exists in Marx's attitude to working-class organizations. He sees both the *League of Communists* and the *International* as foci for the organization of proletarian self-consciousness through working-class association. In his *Herr Vogt* (1860) Marx points out that the *League of Communists* differed basically from all conspiratorial associations in that it wanted to give the working class a consciousness about itself, not to draw it into plots and coups. Marx points out that the *League's* branches established libraries, organized lectures and schooling and tried to create a class out of the miserable rabble created by European industrialization. The underground nature of the *League* resulted not from its own aims, but from the police situation on the continent. The *League* shed its underground habits and came out into the open when it moved its main seat to London after the débâcle of 1848.[2] Friedrich Lessner, one

---

[1] *Recueil*, II, 236. Marx thus sanctions trade union activities not on their own merit, but because they contribute towards the creation of the political tools necessary for the ultimate victory of the proletariat (cf. *Letters to Kugelmann*, pp. 65–6). This idea is also at the root of Marx's main argument in 1847 against Proudhon's condemnation of trade union activities. The economic conditions create the working class objectively; but it will be created subjectively only by its own activities in trade unions, associations, etc. (*The Poverty of Philosophy*, pp. 194–7).

[2] *Werke*, XIV, 438–9.

of the *League's* old-timers, says in his memoirs that the reorganiza-
tion in 1847 of the *League of the Just* into the *League of Communists*
under Marx's influence eliminated the conspiratorial element.[1]
Nicolaevsky's studies also show that during 1848 Marx virtually dis-
banded the *League* because of Jacobin 'ultra-revolutionary' tendencies.[2] It hardly functioned at all in 1848, was revitalized later in
London by Schapper and Moll, and Marx's activity in Cologne
at that time did not rely on any organization based on the *League*.
Nothing could be more different from Lenin's concept of a revolutionary party than Marx's view of the role of the *League* and the
International. The final split in the *League* in 1850 centred on
Marx's view of the *League* as a basis for long-range social change and
not as the headquarters of a short-sighted, and short-lived, conspiracy.

An interesting insight into the way Marx looked at the application of revolutionary *praxis* to England can be gained from his letter
to the Chartist Congress of 1854 in Manchester:

It is the working millions of Great Britain who first have laid down the
real basis of a new society—modern industry, which transformed the
destructive agencies of nature into the productive power of man. The
English working-classes, with invincible energy, by the sweat of their
brows and brains, have called into life the material means of ennobling
labour itself, and of multiplying its fruits to such a degree as to make
general abundance possible.

By creating the inexhaustible productive powers of modern industry
they have fulfilled the first condition of the emancipation of Labour...

The labouring classes have conquered nature; they have now to
conquer man. To succeed in this attempt they do not want strength, but
the organisation of their strength, organisation of the labouring classes on
a national scale.[3]

Marx succinctly points to the difference between such a view of
social action and the traditional conspiratorial attitude when he
writes in 1870 that:

the members of the *International* in France proved to the French government what is the difference between a conspiratorial group and a real

---

[1] F. Lessner, 'Before 1848 and After', in *Reminiscences about Marx and Engels* (Moscow,
n.d.), p. 152.
[2] B. Nicolaevsky and O. Maenchen-Helfen, *Karl Marx, Man and Fighter* (London,
1936), pp. 153–4; *Karl und Jenny Marx* (Berlin, 1933), Appendix.
[3] *On Britain*, p. 417.

147

working-class association. For the police had just arrested all the members of the committees in Paris, Lyons, Rouen and Marseilles—and immediately a double number of committees announce themselves in all the newspapers as the more obstinate continuators of the arrested members.[1]

The theoretical background to this view is, of course, to be found in Theses IX–XI on Feuerbach. Marx argues that all epistemological theories hitherto propounded either held that ultimate reality is impenetrable to human cognition, or suggested that consciousness is a mere reflection of reality. Both theories, i.e. classical idealism and classical materialism, could not therefore overcome the gap between subject and object. Lukács has rightly pointed out that Marx's major contribution to this discussion was to see in the revolutionary *praxis* of the proletariat a new form of consciousness. He saw a consciousness that implies an immediate change of reality within which the subject is ultimately identical with the object. When the worker comprehends that under capitalist production he is degraded to the status of a mere object, of a commodity, he ceases to be a commodity, an object, and becomes a subject. Reaching an adequate comprehension of the world changes the world itself most radically.[2] It is, of course, an open question whether only the proletariat qualifies for this kind of new epistemology, and Marx never satisfactorily discussed this.

According to Marx, the worker's self-definition and his self-knowledge analyse the objective conditions within which he lives. Conversely, a change in these conditions is, of course, a change in the human beings that comprise the proletariat. History has always grown out of human endeavour, but according to Marx this relationship has not been adequately grasped till now. Therefore man has been enslaved by the foreign powers and objects created by his practical activities. Only now can man recognize the world as his province and claim it for himself, understanding that 'man is not an abstract being, squatting outside the world. Man is the human world,

---

[1] Marx to Engels, 18 May 1870 (*Briefwechsel*, IV, 396). At a meeting in 1871 commemorating the seventh anniversary of the International Marx said similarly: 'The International did not propose any new belief. Its aim was to organise the forces of labour and to connect and integrate the different movements of the workers' (*Werke*, XVII, 432).

[2] Lukács, *Geschichte und Klassenbewusstsein*, p. 82.

Unity of theory and praxis

the state, society'.[1] Revolutionary *praxis* is an active and social epistemology; the unity of theory and practice emancipates man from the contemplative, alienated existence that was forced on him. This view of *praxis* also enables Marx to judge the adequacy of other socialist theories. The major defect of so-called 'utopian' socialism lies in its epistemological shortcomings. This socialism, according to Marx, must still envision future society because it has not yet grasped that, because of such an attitude, the future will always elude it. Revolutionary socialism, however, is different: 'But in the measure that history moves forward, and with it the struggle of the proletariat assumes clearer outlines, they no longer need to seek science in their minds; they have only to take note of what is happening before their eyes and to become its mouthpiece.'[2]

The revolution thus expresses the radical need to subject the conditions of life to the conscious power of man who had created them. It also integrates man with the circumstances of his life through their conscious direction and mastery. Hegel's theory of identity receives an eschatological dimension, but this identity is not expressed any more through consciousness but through action that creates objects for consciousness.

The understanding of existing reality is therefore a necessary condition for the possibility of revolutionizing it. As will be set out in the next chapter, only an understanding of the internal mechanism of capitalism makes the transition to socialism possible. Hence a theoretical analysis of the structure of the capitalist economy is undoubtedly the revolutionary praxis *par excellence*. The cycle is closed.

---

[1] *Early Writings*, p. 43.
[2] *The Poverty of Philosophy*, p. 140. Cf. *Communist Manifesto, Selected Works*, I, 61–2. It can, however, be argued that much as this criticism may apply to most of the so-called 'utopian' socialists, it does not really come to grips with the Saint-Simonian analysis and vision of history.

6

THE REVOLUTIONARY DIALECTICS
OF CAPITALIST SOCIETY

HISTORICAL ORIGINS AND THEORETICAL MODELS

Marx's decision to devote most of his life to a systematic study of capitalism, contenting himself with occasional remarks about the structure of socialist society, can be explained by methodological considerations. As 'utopian' socialism, because of its failure to grasp the nature of existing reality, also cannot come to grips with the future, so Marx's claim to understand the present gives him a clue to the ultimate trends of history operating within capitalist society. Utopianism develops 'scientific' theories, which exist 'only in the head of the thinker', because it does not have reality as its object.[1] In the *Critique of the Gotha Programme* Marx refers to the same epistemological argument when saying that he does not deal with an *a priori* concept of communism, but with communist society 'as it has just emerged after prolonged birth pangs from capitalist society'.[2]

Marx's approach to communism demonstrates his belief that the crystallization of socialist forms of society cannot be achieved through a deterministic teleology, but grows out of the causal analysis of existing social forces. If communism cannot be understood otherwise than by its emergence from capitalist society, then the study of capitalism provides the best means to comprehend the development that will ultimately bring communism about. Moreover the emergence of communism from the womb of capitalist society draws attention to the dialectical relationship between the two societies. The possibility for a development in the direction of communism thus depends on a prior development of capitalism. As will be shown later in this chapter, communism is nothing else than the dialectical abolition (*Aufhebung*) of capitalism, postulating the realization of those hidden potentialities which could not have been historically realized under the limiting conditions of capitalism.

---

[1] *The German Ideology*, pp. 501-3.
[2] *Selected Works*, II, 23-4.

Historical origins and theoretical models

Capitalism thus creates urges that it cannot itself satisfy and it is in this sense that Marx refers to its digging its own grave.

Therefore Marx knows no short cuts to socialism. True, he sometimes hesitates when asked to name the country that will be the first to experience a socialist revolution. Twice at least Marx seems to have been inclined to suggest that the revolution will break out first in countries with less developed industrial structures, and not in the most highly industrialized areas. In 1847, in the *Communist Manifesto*, Marx envisages the revolution breaking out first in still under-developed Germany, whereas in 1882, in the Preface to the Russian edition of the *Manifesto*, he mentions the possibility that world revolution may be sparked off by a revolution in Russia that will become 'a signal for a proletarian revolution in the West'.[1] But even in these two instances Marx chooses the more under-developed countries not because they are not capitalistic at all (in such a case, of course, the term 'proletarian revolution' would have no meaning), but because he feels that the late development of capitalism in these countries will promote two necessary processes simultaneously: a rapid development of a sophisticated capitalism and the concurrent intensive emergence of a proletariat. If this double pressure is too heavy, a society thus challenged may not be able to withstand it.

This also explains Marx's reiterated insistence that his historical account of the genesis of capitalism in the West in *Das Kapital* should not be read as a universal law of development. In an unpublished letter to the Russian journal *Otechestvenniye Zapiski*, published in Geneva, Marx insists in 1877 that:

The chapter on primitive accumulation does not pretend to do more than trace the path by which, in Western Europe, the capitalist order of economy emerged from the womb of the feudal order of economy.

But that is too little for my critic. He feels he absolutely must metamorphose my historical sketch of the genesis of capitalism in Western Europe into a historico-philosophic theory of the general path every people is fated to tread, whatever the historical circumstances in which it

[1] *Ibid.* 1, 65; *ibid.* p. 24. In the Preface to the Russian edition of the *Manifesto* Marx explicitly refers to a 'rapidly developing capitalist swindle and bourgeois landed property just beginning to develop' in Russia (p. 23). Cf. Marx's 'Afterword' to the second German edition of *Das Kapital* (1873), *Capital*, 1, 15–16.

finds itself, in order that it may ultimately arrive at the form of economy which ensures, together with the greatest expansion of the productive powers of social labour, the most complete development of man. But I beg his pardon. He is both honouring and shaming me too much. Let us take an example.

In several parts of *Capital* I alluded to the fate which overtook the plebeians of ancient Rome. They were originally free peasants, each cultivating his piece of land on his own account. In the course of Roman history they were expropriated. The same movement which divorced them from their means of production and subsistence involved the formation not only of big landed property, but also of big money capital. And so one fine morning there were to be found on the one hand free men, stripped of anything except their labour power, and on the other, in order to exploit this labour, those who held all the acquired wealth in their possession. What happened? The Roman proletarians became not wage labourers, but a *mob* of do-nothings more abject than the former 'poor whites' in the South of the United States, and alongside of them there developed a mode of production which was not capitalist but based on slavery. Thus events strikingly analogous but taking place in different historical surroundings led to totally different results. By studying each of these forms of evolution separately and then comparing them one can easily find the clue to this phenomenon, but one will never arrive there by using as one's master key a general historico-philosophical theory, the supreme virtue of which consists in being super-historical.[1]

Marx thus faces a severe dilemma every time he discusses the possibilities of socialist growth in countries which have not undergone full-fledged industrialization and capitalist transformation. If the possibility of a socialist realization depends on a prior development of capitalism, then the non-existence of a capitalist tradition in any given society precludes, *prima facie*, the possibility of socialist development. To envisage socialism in these countries, one must first enquire whether alternative sources of societal behaviour may contribute to it. Therefore Marx is interested in the Russian village commune (*mir*) not on historical grounds, but for its present, efficacious existence. Marx's hesitations about the potentialities of a

[1] *Selected Correspondence*, pp. 378–9. Cf. Marx's letter to Vera Zasulitch, 8 March 1881 (*ibid.* p. 412), where he says: 'Hence the "historical inevitability" of this movement is expressly limited to the countries of Western Europe.' See R. Kindersley, *The First Russian Revisionists* (Oxford, 1962), pp. 10–16, 237–8.

Historical origins and theoretical models

Russian socialism based on the *mir* are related to the advanced stage of decay this form of common ownership suffered from capitalist development in Russia. For Marx, it is completely irrelevant that village communism may once have existed in Russia; the question is not whether village communism can be resuscitated (it cannot, according to Marx: nothing can), but whether it still exists in the present and how strong it really is. Therefore Marx's letter to Vera Zasulitch and the Preface to the Russian edition of the *Manifesto* do not, after all, endorse the Populist view of the Russian way to socialism. For the Populists, the village commune, even if it no longer exists, should be reconstituted. Marx feels that if the *mir* existed only in the 'book of Haxthausen', then it is defunct, and no romantic idealization will help.[1]

The importance of capitalism for an adequate understanding of socialism is considered by Marx both historically and speculatively. The industrial revolution in its technological aspects does not really hold the centre of Marx's interest. Here as elsewhere the difference between Marx and Engels is significant and striking. One need only compare the highly technologically oriented draft of the *Manifesto*, written by Engels in 1847, and posthumously published as *Grundsätze des Kommunismus*, with Marx's final version of the *Manifesto*, in which technology is a mere side issue.[2] Marx is interested in technology only because he sees in it the most consequential development of man's relation to his world-shaping capacity. Hence he sees capitalism itself as a highly developed stage in the unfolding of man's creative powers—a speculative element missing from Engels' thought. Marx sees of course that the development of machinery has been the main technological achievement of the industrial revolution. But technology is just an expression of man's creative power. This power, including the discovery and development of machinery, would have never come into being had it not been caused by a human need that could have developed only under specific historical circumstances, and had it not realized itself because at

[1] Cf. the various drafts of Marx's letter to Vera Zasulitch (*Marx-Engels-Archiv*, I, 318–41). This is also Marx's view in his letter to *Otechestvenniye Zapiski* (*Selected Correspondence*, p. 377): 'What is my complaint against this writer there? That he discovered the Russian commune not in Russia but in the book of Haxthausen.'
[2] *Grundsätze des Kommunismus*, *Werke*, IV, 363–80.

that point in history favourable conditions made its realization possible.

Thus the historical genesis of capitalism must be explained by a study of the causes which enabled these historical human needs to fulfil themselves. For this reason, Marx, in his account of the historical development of capitalism, emphasizes not the development of machinery but the growth of commodity demand in the later Middle Ages. Demand grew in the wake of an expansion in international trade, was further developed and enhanced by the discovery of new trade routes and new continents and finally caused the development of machinery as the only effective way to ensure a parallel growth in production beyond what man's mere physical power could produce without the mediation of machinery.[1]

Such an explanation still begs the question. The capacity of rising demand to realize itself through the application of man's creative potentialities as manifested in technology still depended on certain prior social circumstances. After all, this was not the first time that demand as satisfied by existing productive forces outgrew supply. It was, however, the first time that the satisfaction of this rising demand could occur through technological innovation, and technological innovation became possible due to the existence of capital accumulation. Thus the industrial revolution for Marx is not the beginning of the capitalist process, but rather its culmination. Capitalism *precedes* industrialization. Industrialization occurs through primary accumulation of capital, and this again occurs under specific circumstances which need study. The question of the origins of capitalism becomes the question of the *conditions which gave rise to primary accumulation and facilitated it*. Hence the origins of capitalism cannot be reduced to a discussion of technological change. Engels, on the other hand, in his *Grundsätze des Kommunismus* hardly sees anything else.

The question of the origins of capitalism has become a search for the elements which encouraged the accumulation of capital at the close of the Middle Ages. Marx answers this most explicitly in a long letter to Engels in 1854. Here he says that what preceded the

[1] *The Poverty of Philosophy*, pp. 153–6; *The Communist Manifesto, Selected Works*, I, 34–6; *Capital*, I, 713 ff.

industrial revolution and made it possible was a socio-political revolution in late medieval Europe: the emergence of a civil society, *bürgerliche Gesellschaft*, i.e. an autonomous sphere of economic activity, unimpeded by political and religious restrictions. The existence of such a sphere of civil society implies the existence of a legitimate social behaviour according to which people are motivated by considerations emancipated from the political and community-oriented demands inherent in the feudal system. Marx ascribes the emergence of civil society to the communal movement of the late Middle Ages, which emancipated the urban corporations and communes from their dependence on the political arrangements of the feudal structure. According to Marx, the communal movement created a sphere of autonomous economic activity, unrestricted by political and religious tutelage which might limit its freedom of economic choice. The struggle of the burghers' communal movement sought to free property from the ethical and social limitations imposed on it by the feudal nexus which saw all property as a trust. It encumbered every object of property with numerous parallel and overlapping claims, making intensive economic activity almost impossible and severely limiting the growth of a market economy. Only the late medieval town developed, in the wake of the communal movement, a concept of property free from feudal, i.e. political and community-oriented, limitations. Not only did this development justify morally the accumulation of property; it also separated the political sphere from the economic and gave rise to legal and institutional arrangements that made the accumulation of capital possible and socially acceptable. Marx further points out that the term *.capitalia* appears for the first time in connection with the communal movement. He also stresses the profoundly revolutionary character of this movement of urban emancipation *vis-à-vis* the feudal order.[1] In a later letter, addressed to Lassalle, Marx supplements these remarks by saying that the final acknowledgment of the demands raised by the communal movement was institutionalized

---

[1] Marx to Engels, 27 July 1854 (*Selected Correspondence*, pp. 105–8). Marx's theory very clearly distinguishes between 'civil society' (*bürgerliche Gesellschaft*) as a sphere of economic activity unlimited by political considerations, and *bourgeoisie* as a social class. In *The Holy Family* Marx made the same distinction when he said (p. 165) that the principle of civil society is historically realized through the *bourgeoisie*.

Revolutionary dialectics of capitalist society

in England with the Settlement of 1660, and later in the Glorious Revolution, when the political limitations on property were abolished and the freedom of inheritance finally established.[1]

According to Marx, the necessary conditions for the emergence of capitalism include the commercialization of land and agriculture.[2] In societies where commercialization of land did not occur, the growth of capitalism has been severely impeded. Countries which did not evolve a civil society were unable to develop on capitalist lines. This failure is most conspicuous in those countries whose political power and the mineral resources at their command should have enabled them to achieve a high degree of capital accumulation. But the lack of the necessary antecedent social orientations meant that natural wealth was not transformed into capital. Not natural wealth itself but its social utilization is the crucial point. Portugal is Marx's most striking example. Portugal did not experience a communal movement and its cities never really emancipated themselves. The conditions for the growth of civil society never emerged. Consequently Portugal did not experience the development of a capitalist mode of production because the preliminary social conditions necessary for the accumulation of capital were lacking.[3]

It is outside the scope of this discussion to enquire whether Marx's analysis can be regarded as the conclusive account of the emergence of capitalism. Certainly contemporary research on this subject can draw on material immensely more variegated than anything available to Marx. It can, consequently, approach the problem with concepts and techniques far more sophisticated. But Marx's approach is none the less informative on at least two counts.

First, this discussion paradoxically suggests that Marx makes the future development of socialism depend not only on a prior development of capitalism, but also on an infra-structure dependent upon medieval feudal society which made the emergence of capitalism itself possible. Thus from an unusual angle European history is seen by Marx as a totality. Consequently, Marx was sceptical about the chances of socialism in countries which have not experienced feudalism.

[1] Marx to Lassalle, 11 June 1861 (*Werke*, XXX, 607).
[2] *Economic-Philosophical Manuscripts, Early Writings*, pp. 110–19, 140–4; *Capital*, I, 717–33. 　　　　　　　　　　　　　　　　[3] *Capital*, III, 327.

Historical origins and theoretical models

Secondly, Marx's account of the emergence of capitalism suggests that the genesis of capitalist society is not determined by the existence of 'productive forces' as mere naturalistic data. The Marxian concept of 'productive forces' includes the historical conditions which crystallize certain material data. Thus the structure of the late medieval town cannot be reduced to its material components. It must include those elements of socio-economic behaviour which made the utilization of the material component possible. Thus Marx's method is not far removed from Max Weber's thoughts on this subject. It would be false to suggest (as has frequently been done) that, whereas Marx reduced everything to material conditions of production, Weber thought that social consciousness determined social change. In this case both Marx and Weber look for the social consciousness which made primary accumulation and growth possible by destroying the ecclesiastical-cum-feudal system of values which stifled them. The difference between the two theories lies in their versions of the origins of this new consciousness. Whereas Weber made this transformation of social consciousness dependent on Protestantism, and Calvinism in particular, Marx traces its origin to the urban communal movement. *Prima facie*, Marx's theory seems to give more satisfactory answers to at least some of Weber's *lacunae* (Antwerp, for example), though the Italian commercial republics pose the same difficulties for Marx as for Weber.

This leads to a crucial question of method, raised by Max Weber himself in his discussion of Marx's methodology. Reading Marx sometimes raises the question whether Marx describes capitalism as a socio-economic structure already functioning in some countries, or whether he deals with a model of capitalism, an 'ideal type' which serves as a criterion for the form of economic organization prevalent in most Western countries. Weber criticizes Marx for using 'capitalism' as an historical reality, without limiting it to a category of historical explanation. If Weber is right, Marx is then guilty of hypostasis. Since this would contradict Marx's own critique of Proudhon's categories and of idealist philosophy in general, it would constitute a serious defect in Marx's methodological apparatus.[1]

[1] M. Weber, 'Die "Objektivität" sozialwissenschaftlicher und sozialpolitischer Erkenntnisse', *Archiv für Sozialwissenschaft und Sozialpolitik*, XIX (1904), 22–87.

Revolutionary dialectics of capitalist society

But a closer scrutiny of Marx's approach yields a more complex and sophisticated attitude than that attributed to him by Weber. Although Marx deals with capitalism as both a theoretical model and an historical reality, it can be shown that this view is not an hypostasis. Marx's attitude toward classical political economy is a case in point. Marx does not see the theories of political economy as a mere reflection of nineteenth-century economic realities. We have already seen that generally he does not think such a mirror-like reflection is epistemologically possible. For Marx, classical political economy does not describe existing economic conditions, but outlines and anticipates a *potentiality*, a possible organizing principle. Marx argues that Ricardo's theory does not adequately describe existing reality. As a postulate, he says, it is a *prognosis* of future developments, and this is its methodological weakness. It claims universal validity in relation to existing economic conditions, but remains by nature prescriptive, posing demands, suggesting the optimum alternative, but never really describing reality itself.[1] If so, then Marx's polemic against this doctrine is not a quarrel with reality but a dissent from a possible prognosis of the future developments of this reality. *Prima facie* there is no ulterior reason for supposing Ricardo's prognosis more adequate than Marx's. Moreover, in his polemic writings Marx starts from the premise that the theories of political economy must be treated as though their postulates have been historically realized and accepted. This enables Marx to claim in *The German Ideology* that the proletariat constitutes the majority of the population,[2] while it is clear that this is not so. Provided, however, that the prognosis of political economy is correct the future development of capitalism *will* lead to a situation in which the proletariat will be in a majority. Similarly, the extreme class polarization theory in *The Communist Manifesto* cannot justifiably claim to be an adequate description of existing conditions; it can, however, be considered a fair account of processes to come if future developments follow the prognosis of classical political economy.[3] If that is so, Marx can safely underline in *The Civil War in France*

---

[1] Cf. the draft of Marx's speech at the Free Trade Congress of Brussels, 1847, printed in *Werke*, IV, 305–8. Marx never delivered the speech at the Congress, but it was published by Engels in *The Northern Star* of 9 October 1847.
[2] *The German Ideology*, pp. 85–6.   [3] *Selected Works*, I, 38 f.

the preponderant strength of the petty-bourgeoisie, which should have been 'eroded' long ago according to the postulates of the *Manifesto*. The one is an historical account, the other an historical prognosis based on political economy. If the theory of classical political economy is tantamount to 'capitalism', it always remains a model for Marx, never a reality.

Nevertheless, at least one passage seems to imply that Marx regards capitalism not as a model but as existing reality. In his Preface to the first edition of *Das Kapital* (1867), Marx writes: 'In this work I have to examine the capitalist mode of production and the conditions of production and exchange corresponding to that mode. Up to the present, their classical ground is England...The country that is more developed industrially only shows to the less developed the image of its own future.'[1]

In so far as Marx regards capitalism as the future form of economic organization for 'less developed' countries (Germany in this case), he uses the term 'capitalism' as a theoretical model. Not so, however, when he says that England is the homestead of realized capitalism. Here one feels that Weber's objection to Marx's hypostatic use of the term is valid.

A closer look at the passage in question points in another direction. In the Preface to *Das Kapital* Marx does present England as the *existing* historical model of capitalism, but the whole Preface traces the politico-economic mechanisms which change capitalism internally in England through the introduction into the economic system of elements beyond capitalism and opposed to *laissez faire*. These elements subvert the purity of 'ideal-type' economic liberalism and capitalism and channel the development of capitalist society into other forms of social and economic organization. Marx recounts in some detail (and with much relish) these post-capitalistic elements: factory laws, which set a legal limit on the working day and thus undoubtedly infringe on the *laissez faire* model of freedom of contract; royal commissions on sanitation and housing, which bring the state into direct involvement with some aspects of economic activity. All of these elements introduce into the free market economy aspects of community-oriented considerations, and con-

[1] *Capital*, I, 8–9.

159

tribute further to social change. Summarizing the impact of these changes on the structure of capitalist society, Marx says in the Preface to *Das Kapital*: 'Let us not deceive ourselves on this. . . In England the process of social upheaval [*Umwälzungsprozess*] is palpable. When it has reached a certain point, it must react on the Continent.'[1]

Historically, Marx is thus fully aware that British factory legislation infringes on the capitalist model and changes capitalism from within. Methodologically, this passage suggests that Weber might not have grasped the dialectical overtones of Marx's use of the term capitalism. England, the country of the realized model, has already moved beyond the model. The model cannot ultimately exist as an historical reality. Since all historical reality is always in a process of becoming, the model is either a criterion for a reality developing towards it—or, if adequacy between model and reality is maximized, internal circumstances have given rise to a reality that has overtaken the model and moved farther and farther away from it.

The dialectical point is that this emergence of newer forms is derived from the immanent logic of the initial premises of the model itself. Again, *Aufhebung*, meaning both realization and overcoming, here as elsewhere in Marx's thought provides the key to the understanding of Marx's meaning. England, having realized the capitalist model has moved already beyond the point at which the model can serve as an adequate explication of its mode of production. This *List der Vernunft* makes the very act of writing *Das Kapital* an index to the decomposition of capitalist society. That such a treatise could be written not as a postulate of political economy but as a description of the working of a capitalist system means that historical reality has already transcended the capitalist model and is approaching new shores. The owl of Minerva, after all, spreads its wings only with the setting of dusk.

That reality is being recognized clearly indicates that it is being changed, not least by the act of cognition itself. For this reason Marx sees, even before 1848, the Repeal of the Corn Laws as a Pyrrhic victory for the bourgeoisie.[2] Repeal abolished the last mercantilistic,

---

[1] *Capital*, 1, 9. The standard English translation has rendered *Umwälzungsprozess* as 'social disintegration', which is really quite unacceptable.

[2] This is the general tone of the congratulatory address of the German Communist society in Brussels, drafted by Marx and sent on 7 July 1846, to Feargus O'Connor

pre-capitalist encumbrance on the free play of market-economy. Now the way was open to an unfettered expansion of capitalism. Such a development could not but lead to the intensive emergence of the proletariat and the imposition of novel, revolutionary limitations on the economic activity of the market. This is what Marx seems to have had in mind in his Preface to *A Contribution to the Critique of Political Economy* when he said that no social order ever perishes before all the productive forces for which it has room have developed. The Repeal of the Corn Laws was the high tide of the bourgeoisie's influence on the affairs of state. The immediate results of Repeal were beneficial to the bourgeoisie and detrimental to the workers; none the less Marx welcomes it, for only now will economic activity be regulated according to the capitalist free market model. Only now will it develop those forces that will change it from the inside. So long as any limits on the free functioning of the model exist, it cannot develop towards change. For this reason Marx heartily welcomed the Repeal of the Corn Laws while most other socialists bitterly resented it.

Marx reiterates this view in the *Inaugural Address* of the International (1864). Here he sees the Ten Hours Bill enacted in the meantime as definite proof that capitalism is changing internally. Strictly speaking, for Marx the heyday of unfettered capitalism, when economic activity, at least in England, was not encumbered by any limitation at all, pre- or post-capitalist, was short: from the Repeal of the Corn Laws to the introduction of the Ten Hours Bill.[1] In the *Inaugural Address* Marx goes to some length to show that the bourgeois economists who objected to the Ten Hours Bill on *laissez faire* ground understood only too well that the Bill was a severe blow to the concept of a free market economy. Dialectically, Marx sees the Ten Hours Bill as a direct outcome of the Repeal of the Corn Laws. Only after external hindrances were abolished, could capitalism develop towards internal change.

If this systematically proves that the road to socialist development lies within capitalist society itself, then the analysis of capitalism as

on his winning Nottingham against J. C. Hobhouse (*Werke*, IV, 24); see also Marx's speech of 1847 on Free Trade, as well as his lecture to the Democratic Association of Brussels in January 1848 (*ibid*. pp. 444–58). Cf. *The Class Struggle in France, Selected Works*, I, 211.   [1] *Selected Works*, I, 382.

a concept and of the historical phenomena connected with it is a *conditio sine qua non* for understanding the possibilities of socialist growth. The following discussion will cull from Marx's numerous writings on this subject only those aspects that point to Marx's view that the *differentia specifica* of capitalism significantly facilitate the possibility of development toward socialism.

THE UNIVERSALITY OF CAPITALISM

Three aspects characterize capitalism according to Marx: the rationalization of the world, the rationalization of human action and the universalization of inter-human contact. The similarities between this view and Weber's 'ideal type' of capitalism have already been pointed out, as have also been the parallels between some aspects of Marx's view on alienation and the 'this-wordly *askesis*' implied, according to Weber, in the capitalist ethos.[1]

The rationalization of the world and the rationalization of human action are, of course, interdependent. Marx points out again and again that classical political economy, that untarnished 'ideal type' of capitalist economic activity, has revealed that the true nature of property lies in labour. This, according to Marx, has unmasked the mystifications which had surrounded property over the generations. No longer does the essence of property reside in precious metals or in land. Marx credits Adam Smith with this shift of emphasis from external factors to the true origins of property in man's subjectivity and designates him the 'Luther of political economy'.[2]

The whole world is thus divested of its myths. Under capitalism, men are brought to face the harsh realities of this world. This demystification of the world is described in some detail in *The Communist Manifesto*, and this passage shows that Marx's view of capitalism is far from a mere moralistic negation of it:

The bourgeoisie, wherever it has got the upper hand, has put an end to all feudal, patriarchal, idyllic relations. It has pitilessly torn asunder the motley feudal ties that bound man to his 'natural superiors', and has left remaining no other nexus between man and man than naked self-interest, thán callous 'cash payment'. It has drowned the most heavenly ecstasies

[1] G. Lukács, *Geschichte und Klassenbewusstsein*, pp. 104–10.
[2] *Early Writings*, p. 147.

Universality of capitalism

of religious fervour, of chivalrous enthusiasm, of philistine sentimentalism, in the icy water of egotistical calculation. It has resolved personal worth into exchange value, and in place of the numberless indefeasible chartered freedoms, has set up that single, unconscious freedom—Free Trade. In one word, for exploitation, veiled by religious and political illusions, it has substituted naked, shameless, direct, brutal exploitation.

The bourgeoisie has stripped of its halo every occupation hitherto honoured and looked up to with reverant awe...

The bourgeoisie has torn away from the family its sentimental veil, and has reduced the family relation to a mere money relation...

All that is solid melts into the air, all that is holy is profaned, and man is at last compelled to face with sober senses, his real conditions of life and his relations with his kind.[1]

This world, with all human relations stripped of their pretensions and, for the first time in history, reduced to their true reality, is also the world of man's total alienation. Within the capitalist world two ideas dwell side by side: that man's world is nothing but his *praxis* and that man is impotent to act according to this knowledge. Demystification and alienation are thus two sides of the same coin.

Everything becomes an object for exchange, even those qualities hitherto considered man's inalienable property.[2] None the less, capitalism does express the truth of human existence, albeit in an alienated form. As the bourgeois-capitalist world is based on the recognition that property is objectified labour, the principles of capitalism (though not its practice) are thus identical with man's ability to shape and change his own world. Progressive and dynamic, capitalist production is always revolutionizing its own modes of production. It will ultimately undermine its own conditions of existence, because, dialectically, the demystification of the world by capitalism enables the bourgeoisie to penetrate the hidden secret of human existence: the bourgeoisie 'has been the first to show what man's activity can bring about'.[3]

The bourgeoisie has liberated man from his personal dependence upon other men: but it has replaced this by a dependence of man on

---

[1] *Selected Works*, I, 36–7.
[2] *The Poverty of Philosophy*, p. 36. The connection between 'alienation' in the Marxian sense and the linguistic tradition which relates the verb 'to alienate' (*alienare, veräussern*) to selling is now being studied by one of Lukács' disciples, István Mészáros of the University of Sussex. [3] *Selected Works*, I, 37.

objects which are only his alienated projections. Nevertheless, it has thus enabled man to find his roots within himself. It has finally become evident, again in a perverted and alienated form, that the world is an arena of man's self-realization and self-determination. Even the individualistic, self-satisfying atomistic model of man, one of the illusions of the bourgeois *Weltanschauung*, still tries, according to Marx, to express man's emancipation from personal dependence. Even if this emancipation is limited and formal, it remains a necessary premise for the ultimate unfolding of the final and real emancipation. Hegel saw the passage from personal-concrete dependence to general dependence upon the idea of universality as the final emancipation from arbitrariness and the ultimate expression of freedom. Marx does not accept this formulation, yet he sees in it a vital phase for the emergence of a potentiality hidden while the forms of dependence were personal. The abstract cash nexus is thus the last form of human subjection.[1]

The disappearance of personal dependence made the patterns of dependence universal. This aspect of the depersonalization of human relations also contributes, according to Marx, towards their further rationalization. In capitalist society relations of dependence are anonymous, general and abstract: no longer does serf *A* depend on knight *B*, but a group of people depends as a group, hence as a class, upon another group, which thus constitutes another class; hence the growing importance of class relations *per se* in modern times. Only this universality of dependence enables Marx methodologically to discuss such concepts as 'average wage' and to perceive the social average as the regulator of inter-human relations:

But the worker, whose sole source of livelihood is the sale of his labour power, cannot leave the *whole class of purchasers, that is, the capitalist class*, without renouncing his existence. He belongs not to this or that capitalist but to the *capitalist class*, and, moreover, it is his business to dispose of himself, that is, to find a purchaser within this capitalist class...

This wage minimum, like the determination of the price of commodities by the cost of production in general, does not hold good for the *single individual* but for the *species*. Individual workers, millions of workers, do not get enough to be able to exist and reproduce themselves; *but the*

---

[1] Cf. Engels to Marx, 19 November 1844 (*Briefwechsel*, I, 8–9).

wages of the whole working class level down, within their fluctuations, to this minimum.[1]

This also frustrates all pre-capitalist attempts to fit the previous personal forms of dependence into a context of universal significance. The situation of the slave could never have been conceived as a paradigm for the totality of human relations; slavery was ultimately a personal and accidental affair. Precisely because the worker becomes a commodity, reaches the rock bottom of destitution and dehumanization, can a universal meaning be bestowed on his position. Only alienation universalizes the worker. That only a universal mode of production can give rise to a class of universal significance leads to political consequences: this relationship links capitalism, as a universal mode of production, and parliamentarism. As particular, personal-concrete dependence was accompanied by a system of government both autocratic and absolutist, so universal dependence, capitalism, is accompanied by parliamentarism as a political system reflecting abstract universality.[2]

This universality needs a geographical dimension. Marx shows how civil society creates the needs satisfaction of which requires a universal market. From this emerges a world-wide unity in the modes of production and the style of life, further developed and accentuated by each successive expansion of capitalist, European civilization. The uniqueness of Western civilization, according to Marx, lies in its capacity for universalization; no other human society developed this capacity. This unique strain in modern Europe developed, within capitalism, man's creative powers to hitherto unknown limits. This is, according to Marx, the civilizing role of the bourgeoisie, which draws all non-European nations into its orbit:

The need for a constantly expanding market for its products chases the bourgeoisie over the whole surface of the globe. It must nestle everywhere, settle everywhere, establish connexions everywhere.

The bourgeoisie has through its exploitation of the world-market given a cosmopolitan character to production and consumption in every country...All old-established national industries have been destroyed

[1] *Wage Labour and Capital, Selected Works*, I, 83, 89.
[2] *The 18th Brumaire, ibid.* pp. 287–8.

or are daily being destroyed. They are dislodged by new industries, whose introduction becomes a life and death question for all civilised nations, by industries that no longer work up indigenous raw material, but raw material drawn from the remotest zones; industries whose products are consumed, not only at home, but in every quarter of the globe. In place of the old wants, satisfied by the products of the country, we find new wants, requiring for their satisfaction the products of distant lands and climes. In place of the old local and national seclusion and self-sufficiency, we have intercourse in every direction, universal inter-dependence of nations. And as in material, so also in intellectual production. The intellectual creations of individual nations become common property. National one-sidedness and narrow-mindedness become more and more impossible, and from the numerous national and local literatures there arises a world literature.

The bourgeoisie, by the rapid development of all instruments of production, by the immensely facilitated means of communications, draws all, even the most barbarian, nations into civilisation. The cheap prices of its commodities are the heavy artillery with which it batters down all Chinese walls, with which it forces the barbarians' intensely obstinate hatred to foreigners to capitulate. It compels all nations, on pain of extinction, to adopt the bourgeois mode of production; it compels them to introduce what it calls civilisation into their midst, i.e. to become bourgeois themselves. In one word, it creates a world after its own image.

The bourgeoisie has subjected the country to the rule of the towns. It has created enormous cities, has greatly increased the urban population as compared with the rural, and has thus rescued a considerable part of the population from the idiocy of rural life. Just as it has made the country dependent on the towns, so it has made barbarian and semi-barbarian countries dependent on the civilised ones, nations of peasants on nations of bourgeois, the East on the West.[1]

As Marx sees it, it was the universal nature of modern industry which turned history into world-history, *Weltgeschichte*. Only where man consciously changes the world is there history. As capitalism means the constant transformation of the whole world, there is now, for the first time, only one, universal history:

Big industry universalised competition...established means of communication and the modern world market...By universal competition it forced all individuals to strain their energy to the utmost...It produced

[1] *The Communist Manifesto, ibid.* pp. 37–8.

166

world history for the first time, insofar as it made all civilised nations and every individual member of them dependent for the satisfaction of his wants on the whole world, thus destroying the formal natural exclusiveness of separate nations.[1]

This is also the theoretical background for Marx's doctrine that communism, which is the ultimate outcome of this universality, must also be realized universally and that any particularistic, national communism is doomed to failure:

Empirically, communism is only possible as the act of the dominant people 'all at once' and simultaneously, which presupposes the universal development of productive forces and the world intercourse bound up with communism.....

The proletariat can thus only exist world-historically, just as communism: its activity can only have a 'world historical' existence. [This is] world-historical existence of individuals, i.e. existence of individuals which is directly linked up with world history.[2]

Almost forty years later, in 1882, when Marx envisaged the possibility that the revolution might break out first in Russia he made this possibility depend on the proviso: 'if the Russian Revolution becomes the signal for a proletarian revolution in the West.'[3] Socialism in one country, according to Marx, is conceptually and historically a self-destroying hypothesis; and it is easy to show that this belief was also at the root of Marx's quarrel with Lassalle.

Marx holds that, so long as this universality of the market has not reached its ultimate geographical limit, capitalism has not yet reached its apex. Only when this process reached its culmination with the opening of Japan and China to Western trade and the discovery of gold in Australia and California, only then could the internal process of decomposition and change be expected to start.[4] The temporal overlap of the Repeal of the Corn Laws and the final

[1] *The German Ideology*, pp. 75-6. Cf. also Marx's article in the *Neue Rheinische Zeitung* of 15 December 1848, 'The Bourgeoisie and the Counter-Revolution' (*Selected Works*, I, 66-9).
[2] *The German Ideology*, pp. 46-7.
[3] Preface to the Russian edition of *The Communist Manifesto*, *Selected Works*, I, 24.
[4] Marx to Engels, 8 October 1858 (*Selected Correspondence*, p. 134). Here Marx voices his anxiety lest the development of civil society will not reach full growth in the non-European world. He fears that the European revolution may consequently be 'bound to be crushed in this little corner'.

167

breakthrough to universalism shows, according to Marx, the causal relation between these two aspects of capitalist development. Only since then is the road to change wide open.

These considerations also determine Marx's attitude to European colonial expansion, with special reference to the significance of British rule in India. As early as 1846 Marx emphasized in *The Poverty of Philosophy* that the rising standard of living of the British worker was achieved only at the expense of the horribly low wages paid in India.[1] Yet Marx did not see this as the only influence on his judgment of colonialism. More than a decade later he explicitly points out that, at least since the Revolt, British expenditure in India is so heavy as to make the continuing British rule in India economically prohibitive: India costs Britain more than the income it brings her.[2] Ultimately Marx bases his evaluation of European colonialism on completely different criteria, connected with his view of the civilizing nature of capitalism derived from its capacity for universalization.

Marx dealt with British rule in India in two extremely interesting articles written in 1853 for *The New York Daily Tribune*: 'The British Rule in India' and 'The Future Results of British Rule in India'. What characterizes Marx's approach to Indian society in both articles is his emphasis on the backwardness, isolationism, stagnation and ossification of Indian society in general and the rural Indian village communities in particular:

...We must not forget that these idyllic village communities, inoffensive though they may appear, had always been the solid foundation of Oriental despotism, that they restrained the human mind within the smallest possible compass, making it the unresisting tool of superstition, enslaving it beneath traditional rules, depriving it of all grandeur and historical energies. We must not forget the barbarian egotism which, concentrating on some miserable patch of land, had quietly witnessed the ruin of empires, the perpetuation of unspeakable cruelties, the massacre of the population of large towns, with no other consideration bestowed upon them than on natural events, itself the helpless prey of any aggressor who deigned to notice it at all. We must not forget that this undignified, stagnatory, and vegetative life, that this passive sort of existence evoked

[1] *The Poverty of Philosophy*, p. 133.
[2] Marx to Engels, 9 April 1859 (*Briefwechsel*, II, 462).

on the other part in contradistinction, wild, aimless, unbounded forces of destruction and rendered murder itself a religious rite in Hindostan. We must not forget that these little communities were contaminated by distinction of caste and by slavery, that they subjugated man to external circumstances instead of elevating man to the sovereign of circumstances, that they transformed a self-developing social stage into never changing natural destiny, and thus brought about a brutalising worship of nature, exhibiting its degradation in the fact that man, the sovereign of nature, fell down on his knees in adoration of *Kanuman*, the monkey, and *Sabbala*, the cow.[1]

Marx answers the question of Britain's right to India in a somewhat facile way: Indian history has never been anything but the chronicle of foreign invasions and foreign domination. India has never really been ruled by her own sons. In the nineteenth century, the choice is between England and Russia as potential rulers of India. Marx unequivocally prefers industrial, liberal and bourgeois Britain to under-developed, autocratic Russia, as Britain's level of economic development guarantees the integration of India within the world market and the universalization of European culture.[2] Although Indian agriculture has been cruelly destroyed by the English economic impact, not much in Indian rural society was, according to Marx, worth preserving. The major contribution of European rule has been the introduction into India of industrial production which ended the social stagnation of traditional Indian society. 'Stagnation' in this context is for Marx not a mere economic or technological designation, but an anthropological determination: if man's creative ability is his distinctive trait, then stagnation is the worst adjective that may be attributed to any society.

One condition for modernization created by the British in India was, according to Marx, the introduction of private property into a society ignorant of it. Private property points the way, even in an alienated form, toward emancipation; it lays the foundations for the transition to communism, since private property cannot be abolished unless it has been fully developed. The integration of India into universal history is manifested also through the dialectics of sub-

---

[1] *Selected Works*, I, 350–1.
[2] *Ibid.* pp. 352–3. See G. Lichtheim, 'Marx and the Asiatic Mode of Production', *St Antony's Papers*, XIV (London, 1963), 86–112.

jective intentions and objective consequences. Those who came to India to exploit and conquer her eventually became dependent on her development and well-being:

The political unity of India, more consolidated, and extending farther than it ever did under the Great Moguls, was the first condition of its regeneration. That unity, imposed by the British sword, will now be strengthened and perpetuated by the electric telegraph. The native army, organised and trained by the British drill-sergeant, was the *sine qua non* of Indian self-emancipation, and of India ceasing to be the prey of the first foreign intruder. The free press, introduced for the first time into Asiatic society, and managed principally by the common offspring of Hindoo and Europeans, is a new and powerful agent of reconstruction. The *Zemindars* and *Ryotwar* themselves, abominable as they are, involve two distinct forms of private property in land—the great *desideratum* of Asiatic society. From the Indian natives, reluctantly and sparingly educated at Calcutta, under British superintendence, a fresh class is springing up, endowed with the requirements of government and imbued with European science...That once fabulous country will thus be actually annexed to the Western world.

The ruling classes of Great Britain have had, till now, but an accidental, transitory and exceptional interest in the progress of India. The aristocracy wanted to conquer it, the moneyocracy wanted to plunder it, and the millocracy to undersell it. But now the tables are turned. The millocracy have discovered that the transformation of India into a reproductive country has become of vital importance to them, and that, to that end, it is necessary, above all, to gift her with means of irrigation and of internal communication. They intend now drawing a net of railways over India. And they will do it. The results must be inappreciable.[1]

Marx's ultimate judgment on British rule in India is thus far removed from a purely moralistic anti-imperialist attitude. A strong Hegelian undercurrent of the 'cunning of reason' can be traced in Marx's account:

England, it is true, in causing a revolution in Hindostan, was actuated only by the vilest interests, and was stupid in her manner of enforcing

---

[1] *Selected Works*, I, 353–4. The Hegelian dialectics of the master-slave relationship is very conspicuous here. Cf. Hegel's *Phenomenology of Mind* (Baillie's edition), pp. 231–40. Few of Marx's contemporaries achieved a similar insight into the dialectical vicissitudes of European colonialism. Lenin does not seem to have been aware of these articles of Marx when he wrote his work on imperialism.

Universality of capitalism

them. But that is not the question. The question is, can mankind fulfil its destiny without a fundamental revolution in the social state of Asia? If not, whatever may have been the crimes of England she was the unconscious tool of history in bringing about that revolution.[1]

Marx's account of British rule in India clearly brings out the dialectical position of capitalism as the apex of alienation bearing the seeds of redemption. Imperialism is, indeed, according to Marx, the highest stage of capitalism. Not, as Lenin thought, because it must bring about a world war that will ultimately destroy capitalism and drag victors and vanquished alike into the uplands of socialism, but because there is neither hope nor chance for socialism as the hegemony of social universalism unless its foundations are laid down by capitalism itself. Lenin never bothered himself with such theoretical speculations as those underlying Marx's conclusive remarks about India:

The bourgeois period of history has to create the material basis of the new world—on the one hand the universal intercourse founded upon the mutual dependence of mankind, and the means of that intercourse; on the other hand the development of the productive powers of man and the transformation of material production into a scientific domination of natural agencies. Bourgeois industry and commerce create these material conditions of a new world in the same way as geological revolutions have created the surface of the earth.[2]

This view draws very heavily on Marx's earlier historical analysis of revolutions in *The German Ideology*. Here he points out that all revolutions until now have only shifted the internal distribution of productive relations, without changing this relationship itself; they have transferred control over means of production and property from one class to another, but have not transformed the nature of this control. Because of the universality of capitalism which implies that all men are subsumed under the division of labour, the revolution must now emancipate all men together. As emancipation depends on

---

[1] *Selected Works*, I, 351. Cf. my 'Afro-Asia and the Western Political Tradition', *Parliamentary Affairs*, xv, no. 1 (1962), 58–73.
[2] *Selected Works*, I, 358. In another context Marx says that it is in the nature of the dialectics of historical development that all the tools created by the bourgeoisie and aimed at the perfection of its rule ultimately cause its own internal change and decay (*The 18th Brumaire, Selected Works*, I, 287).

the forces of production, and as all previous productive forces were merely particular, all previous revolutions could not carry out universal postulates. They stopped midway, tangled in class arrangements.[1]

There are two further aspects to the universality of capitalism viewed, according to Marx, as the main lever for ultimate emancipation. On one hand, it polarizes wage labour and capital as two phenomenal manifestations of human labour. On the other hand, the more the development of capitalism intensifies and radicalizes alienation, the more it intensifies the total dependence of man upon man. Capitalism ends the individual, particularistic form of production and imposes specialization and division of labour which are alienated forms of universal human inter-dependence. Socialism is nothing but the emancipation of this universal inter-dependence of man on man from its alienated shell:

Hand in hand with this centralisation, or this expropriation of many capitalists by few, there develop, on an ever-extending scale, the co-operative form of the labour-process, the conscious technical application of science, the methodical cultivation of the soil, the transformation of the instruments of labour into instruments of labour only usable in common, the economising of all means of production by their use as the means of production of combined, socialised labour, the entanglement of all peoples in the net of the world-market, and with this, the international character of the capitalistic regime.[2]

The unfolding of the universality of capitalism is thus immanent in inter-human relations and is not merely of geographical significance. Economically, this ever-increasing tendency in industry means a constant increase in the demand for labour. Thus a gradual rise in the wages of the industrial worker may accompany the pauperization and proletarization of the lower middle classes. But because of the inner connection between capital and labour under the technological conditions of developed industrial society, the relative rise in wages will always be smaller than the increase in the ratio of profitability of capital. Even if, economically and materially, the position of the workers improves, their relative *social* position, i.e. their relation to the non-workers, will still deteriorate. Their stand-

[1] *The German Ideology*, pp. 83-6.   [2] *Capital*, I, 763.

ard of living may rise, but the profits of capital will rise even faster. The reason for this, according to Marx, is simple: the more machinery is used, the greater is the surplus value created by the worker. The more machinery used by the worker, the more power the worker creates for the forces enslaving him:

Even the *most favourable situation* for the working class, the *most rapid possible growth of capital*, however much it may improve the material existence of the worker, does not remove the antagonism between his interests and the interests of the bourgeoisie, the interest of the capitalists. *Profit and wages* remain as before in *inverse proportion*.

If capital is growing rapidly, wages may rise; the profit of capital rises incomparably more rapidly. The material position of the worker has improved, but at the cost of his social position. The social gulf that divides him from the capitalist has widened.[1]

This theoretical distinction between the economic and the social positions of the worker may also put into focus Marx's statement in the *Inaugural Address* of the International, which might otherwise look wild and unsubstantiated:

...No improvement of machinery, no appliance of science to production, no contrivances of communication, no new colonies, no emigration, no opening of markets, no free trade, nor all these things put together, will do away with the miseries of the industrial masses...On the present false base, every fresh development of the productive powers of labour must tend to deepen *social* contrasts and point *social* antagonisms.[2]

The importance of this statement lies in its clear indication that Marx's critique of capitalism is not aimed at capitalism's inability to feed the proletarians physically. Marx never made such an obviously wrongheaded statement, and he never implied that the absolute position of the workers would deteriorate endlessly. Such an assumption is also sheer nonsense on Marx's own premises, since the worker himself is, according to Marx, a commodity bought at a minimal price under optimal supply conditions. This price, though it may fluctuate from society to society and from time to time, still has an absolute minimum—the bare physical subsistence level of the worker and his family. What has no limit at all, is the *ratio* of the

[1] *Wage Labour and Capital, Selected Works*, I, 98; cf. *Early Writings*, pp. 71–2.
[2] *Selected Works*, I, 381 (my italics).

173

gap between the standard of living of the workers and that of the bourgeoisie. This gap may widen even if real wages generally rise. Marx intended to show that even in the most favourable conditions possible under capitalism this gap may constantly increase. Not a mere quantitative factor, it determines the social fabric of society; it relates not to the worker's powers of consumption but to the submission of live labour to 'dead' labour, i.e. to capital. No economic prosperity can, according to Marx, solve *this* problem within capitalist society, as this society is based on the interdependence of the twin concepts of labour and capital.

THE DIALECTICS OF CHANGE: STOCK COMPANIES AND CO-OPERATIVES

We have already noted that on several occasions Marx maintained that the material conditions which will ultimately transform capitalism are immanent in capitalism itself. The *Communist Manifesto* says that the development of big industry cuts the very foundation from under the feet of the bourgeoisie: 'What the bourgeoisie, therefore, produces, is, above all, its own grave-diggers.'[1] In *The German Ideology* the same idea is developed when Marx says that productive relations fetter production itself, giving rise to an immanent demand for a transition to a new form of production.[2] In his comments on Bakunin's *Étatism and Anarchy*, Marx writes in 1874/5 that Bakunin overlooks the fact that socialism must emerge from the womb of bourgeois society;[3] the same expression occurs also in the *Critique of the Gotha Programme*, written at the same period.[4]

The failure to clarify this internal development in these passages gave rise to various interpretations, the most popular being the suggestion that the cyclical crises of capitalism will ultimately bring about its internal total disruption. Despite some possible rhetorical allusions to such a contingency, no analysis of Marx points in this direction; Marx's view was far less mechanistic and attributed much more dialectical significance to the working of the capitalist system.

One way to approach the subject is through Marx's Preface to *A Contribution to the Critique of Political Economy*; here Marx

[1] *Selected Works*, I, 45.   [2] *The German Ideology*, p. 76.
[3] *Werke*, XVIII, 630.   [4] *Selected Works*, II, 23.

The dialectics of change

relates this internal development of capitalism to his hypothesis that capitalism is the last antagonistic form of production:

> The bourgeois relations of production are the last antagonistic form of the social process of production—antagonistic not in the sense of individual antagonism, but of one arising from the social conditions of life of the individuals; at the same time the productive forces developing in the womb of bourgeois society create the material conditions for the solution of that antagonism.[1]

This raises, of course, an acute question of method in Marx's thought: what guarantee has Marx that the capitalist form of production is 'the last antagonistic form of the social process of production'? What assurance that future antagonisms will not divide socialist society as they divided all previous societies? Is there any methodological reason why the dialectics of internal change should cease to work even after socialism has been achieved? As Marx himself said, each class reaches political power by a claim for universality. May not the same be true of the proletariat, i.e. that after achieving power its universality will prove illusory?

Without going into the various polemic answers to this dilemma, it should be noted that the different mechanistic answers given to these questions have engendered such bastard-terms as 'non-antagonistic contradictions' meaningless within Marx's frame of thought. The best way to approach this question would be to suggest that the elements of future society already 'within the womb of bourgeois society' can give some clue to the non-antagonistic nature of future society, provided that the term 'antagonism' be related to man's subsumption under the conditions of production. According to Marx the abolition of capitalist society means the abolition of all antagonisms, because it implies the realization of the hidden tendencies of capitalist society itself. Hence Marx sees this as a new and revolutionary way of abolition. This is also the reason why he feels that socialism does not need a new economic methodology of its own beyond a critique of classical political economy. Socialism seeks an ultimate vindication of the premises of bourgeois economic theory that cannot be realized within bourgeois society itself. In the

[1] *Selected Works*, I, 363-4.

Revolutionary dialectics of capitalist society

Grundrisse Marx says that, because of the universality of capitalism, the categories of classical political economy, although products of given historical conditions, imply an understanding of the productive process broader and more adequate than all previous, partial systems of economic theory.[1] It was, incidentally, Lassalle who grasped this when he told Marx that he was 'Ricardo turned socialist, Hegel turned economist'.[2]

Marx points out that the capitalist form of production necessarily stresses the need for social togetherness and mutual co-operation in the productive process. This statement contradicts the individualistic model on which capitalist economic theory operates, and this antagonism between capitalist theory and practice ultimately causes the capitalist mode of production to fetter its own development. The antagonism can be resolved only in socialism. That capitalism gives partial, distorted expression to the organizing principles of future society is also revealed by Marx's seeing one of the main postulates of socialism, the disappearance of the differences between town and country, as one of the great contributions of capitalism to world history. In *The German Ideology* Marx also points out that urbanization under capitalism not only bridges the gap between town and country, but also intensifies social mutuality within the capitalist system itself.[3]

But there is more in Marx's writings than just this theoretical hypothesis: there are clear indications about the precise material conditions that will ultimately become the 'grave-diggers' of capitalist society.

The first hint can be found in a letter of Marx to Engels in 1858, where he sets forth the structure of his book on the critique of political economy. The chapter on capital, Marx explains, will be treated under four headings: (*a*) capital in general; (*b*) competition; (*c*) credit; and lastly '(*d*) share capital as the most perfect form, turning over [*überschlagend*] into communism, together with all its contradictions'.[4]

Towards the end of *Das Kapital*, I, Marx details what he had in

---

[1] *Grundrisse*, pp. 25–6. [2] Lassalle, *Nachlass*, III, 29.
[3] *Selected Works*, I, 38; *The German Ideology*, p. 40.
[4] Marx to Engels, 2 April 1858 (*Selected Correspondence*, p. 126). The English translation of *überschlagend* as 'leading to' is quite inadequate.

176

mind when he said that the most sophisticated form of capitalist private property is already turning into communism. Here he postulates a new kind of individual property which will do away with capitalist property yet differ from all previous forms of property. This 'individual property' is characterized by the internal contradictions of capitalist property:

The capitalist mode of appropriation, the result of the capitalist mode of production, produces capitalist private property. This is the first negation of individual private property, as founded on the labour of the proprietor. But capitalist production begets, with the inexorability of a law of Nature, its own negation. It is the negation of the negation. This does not re-establish private property for the producer, but gives him individual property based on the acquisitions of the capitalist era: i.e. on co-operation and the possession in common of land and of the means of production.[1]

This cryptic Hegelian code ('negation of the negation') is deciphered by Marx only towards the end of *Das Kapital*, III. In ch. XXVII, inconspicuously entitled 'The Role of Credit in Capitalist Production', Marx sets out his most comprehensive description of the future development of capitalism and its internal change into a socialized system of production. This is without doubt one of the most significant insights into capitalism offered by Marx. It owes its unfamiliarity to its obscure context. Marx summarizes his analysis as follows: 'The capitalist stock companies, as much as the co-operative factories, should be considered as transitional forms from the capitalist mode of production to the associated one, with the only distinction that the antagonism is resolved negatively in the one and positively in the other.'[2]

The detailed description of this process shows how much Marx's thinking is again determined by the dialectical meaning of *Aufhebung*. The 'negation of the negation' at the end of *Das Kapital*, I, points, of course, in the same direction. It is worthwhile to quote Marx's account at some length, as it shows how Marx sees the alternative to capitalism as emerging from the immanent development of capitalism itself. Marx shows how large-scale industry will not be able to finance itself from individual investments, but will

[1] *Capital*, I, 763.   [2] *Ibid.* III, 431.

177

have to be financed by a sale of shares to the anonymous public. The consequences, according to Marx, will be as follows:

Transformation of the actual functioning capitalist into a mere manager, administrator of other people's capital, and of the owner of capital into a mere owner, a mere money-capitalist. Even if the dividends which they receive include the interest and the profit of enterprise, i.e. the total profit (for the salary of the manager is, or should be, simply the wage of a specific type of skilled labour, whose price is regulated in the labour-market like that of any other labour), this total profit is henceforth received only in the form of interest, i.e., as mere compensation for owning capital that now is entirely divorced from the function in the actual process of reproduction, just as this function in the person of the manager is divorced from ownership of capital. Profit thus appears...as a mere appropriation of the surplus-labour of others, arising from the conversion of means of production into capital, i.e. from their alienation vis-à-vis the actual producer, from their antithesis as another's property to every individual actually at work in production, from manager down to the last day-labourer. In stock companies the function is divorced from capital ownership, hence also labour is entirely divorced from ownership of means of production and surplus-labour. This result of the ultimate development of capitalist production is a necessary transitional phase towards the reconversion of capital into the property of producers, although no longer as the private property of the individual producers, but rather as the property of associated producers, as outright social property. On the other hand, the stock company is a transition toward the conversion of all functions in the reproduction process which still remain linked with capitalist property, into mere functions of associated producers into social function...

This is the abolition [*Aufhebung*] of the capitalist mode of production within the capitalist mode of production itself, and hence a self-dissolving contradiction, which *prima facie* represent a mere phase of transition to a new form of production. It manifests itself as such a contradiction in its effects. It establishes a monopoly in certain spheres and thereby requires state interference. It reproduces a new financial aristocracy, a new variety of parasites in the shape of promoters, speculators and simply nominal directors; a whole system of swindling and cheating by means of corporation promotion, stock issuance, and stock speculation. It is private production without the control of private property.[1]

[1] *Capital*, III, 427–9. According to Engels (Preface to *Capital*, II, 2–3) these sections were written by Marx during 1864–5. Engels' lengthy remark accompanying this passage

The dialectics of change

The text does not need any gloss. Still, the several conclusions that follow should be made explicit. First, this text proves that Marx's analysis of capitalism was not confined to so-called 'primitive' or early capitalism, which united direct ownership and effective control. Clearly the view that Marx never envisaged a more sophisticated form of capitalism, with legal ownership divorced from effective control, is utterly false. On the contrary, Marx was one of the first to predict this development as a necessary outcome of the internal needs of ever-growing capitalist expansion.

Secondly, the claim that James Burnham's theory of the Managerial Revolution has made Marx's analysis dated and obsolete is nonsense. The Managerial Revolution was foreseen by Marx as early as 1864. He saw in it nothing less than the internal development of capitalism, leading ultimately to its *Aufhebung*.

Thirdly, a careful reading of the passage suggests that Marx tries to relate the theory propounded here to his theory of alienation. The separation of ownership from control and management must also be viewed as the climax of alienation. Not only is the worker alienated from his labour; even the capitalist is alienated, in the more sophisticated form of capitalist society, from his capital.

Marx's comments on the stock companies are followed by what seems to him a parallel development: the co-operative movement. At about the same time that this chapter of *Das Kapital*, III, was written. Marx said in his *Inaugural Address*:

But there was in store a still greater victory of the political economy of labour over the political economy of property. We speak of the co-operative movement, especially the co-operative factories, raised by the unassisted efforts of a few bold 'hands'. The value of these great social experiments cannot be over-rated. By deed, instead of by argument, they have shown that production on a large scale, and in accord with the behest of modern science, may be carried on without the existence of a

(*Capital*, III, 428–9) clearly suggests that he has not grasped the immense methodological significance of Marx's analysis. Some public debate about the merely formal control of the share owners in stock companies can already be discerned at the time of Marx's writing these passages, and there was some public pressure to reinforce the share-holders' control through more effective legislation. But even John Stuart Mill, who dealt with this problem, never saw in it anything more than an administrative and legal dilemma. He did not perceive in it anything that could ultimately lead to a structural change in capitalism. Cf. J. S. Mill, *Principles of Political Economy*, People's Edition (London, 1861), pp. 580–1.

179

class of masters employing a class of hands; that to bear fruit, the means of labour need not be monopolised as a means of dominion over, and of extortion against, the labouring man himself; and that, like slave labour, like serf labour, hired labour is but a transitory and inferior form, destined to disappear before associated labour plying its toil with a willing hand, a ready mind, and a joyous heart. In England, the seeds of the co-operative system were sown by Robert Owen...

At the same time, the experience of the period from 1848 to 1864 has proved beyond doubt that, however excellent in principle, and however useful in practice, co-operative labour, if kept within the narrow circle of the casual efforts of private workmen, will never be able to arrest the growth in geometrical progression of monopoly, to free the masses, nor even to perceptibly lighten the burden of their miseries...To save the industrious masses, co-operative labours ought to be developed to national dimensions, and consequently, to be fostered by national means.[1]

Marx's praise is mixed with criticism, but the praise was not just lip-service to the co-operative elements in the *International*. As is clear from *Das Kapital*, III, where considerations of rhetoric and internal working-class politics could not have played any role, the co-operative movement, just like the stock company, indicates for Marx the ultimate trends governing capitalist society. Like stock companies, co-operation created a new kind of property—social property—which, though still expressed within the conceptual framework of private property, is in truth a novel and revolutionary phenomenon. This comes out very clearly from Marx's remarks about the co-operative factories in *Das Kapital*, III:

The co-operative factories of the labourers themselves represent within the old form the first sprouts of the new, although they naturally reproduce, and must reproduce, everywhere in their actual organisation all the short-comings of the prevailing system. But the antithesis between capital and labour is overcome [*aufgehoben*] within them, if at first only by way of making the associated labourers into their own capitalist, i.e., by enabling them to use the means of production for the employment of their own labour. They show how a new mode of production naturally grows out of an old one, when the development of the material forces of production and of the corresponding forms of social production have reached a particular

[1] *Selected Works*, I, 383–4.

stage. Without the factory system arising out of the capitalist mode of production there could have been no co-operative factories.[1]

This is then at the root of the transition from capitalism to socialism: socialism is in practice nothing but what capitalism is potentially. The universalism of future society is, philosophically, nothing but retention of the Hegelian concept of the state, emancipated from the historical forms which inclined it towards political conservatism. Whether manifested in the mode of production or in the historical subject, the proletariat, this universality is ultimately possible because 'what we have to deal with here is a communist society just as it emerges from capitalist society'.

Finally, this account of the future development of capitalist society may also suggest a way out of the dilemma bedevilling Marxists for several generations and recently taken up again by Oscar Lange.[2] According to Lange, the uniqueness of the proletarian revolution lies in its preceding the emergence of socialist economic conditions, whereas all previous revolutions have only legitimized politically socio-economic changes which had already occurred. In the case of socialism, it is the aim of the socialist revolution to make these conditions possible politically.

This explanation is at considerable variance with Marx's views in the cited passages of *Das Kapital*, III. According to Marx, the recourse to political power can never do more than realize potentialities already existing within the socio-economic structure. Political power, according to Marx, can never create anything *ex nihilo*. That Marx specifically named the stock companies and the co-operative factories as two examples of the process through which the hidden transition from capitalism to socialism is already occurring seems to contradict Lange's notion that in this respect the socialist revolution behaves differently from previous revolutions. Political power may be crucial for the realization of potentialities, but it does not create the new structures realized. It perfects existing reality, giving dominance to what may still be marginal in existing society, but it can never be the prime mover. Like other followers of

[1] *Capital*, III, 431.
[2] O. Lange, *Problems of Political Economy of Socialism* (Calcutta, 1962), pp. 13 f.

181

Revolutionary dialectics of capitalist society

Lenin, Lange shares his view about the omnipotence of politics, which is at variance with Marx's opinions.

The same considerations as those behind Marx's views in *Das Kapital*, III, also prompted him to support as early as 1846 the American Homestead Act movement and to oppose those among the German left-wing emigrés in the United States who viewed with suspicion this widening of the social base of private property.[1] Marx, on the contrary, thought that where no private property exists its dialectical abolition by universalization is *ipso facto* impossible. Therefore a further widening of the social base of private property should be welcome, since ultimately the abolition of private property universalizes the principle on which it is based.

When Marx suggests that capitalism is necessary for the development towards socialism he does not, however, imply a deterministic concept of necessity. Capitalism is necessary in so far as the next stage dialectically unfolds the principles inherent in capitalism itself. For the realization of these principles, their present economic and political form must be overcome. In this sense Marx views capitalism as an intrinsic contradiction.

This again shows that Marx's attitude to his contemporary world is always ambivalent. It may well be that, like Hegel, Marx ultimately felt that only when a form of life has reached its apex does the ideal appear over against the real. The socialist vision never appears to Marx a mere antithesis of capitalism: it is virtually incapable of realization unless it will emerge, phoenix-like, from the ashes of capitalist society itself—an insight which other socialists never really shared with Marx, with the possible exception of Saint-Simon.

Marx's attitude to political liberalism can perhaps be better understood against the background of these considerations. It is sometimes overlooked that all the socialist schools so savagely attacked by Marx had one trait in common: 'True Socialists' and Proudhonists, Lassalleans and Bakuninists were all more than sceptical about political liberalism. This scepticism, turned into radical and uncritical hatred, sometimes brought them into direct or indirect

[1] Cf. the circular of the German Communist Corresponding Society of Brussels, drawn up by Marx in May 1846 (*Werke*, IV, 3–17).

alliance with the aristocracy and the autocracy of the Ancien Régime against the common enemy—the bourgeoisie and political liberalism. Marx with all his critique of bourgeois liberalism, always supports political liberalism against the traditional Right, not because of any deterministic attitude which sees history moving constantly 'leftward', but for completely different reasons. For Marx, socialism grows out of the contradictions inherent in bourgeois society and political liberalism. A socialism that would grow, like Lassallean socialism, out of an alliance with the Right after both have overthrown political liberalism, will necessarily carry with it some of the characteristics of its authoritarian ally. Not only because allies naturally influence each other, but also because the destruction of the bourgeoisie and the stifling of political liberalism with the help of the right wing will prematurely kill the only forces capable of creating the economic and conceptual basis for socialism itself.[1]

Marx's criticism of these doctrines acknowledges the danger that such uncritical enmity of all socialist schools toward the bourgeoisie and capitalism makes them purblind to the forces that shape reality and to the socialist vision and the possibilities of its realization. Marx ultimately maintains that only a socialism that knows a fully differentiated system of private property can abolish it and replace it by a new, non-possessive relationship between man and man and between man and his artifacts. Only a socialism that has wrestled with the capitalist, bourgeois abstraction about an individual's total separation from his fellow-creatures can set up against this abstraction the alternative of an essential unity of the individual and society. Only a socialism that knows how abstract and empty are the Rights of Man in alienated society—and total alienation exists only in capitalist society—can try to evolve a social system to realize the content of these rights while abolishing their external form as just another expression of alienation. According to Marx, any breakthrough to the final end not mediated through this dialectical ambivalence is doomed to end either in Cloud Cuckoo Land or in a new authoritarianism that will not begin to grasp what freedom really is.

[1] Cf. M. Rubel, 'Marx's Conception of Democracy', *New Politics*, i, no. 2 (1962), 78–90. On Marx and the Lassalleans, see R. P. Morgan, *The German Social Democracy and the First International* (Cambridge, 1965), pp. 1–97.

No doubt many of Marx's arguments against Bakunin, stripped of their propagandistic excesses, their personal venom and their Russophobia, can be reduced to the scepticism of Marx, a son of Western civilization aware of the limits as well as the achievements of his society, towards someone from a society that has never experienced modern liberalism and therefore dismisses liberalism entirely without perceiving that one cannot establish socialism except by simultaneously realizing and destroying liberalism. When Marx referred to Lassalle as 'Workers' dictator' he had in mind the same dialectics: a socialist system that will have to rely on Bismarck and Prussian autocracy in order to destroy liberalism will end as a socialist replica of Bismarck and Prussia. Nothing could be more self-destroying.

7

THE FRENCH REVOLUTION AND THE TERROR: THE ACHIEVEMENTS AND LIMITS OF POLITICAL REVOLUTION

We have already seen how Marx's historical prognosis makes the future development of capitalism towards socialism depend on the prior existence of conditions which make this social change possible. The criteria for this method of historical explanation are applied by Marx to two other historical phenomena as well: the French Revolution and the revolutions of 1848.

Marx formed his opinion about the French Revolution as early as 1843. In *On the Jewish Question* Marx says that the modern state reached in the French Revolution its emancipation and differentiation from socio-economic life. All political, community-oriented limitations on economic activity were swept away in 1789, and civil society became independent of the political sphere within which it had been embedded in medieval times. This achievement signifies the emergence of the tension between civil society and the state, which institutionalizes the alienation of man from his universality.[1] In *The Holy Family* Marx supplements this argument by saying that this separation, though formally declared in 1789, was fully established only by the July Revolution of 1830.[2]

Marx does not limit his explanation of the French Revolution to an analysis of its historical impact. Dialectically, the French Revolution has two aspects. Subjectively, it was nothing but an expression of the will of the bourgeoisie to shape the political world according to the principles of civil society, and these goals were finally vindicated, according to Marx, under the Directoire and Napoleon. But objectively, the social order promoted by the bourgeoisie also implies universal criteria bound in the long run to undermine this social order itself. Thus the French Revolution bred its own destruction. Since the abolition of feudalism and the guild system each individual, including members of the proletariat,

---

[1] *Early Writings*, pp. 27-9.   [2] *The Holy Family*, p. 167.

could emancipate himself. Society grew more open, and each individual could affirm his liberty by becoming a bourgeois. But by definition, the existence of one person as a bourgeois presupposes the existence of other people as non-bourgeois. Hence the practice of the bourgeois revolution gives the lie to its theory: everyone *could* become a bourgeois precisely because not everyone *would* become one. The bourgeois revolution could never encompass all humanity, though its justification lay precisely in this universal postulate.[1]

Since the bourgeois revolution cannot thus realize its principles, their vindication must be achieved beyond civil society. Here Marx sees in the universalistic principles of the French Revolution a significance transcending the subjective intentions of the bourgeoisie. He sees these universalistic principles as forerunners of a communist order that will bring this universalism to its logical conclusion. Thus communism is the true *Aufhebung* of the principles of 1789:

> The French Revolution brought forth ideas which led beyond the *ideas* of the entire old world system. The revolutionary movement which began in 1789 in *Cercle social*, which in the middle of its course has as its chief representatives *Leclerc* and *Roux* and which finally was temporarily defeated with *Baboeuf's* conspiracy, brought forth the communist idea which *Baboeuf's* friend *Buonarroti* re-introduced into France after the Revolution of 1830. This idea, consistently developed, *is the idea of the new world system.*[2]

There is little doubt that Marx had a clearer insight into the internal contradictions of the French Revolution than did most of his contemporaries. While some, like Bauer, saw in the bourgeois revolution only the separation of state from religion, others, like Louis Blanc, saw 1793 as distinctly different from 1789; Marx saw the social as well as the political significance of 1789, and made its subsequent history conform to an adequate pattern of historical explanation.[3]

Marx reaffirms this analysis of the French Revolution in a news-

---

[1] *The German Ideology*, p. 62.   [2] *The Holy Family*, p. 161.
[3] B. Bauer, *Die bürgerliche Revolution in Deutschland* (Berlin, 1849); L. Blanc, *Histoire de la Révolution française* (Paris, 1866).

paper article in 1847, when he says that in both the Puritan and French Revolutions republicanism necessarily led to a communist view:

The first appearance of a real active communist party occurs within the bourgeois revolution, at the moment at which constitutional monarchy has been vanquished. The most consequent republicans, the Levellers in England, Baboeuf, Buonarroti etc. in France, are the first who proclaim these 'social problems'.[1]

This theoretical deduction of communism from republicanism still does not mean that communist ideas can be realized within the historical context of the French Revolution. On the contrary, any attempt to realize communism during the French—or Puritan—Revolution is, according to Marx, doomed to failure. The existence of communist ideas precedes the conditions necessary for their realization, as the ideas of a civil society preceded the full growth of the bourgeoisie. Conditions, Marx says, never give rise to ideas; they just make their realization possible. The *idea* of communism, after all, is as old as Plato, the medieval monasteries, and Thomas More.

This view of the significance of the French Revolution for communism is accompanied in Marx's work by what might be considered a surprising attitude to the reign of terror and the Jacobin dictatorship. Marx's position on this is unique in that, though he naturally sympathizes with the Jacobins, he regards them as utterly misguided and muddle-headed and considers their recourse to terrorism immanent in their basic fallacy. Marx denounces Jacobin terror unequivocally, and the Jacobin dictatorship does not and cannot serve him in any way as a model for a future communist revolution. Yet he does not oppose Jacobin terror on moralistic grounds. His opposition is immanent in his systematic thought about the nature of social change. This problem in Marx's thought has never been thoroughly investigated, and even the Kautsky–Lenin controversy about political terror, in which both protagonists quoted

---

[1] *Deutsche Brüsseler Zeitung*, 11 November 1847 (*Werke*, IV, 341). In a letter to Engels of 25 March 1868, Marx again says that the tendency towards socialism is a reaction to the French Revolution derived from its own premises (*Selected Correspondence*, p. 242).

liberally from Marx, was conducted under such political pressure that it hardly helped to bring out the Marxian analysis itself.[1]

Marx explains the reign of terror as derived from the Jacobin attempt to realize a political order still lacking its socio-economic preconditions. Consequently the Jacobins were driven to apply merely political measures more and more similar to quasi-classical republicanism and more out of touch with the contemporary world. That terror became the only avenue still open to them indicates their inability to bring about the desired change. Recourse to terror is, according to Marx, an ultimate proof that the aims the revolution wishes to achieve cannot be achieved at present. Terror is less a means towards the realization of a revolutionary aim than a mark of failure.

This view characterizes Marx's attitude to terror through all his life, from his very earliest writings. In his first printed article, *Notes about the New Prussian Censorship Regulations* (1842), Robespierre's name occurs for the first time. Marx's main argument against censorship is that it is aimed not at one's actions but at one's thoughts. This violates, according to Hegel's *Philosophy of Right*, the nature of law as an expression of rational, objective norms and not of subjective tendencies. Hence Marx opposes the censorship of the press as 'terroristic', since it seeks to intimidate man's thought and not to punish him for acts he committed. In this context Robespierre's name comes up:

The writer is exposed to the most dreadful terrorism, the jurisdiction of suspicion. Tendencious laws, laws that do not supply objective norms, are laws of terrorism, as they were thought out by the necessity of the state under Robespierre and by the corruption of the state under the Roman emperors. Laws that take as their criteria not action as such, but the state of mind of the actor, are nothing else than the positive sanction of lawlessness.[2]

While discussing the French Revolution in *On the Jewish Question*, Marx gives a further insight into these considerations. The French Revolution separated the state from civil society, but Jacobin

[1] K. Kautsky, *Terrorism and Communism* (London, 1920); V. I. Lenin, *The Proletarian Revolution and the Renegade Kautsky, Selected Works* (London, 1946), VII, 113–217.
[2] *Werke*, I, 14. This again proves the basic fallacy of the view of the early Marx as a 'Jacobin democrat'.

government behaved as if this separation had not taken place, forgetting that the existence of each sphere was made possible by its differentiation from the other. Seen from this angle, Jacobin terror is to Marx an attempt of the political state, emancipated and separated from civil society, to re-impose itself on civil society, to crush the private and particular interests realized in civil society. The Jacobin dictatorship attempts to overcome the antagonism between state and civil society by force, and the failure of such an attempt is immanent: the dichotomy between state and civil society cannot be overcome by the politization of civil society but only through a synthesis of particularism and universalism brought about by the recognition of the universality of the individual. The Jacobin *tour de force* not only failed to impose the political state on civil society: dialectically, particularism triumphed and forced the state to subserve its aim. The restoration implied by the Directoire was already inherent in the one-sidedness of Jacobin terror and its necessary failure:

Certainly, in periods when the political state as such comes violently to birth in civil society, and when men strive to liberate themselves through political emancipation, the state can, and must, proceed to *abolish and destroy religion*; but only in the same way as it proceeds to abolish private property, by declaring a maximum, by confiscation, or by progressive taxation, or in the same way as its proceeds to abolish life, by the *guillotine*. At those times when the state is most aware of itself, political life seeks to stifle its own prerequisites—civil society and its elements—and to establish itself as the genuine and harmonious species-life of man. But it can only achieve this end by setting itself in *violent* contradiction with its own conditions of existence, by declaring a *permanent* revolution. Thus the political drama ends necessarily with the restoration of religion, of private property, of all the elements of civil society, just as war ends with the conclusion of peace.[1]

This Jacobin attempt to force the state on socio-economic conditions and thus direct them according to its political will grew,

---

[1] *Early Writings*, p. 16. There is a strong affinity between this description and the chapter on the terror in Hegel's *Phenomenology* (pp. 599–610 in Baillie's edition). Marx's critique of the Jacobin attempt of a politization of all spheres of life is surprisingly similar to Talmon's argument against totalitarian democracy, which makes politics all-inclusive and subsumes human life under political existence and activity (J. L. Talmon, *The Origins of Totalitarian Democracy*, London, 1952).

according to Marx, out of the Jacobin incomprehension of economic circumstances. The Jacobins saw economics as a side-issue, to be mastered by political measures that would ultimately express a political will. The Jacobins thus reduced political power to a subjective expression of preferences, devoid of all contact with the objective realities of the socio-economic world. They reduced political power to sheer arbitrariness. Marx brings this out distinctively in a newspaper article of 1844:

> The classical period of political reason [*Verstand*] is the French Revolution. Far from seeing in the very principle of the state the source of social want, the heroes of the French Revolution see social wants as the source of all political disorder. Thus Robespierre sees in great poverty and great richness only a stumbling-block to pure democracy. He wants therefore to establish a universal Spartan frugality. According to him, will is the principle of politics. The more one-sided and hence the more accomplished is the political reason, the more does it believe in the omnipotence of the will, the more blind is it to the natural and spiritual limits of the will, the more incapable is it to discover the roots of the social evil.[1]

Terror is thus a subjectivist fallacy, abstracted from the real economic and social circumstances. Hence it can never win. That Jacobinism is out of touch with reality is stated by Marx in another way as well: the classic *polis* is the model of Jacobin republicanism, as it implies the subsumption of the economic under the political sphere. But the anachronism of this model makes the Jacobin attempt utterly helpless. Since the Jacobins, according to Marx, lack any understanding of history, they overlook the significance of economic processes. In Athens and Rome socio-economic life, i.e. civil society, could come under political domination because at that stage the differentiation between the two spheres had not yet really taken place. In the modern world where life is divided into private and public spheres, such a subsumption is utterly impossible. For Marx, the universality bound ultimately to be realized through communism is a dialectical totality that preserves the previous achievements of civil society, whereas the Jacobin general will is one-sided. Marx's universality abolishes civil society, Robespierre's only negates it. In Rousseau's language, the Jacobins try to eliminate

[1] *Vorwärts*, 7 August 1844 (*Werke*, 1, 402).

The French Revolution and the terror

volonté des tous in order to reach *volonté générale*, whereas Marx sees no other way to arrive at the *volonté générale* except through a dialectical incorporation and transcendence of *volonté des tous*. While the Jacobins try to restore the *polis*, Marx holds that you can never step twice into the same river:

Robespierre, Saint Just and their party fell because they confused the ancient, realistic and democratic republic based on real slavery with the modern spiritualist democratic representative state which is based on emancipated slavery, on civil society. What a terrible mistake it is to have to recognise and sanction in the Rights of Man modern civil society, the society of industry, of universal competition, of private interest freely following its aims, of anarchy, of self-alienated natural and spiritual individuality, and yet subsequently to annul the manifestations of the life of that society in separate individuals and at the same time to wish to model the political head of the society after the fashion of the ancients...
Terror wished to sacrifice [civil society] to an ancient form of political life.[1]

Under the impact of his later economic and historical studies Marx subsequently reiterates his verdict on terrorism in terms of economic development rather than Hegelian speculation, yet his views remain basically the same. In 1847 Marx warns against a premature rising of the proletariat that will ultimately have to rely on political measures:

If the proletariat brings down the domination of the bourgeoisie, its victory will be merely ephemeral, only a moment in the service of the bourgeoisie (just like *anno* 1794), so long as within the process of history, within its 'movement', those material conditions have not been created that make necessary the abolition of the bourgeois mode of production and therefore also the definitive fall of political bourgeois domination.[2]

Marx judges Baboeuf's conspiracy in *The Communist Manifesto* in the same way. He adds that a communist revolution that would try to realize itself by merely political means will never go beyond formalistic egalitarianism based on an asceticism unaware of the enormous creative potentialities offered by civil society:

The first direct attempts of the proletariat to attain its own ends, made in times of universal excitement, when feudal society was being overthrown,

---

[1] *The Holy Family*, pp. 164–5.
[2] *Deutsche Brüsseler Zeitung*, 11 November 1847 (*Werke*, IV, 338–9).

these attempts necessarily failed, owing to the then underdeveloped state of the proletariat, as well as to the absence of the economic conditions for its emancipation, conditions that have yet to be produced, and could be produced by the impending bourgeois epoch alone. The revolutionary literature that accompanied these first movements of the proletariat has necessarily a reactionary character. It inculcated universal asceticism and social levelling in its crudest form.[1]

That these premature breakthroughs ultimately helped the bourgeoisie, not the proletariat, Marx maintains towards the end of 1848:

In both revolutions (1648, 1789) the bourgeoisie was the class that really led the movement. The proletariat and those factions that did not belong to the bourgeoisie either did not yet possess interests which were indistinguishable from those of the bourgeoisie, or did not constitute independently developed classes or class-groups. Hence each time they oppose the bourgeoisie, as during 1793–94 in France, they actually fight for the implementation of the interests of the bourgeoisie, though not in the manner of the bourgeoisie. The whole of French terrorism was nothing else than a plebeian manner to put an end to the enemies of the bourgeoisie...[2]

This also helps Marx to avoid analogies between 1793 and 1848. The Jacobins can in no way inspire a communist revolution; on the contrary. Even more important are the sociological implications separating Marx from the Jacobins: the Jacobins still believed in a breakthrough carried out by marginal radicalized groups, *sans-culottes* or *enragés*. Marx thinks of distinct class organizations. The Blanquists are to Marx descendants of Jacobins who have neither learned nor forgotten anything.[3]

The same theme recurs frequently in Marx's writings. Arguing against Bakunin, Marx says in 1853 that revolutionary enthusiasm does not guarantee right thinking, since 'revolutionary feeling' brought forth the *lois de suspects* of Jacobin terror. The strongly anti-subjectivist line, which Marx inherited from Hegel, is again evident here.[4] In a letter to Engels in 1865 Marx remarks that Robespierre did nothing to abolish the 1789 laws of association which had out-

---

[1] *Selected Works*, I, 61. Marx also criticizes in identical form the crudity of communism in its first stages (*Early Writings*, pp. 153–4).
[2] 'Die Bourgeoisie und die Kontrerevolution', *Neue Rheinische Zeitung*, 15 December 1848 (*Werke*, VI, 107).   [3] *Werke*, VII, 276.   [4] *Ibid.* IX, 301.

lawed working-class organizations and trade unions. In the final balance, nothing in Jacobin rule gave it any real anti-bourgeois character.[1]

Hence it comes as no surprise that Marx complimented the Paris Commune of 1871 on its refusal to establish a reign of terror.[2] This seems to be more than special pleading on behalf of the Commune: for Marx this was a point of principle. If a revolution can be carried out, it can be carried out without terror. What one wishes to accomplish through terror cannot ultimately be accomplished under the given circumstances. From this point of view Kautsky was right when he read Marx as meaning that the recourse to terror is by itself a sign of weakness and frustration.[3] What Marx may have overlooked here was the possibility that through terror a revolutionary régime may succeed in holding on to its *political* power. None the less, political power retained through terror would be unable to emancipate itself from its terroristic birth marks, and would certainly cease to implement those ends for which it had been instituted. The retention of political power would under such circumstances become an end unto itself.

The Jacobin experience thus gains a wider significance: when Marx terms the Jacobin kind of revolution a merely 'political' revolution, he refers to two aspects at once. Such a revolution limits itself to the capture of political power without enquiring whether the socio-economic conditions make the retention of that power feasible. Yet such a process constitutes an attempt by the political sphere to force itself on civil society and to try to organize it according to its principles. This means the subsumption of all the spheres of private life under a political universality abstracted from its concrete conditions.

The dangers inherent in such a gap between political power and social circumstances were underlined by Marx in 1843 in his essay

---

[1] Marx to Engels, 30 January 1865 (*Selected Correspondence*, p. 193); Engels very aptly remarks in 1870 that 'we take [the Reign of Terror] to mean the rule of people who inspire terror. On the contrary, it is the rule of the people who themselves are terror-stricken. Terror implies mostly useless cruelties perpetrated by frightened people in order to reassure themselves' (Engels to Marx, 4 September 1870 (*ibid.* pp. 302–3)).
[2] *Selected Works*, I, 528–9.
[3] Kautsky, *op. cit.* p. 38. Cf. R. Luxemburg, *The Russian Revolution*, ed. Bertram D. Wolfe (Ann Arbor, 1961).

The French Revolution and the terror

Introduction to a Critique of Hegel's Philosophy of Right.[1] In a newspaper article of the following year Marx says that the merely political revolution is nothing but the ultimate radicalization of the dichotomy between the particular and the universal; it finally proves that merely political universality is illusory, since it shows that the state can realize its universality only by disregarding the particularistic content of civil society and abstracting from it. Such a one-sided universality does not constitute a synthesis that incorporates and overcomes particularism.[2]

From this Marx concludes that any merely political insurrection of the proletariat trying to create politically conditions not yet immanently developed in the socio-economic sphere is doomed to fail. Hence Marx's stubborn opposition, throughout his life, to a political *émeute* of the working class. The political sphere cannot, according to Marx, impose itself on civil society unless civil society has already developed within itself the elements that make this *tour de force* unnecessary. Marx's general view that political arrangements have their root in the conditions of civil society has been projected onto the strategy of revolution; politics by itself is impotent.[3]

This explains Marx's position in 1848. Despite his seeing in the political upheavals of this year a chance to create the circumstances for a socialist revolution, he consistently opposes all radical attempts at armed insurrection. A political revolution cannot bring down the walls of social reality. At the end of June 1848 Marx concludes his observations on the failure of the Jacobin-Blanquist *émeutes* in Paris by calling it not a defeat of the proletariat but a defeat of the republican Jacobin illusions, which fooled the workers into thinking that the failure of 1793 could become the success of 1848.[4] Two years later, when the need for immediate political consolation might have relaxed, Marx still holds the same view; summarizing 1848, and the June insurrection in particular, he says in *The Class Struggle in France*:

What succumbed in these defeats was not the revolution. It was the pre-revolutionary traditional appendages, results of social relationships which

[1] *Early Writings*, pp. 55–6. [2] *Vorwärts*, 8 August 1844 (*Werke*, I, 401, 407).
[3] *Selected Works*, I, 362.
[4] *Neue Rheinische Zeitung*, 29 June 1848 (*Werke*, V, 133–7).

had not yet come to the point of sharp class antagonisms—persons, illusions, conceptions, projects from which the revolutionary party before the February Revolution was not free, from which it could be freed not by the *victory of February*, but only by a series of defeats.[1]

Marx passes the same verdict on the radical insurrection in Germany, especially the Baden revolt of Friedrich Hecker, who was greatly influenced by French Jacobinism:

Friedrich Hecker expects everything to happen as a consequence of the magical activity of single personalities; we expect everything from the collisions that are consequences of economic conditions...For Friedrich Hecker the social questions are consequences of political struggles, for the *Neue Rheinische Zeitung* the political struggles are only a phenomenal form of social collisions. Friedrich Hecker could have been a good tricolor republican; the real opposition of the *NRZ* starts only with the tricolor republic.[2]

The ultimate subjectivism of Jacobinism also provides Marx's main argument against the Blanquist elements in the League of Communists. At the crucial meeting in London on 15 September 1850, when the League split into the Marx–Engels faction and the Willich–Schapper faction, Marx characterized his Blanquist opponents as follows:

Instead of the universal view of the *Manifesto* there comes the German national one, and the national feelings of the German artisan are being flattered. Instead of the materialistic view of the *Manifesto* they bring forth the idealist one. Instead of the real conditions they point to the *will* as the major factor in the revolution.

While we tell the workers: 'You have to endure and go through 15, 20, 50 years of civil war in order to change the circumstances, in order to make yourselves fit for power'—instead of that, you say: 'We must come to power immediately, or otherwise we may just as well go to sleep'. In the same way as the word 'People' has been used by the Democrats as a mere phrase, so the word 'Proletariat' is being used now...

As far as enthusiasm is concerned, one doesn't need to have much of it in order to belong to a party that is believed to be about to come to power. I have always opposed the ephemeral notions of the proletariat. We devote

[1] *Selected Works*, I, 139. Cf. also the last advice of the *NRZ*, on the day of its closing down, urging the workers *not* to revolt (19 May 1849; *Werke*, VI, 519).
[2] *Neue Rheinische Zeitung*, 29 October 1848 (*Werke*, V, 443).

ourselves to a party which is precisely far from achieving power. Would the proletariat have achieved power, then it would have enacted not proletarian, but petty-bourgeois legislation. Our party can achieve power only if and when conditions permit it to realise its *own* views. Louis Blanc serves as the best example of what can be achieved when one attains power prematurely.[1]

Marx's remarks about some of Willich's subsequent attempts at insurrection follow these premises: they will collapse immediately, or they will lead to political terrorism because of the incongruence between the political will and the objective conditions of civil society.[2]

These considerations can also explain the perplexing tone of Marx's *Address of the Central Committee of the Communist League* of March 1850.[3] This *Address* has been used· repeatedly to prove Marx's basically Blanquist attitude at that time. Yet such an explanation fails to explain why Marx totally altered his views between March and September 1850, when he caused the split in the League precisely because he opposed the Blanquist elements. Such an explanation also seems to be misled by Marx's rhetoric which here disguises his analytical insights.[4]

The *Address* is couched in somewhat violent language because any other tone would not have evoked a response from the defeated remnants of the League of Communists in Germany. Marx also had to pay lip-service to the Blanquist elements still members of the League. In content, however, this *Address* is in no way a blueprint for a proletarian revolution, but is intended as a guide in case the petty bourgeoisie rather than the proletariat should start a radical insurrection. Marx seeks to help the League in Germany if it should find itself in a situation not of its own making. For such an emergency

---

[1] *Werke*, VIII, 598–601. Cf. L. D. Easton, 'August Willich, Marx and Left-Hegelian Socialism', *Cahiers de l'ISEA*, no. 9 (August, 1965), pp. 101–37; W. Blumenberg, 'Zur Geschichte des Bundes der Kommunisten', *International Review of Social History*, IX (1964), 81–121; S. Na'aman, 'Zur Geschichte des Bundes der Kommunisten in der zweiten Phase seines Bestehens', *Archiv für Sozialgeschichte*, V (1965), 5–82.

[2] *Enthüllungen über den Kommunistenprozess zu Köln*, *Werke*, VIII, 461, 574–5; *Der Ritter vom edelmutigen Bewusstsein*, *Werke*, IX, 514 f.

[3] *Selected Works*, I, 106–17.

[4] Mehring, *Karl Marx*, pp. 202–4; J. Plamenatz, *German Marxism and Russian Communism* (London, 1954), p. 127.

he sends instructions to show members of the League how to avoid identification with the radical petty-bourgeois left and develop a revolutionary activity relevant to actual circumstances and invulnerable to putschistic revolutionarism. The whole *Address* lists suggestions aimed at securing the social and organizational basis of proletarian activity in the event of a petty bourgeois revolution. Marx thus urges the organization of proletarian associations so that they could become a real power if and when the revolution breaks out. Nowhere does he urge Communists to start that revolution themselves. He offers no directives for an *émeute*, a *putsch* or a *coup*. The closing passages of the *Address*, resigned in tone, stress the importance of the emergence and creation of class consciousness and envisage a lengthy revolutionary struggle, quite reminiscent of the '15, 20, 50 years' mentioned by Marx a few months later in his 15 September speech:

If the German workers are not able to attain power and achieve their own class interests without completely going through a lengthy revolutionary development, they at least know for a certainty this time that the first act of this approaching revolutionary drama will coincide with the direct victory of their own class in France and will be very much accelerated by it.

But they themselves must do the utmost for their final victory by clarifying their minds as to what their class interests are, by taking up their position as an independent party as soon as possible and by not allowing themselves to be seduced for a single moment by the hypocritical phrases of the democratic petty bourgeoisie...[1]

These considerations must have been behind Marx's protracted and jejeune polemic in the 'fifties with the German radical democratic politician Karl Vogt. Otherwise one can hardly understand why Marx inflated so tremendously something which at least appeared trivial. Vogt, in exile in Geneva, published in 1859 a book about an obscure libel case he was conducting against a German newspaper. In this book he called Marx the chief of a putschistic conspiracy, busily working at subversion and preparing for a violent take-over of power.[2] Marx spent several months in collecting

---

[1] *Selected Works*, I, 116–17.
[2] C. Vogt, *Mein Prozess gegen die 'Allgemeine Zeitung'*, (Genf 1859), p. 136; Anhang, pp. 31–2.

historical and legal material to refute this charge, and ultimately published his findings as a book of several hundred pages under the title *Herr Vogt*. Such massive retaliation by Marx can be understood only as part of his wider aims which saw in the League of Communists not just one more conspiratorial group aiming at a violent overthrow of political power but a novel phenomenon. Marx may have understated the case when he referred to the League of Communists as a 'propaganda association',[1] but basically his implication is valid. Marx saw the uniqueness of the League in its attempts to form the organizational and cognitive basis that will bring in its wake the change in the political and social structure. By lumping the League together with the dozens of conspiratorial societies which flourished in the undergrowth of the revolutionary movement, Vogt trivialized what Marx considered his major contribution to the working-class movement: the understanding in depth of social processes, coupled with the propagation of this understanding among the proletarians.[2] Marx rightly understood that Vogt's success in identifying him in this uncritical way with the Jacobin tradition would be the worst blow ever aimed at his theory.

The internal need of the working-class movement to emancipate itself from terrorism and Jacobinism appears in Marx's activity in the *International* as well. It explains Marx's strong condemnation of the terroristic anti-Bonapartist activity of the radical Blanquist French section of the International under the leadership of Félix Pyat.[3] In an annual report to the General Council of the International, published in the *International* press, Marx says in September 1868 that the French secret police considers the International just another conspiratorial association. They miss the real danger which the *International* poses to the Bonapartist régime.[4] On 3 May 1870 the General Council again dissociates itself from the conspiratorial tendencies and declares that the proletariat never really needs a conspiracy: its conspiracy is always public.[5]

[1] *Herr Vogt, Werke*, XIV, 438.
[2] Cf. the already quoted letter to Feuerbach of 11 August 1844 (*Werke*, XXVII, 425–7).
[3] See Marx's motion for a vote of censure on this, approved by the General Council on 7 July 1866 (*The General Council of the International 1866–1868*) [Moscow, n.d.], p. 224.
[4] *Werke*, XVI, 319.   [5] *Ibid.* p. 422.

These attitudes determined the path along which Marx tried to guide the *International* during the critical years 1870–1. The *First Address of the International on the Franco-Prussian War*, 23 July 1870, reaffirms this anti-putschist attitude.[1] It is even stronger in the *Second Address*, drafted by Marx and endorsed by the General Council on 9 September 1870, after the abdication of Napoleon III and the formation of the Provisional Government under Thiers. Marx could not have used harsher and stronger language against Thiers' government, yet he urged the workers not to fall into the traditional trap of French radicalism, the attempt to re-enact the 1793 fiasco all over again. His condemnation of working-class insurrection could not be more explicit:

We hail the advent of the Republic in France, but at the same time labour under misgivings which we hope will prove groundless. That Republic has not subverted the throne, but only taken its place become vacant. It has been proclaimed not as a social conquest, but as a national measure of defence. It is in the hands of a Provisional Government composed partly of notorious Orléanists, partly of middle-class Republicans, upon some of whom the insurrection of June, 1848, has left its indelible stigma. The Orleanists have seized the strongholds of the army and the police, while to the professed Republicans have fallen the talking departments. Some of their first acts show that they have inherited from the Empire, not only ruins, but also its dread of the working class...

The French working class moves, therefore, under circumstances of extreme difficulty. Any attempt at upsetting the new Government in the present crisis, when the enemy is almost knocking at the doors of Paris, would be a desperate folly. The French workmen must perform their duties as citizens; but, at the same time, they must not allow themselves to be deluded by the national *souvenirs* of 1792, as the French peasants allowed themselves to be deluded by the national *souvenirs* of the First Empire. They have not to recapitulate the past, but to build up the future. Let them calmly and resolutely improve the opportunities of Republican liberty, for the work of their own class organisation. It will give them with fresh Herculean powers for the regeneration of France, and our common task—the emancipation of labour. Upon their energies and wisdom hinges the fate of the Republic...

Vive la République![2]

---

[1] *Selected Works*, I, 486–90.   [2] *Ibid.* pp. 496–8.

The French Revolution and the terror

Indeed, three days earlier, on 6 September 1870, Marx tried to prevent the outbreak of a misdirected Blanquist insurrection in Paris; in a letter of that date he tells Engels:

I have just sat down to write to you when Serraillier comes in and informs me that he is leaving London for Paris tomorrow, but will stay there for only a few days. Main object: to settle the affairs of the International there (Conseil Fédérale de Paris). This is now even more necessary, since the whole French Branch [of the International in London] escapes now to Paris, in order to do there all kinds of follies in the name of the International. They wish to bring down the Provisional Government, to establish a Commune de Paris, nominate Pyat as French Ambassador to London etc.[1]

We shall see in the next chapter to what extent Marx changed his attitude to the Paris Commune once the insurrection had broken out. Yet at no stage did he believe that the Commune could succeed and survive, nor did he ever say anything of this sort even in his eulogy of the Commune in *The Civil War in France*. Marx always believed that the Commune, as a purely political insurrection, never had a chance. In a ruthless, though private, communication Marx summarized this in 1881 in a letter to a Dutch socialist:

One thing you can at any rate be sure of: a socialist government does not come into power in a country unless conditions are so developed that it can immediately take the necessary measures for intimidating the mass of the bourgeoisie sufficiently to gain time—the first *desideratum*—for permanent action.

Perhaps you will refer me to the Paris Commune; but apart from the fact that this was merely the rising of a city under exceptional conditions, the majority of the Commune was in no way socialist, nor could it be. With a modicum of common sense, however, it could have reached a compromise with Versailles useful to the whole mass of the people—the only thing that could have been reached at the time. The appropriation of the Bank of France alone would have been enough to put an end with terror to the vaunt of the Versailles people, etc. etc.[2]

[1] Marx to Engels, 6 September 1870 (*Briefwechsel*, IV, 453). Unfortunately the otherwise excellent study by H. Collins and C. Abramsky, *Karl Marx and the British Labour Movement* (London, 1965), in quoting this letter on p. 185 omits some of the central clauses of this sentence.

[2] Marx to Ferdinand Domela-Nieuwenhuis, 22 February 1881 (*Selected Correspondence*, p. 410). Collins and Abramsky (*op. cit.* p. 195) again omit the crucial clause 'the majority of the Commune was in no way socialist, nor could it be'.

The French Revolution and the terror

Had we not possessed Marx's pre-Commune letters, this might have looked like hindsight; but it is not. For Marx the majority of the Commune was interested in political power *per se*, not in society. Hence they were not socialists, 'nor could they be'.[1]

Marx summarized his attitude to the Blanquist-Jacobin *conspirateurs* in an article written in 1850, during his quarrel with the Willich–Schapper group. His characterization of the *conspirateur* is of some interest:

It is self-evident that these *conspirateurs* do not limit themselves to the mere task of organising the proletariat; not at all. Their business lies precisely in trying to pre-empt the developing revolutionary process, drive it artificially to crisis, to create a revolution *ex nihilo*, to make a revolution without the conditions of a revolution. For them, the only necessary condition for a revolution is an adequate organisation of their conspiracy. They are the alchemists of the revolution, and they share all the woolly-mindedness, follies and *idées fixes* of the former alchemists. They throw themselves on discoveries which should work revolutionary wonders: incendiary bombs, hell-machines of magical impact, *emeutes* which ought to be the more wonder-making and sudden the less they have any rational ground. Always busy and preoccupied with such absurd planning and conniving, they see no other end than the next toppling-over of the existing government. Hence their deepest disdain for the more theoretical enlightment of the workers about their class-interests. Hence their not proletarian, but rather plebeian, anger at those gentlemen in black coats (*habits noirs*), the more or less educated people, who represent this side of the movement, and from whom they never manage to free themselves wholly as the official representatives of the party.[2]

The Jacobin legacy is thus a trauma from which the working-class must, according to Marx, emancipate itself.

---

[1] Engels, on the other hand, did not share Marx's doubts about the Commune. For him, it was much simpler. 'Had the Paris Commune just exercised a little bit more authority and centralization, then it would have triumphed over the bourgeois' (Engels to Terzaghi, 14 January 1872, *Werke*, XXXIII, 372).

[2] *Werke*, VII, 273–4.

8

THE NEW SOCIETY

UNIVERSAL SUFFRAGE AND 'AUFHEBUNG DES STAATES'

The major difficulty in understanding Marx's postulate about the abolition of the state is a result of overlooking the dialectical overtones of the term *Aufhebung*. To this one should add Marx's own admission that even in its higher stage socialist society will require direction and planning at least in economic production, since socialism implies the subjection of man's creative powers to his conscious direction.[1] In *The Civil War in France* Marx refers to a 'national delegation' due to have been established by the Commune, and nowhere does he imply that this new body should ultimately disappear.[2] It is only natural that such statements have caused some consternation. They have given rise to the idea that after all the abolition of the state may have, strictly speaking, no concrete meaning: all it aims at is replacing the coercive power of the state by a legitimate form of social authority. But such an authority, it has been argued, might interfere in the life of the individual even more than the existing, largely minimalist state. The difference between this social authority and the state as we know it today would lie in the derivation of the legitimacy of the new authority from internal identification rather than external coercion.[3] Marx, then, seems to have been the last of the Lutherans.

Part of the difficulty may be avoided by pointing out that there is a marked difference between the terms Marx and Engels used when discussing the ultimate disappearance of the state under socialism. While Engels in the famous passage in his *Anti-Dühring* speaks about the state 'withering away' (*der Staat wird nicht 'abgeschafft', er stirbt*

---

[1] *The German Ideology*, pp. 91–2; *The 18th Brumaire, Selected Works*, I, 340; *Capital*, III, 798–9.

[2] *Selected Works*, I, 376. Lenin, on the other hand (*State and Revolution*, pp. 64–71), argues that this 'residual state' will also disappear. Though this may be an interesting gloss of Lenin on Marx's text, it was never clearly said by Marx himself.

[3] This has been most convincingly argued by Thilo Ramm, 'Die künftige Gesellschaftsform nach der Theorie von Marx und Engels', *Marxismusstudien*, II, 77–119.

Universal suffrage

ab),[1] Marx always refers to the abolition and transcendence (*Auf-hebung*) of the state. *Absterben des Staates* and *Aufhebung des Staates* are clearly two different terms deriving from quite different intellectual traditions: while Engels' *Absterben* is a biological simile, Marx's *Aufhebung* is a philosophical term with clear dialectical overtones.

For the first time Marx refers to the *Aufhebung des Staates* in his various 1843 essays. As we have already seen, he conceives the modern state as a perpetual tension between the idea of universality, ideally a bulwark against the particularistic interests of civil society, and these antagonistic interests themselves. From this point of view Marx always sees the state differently from Engels (and Kautsky and Lenin who largely follow Engels). For Engels the state is nothing more than an external organization for coercion mechanistically directed by the dominant economic powers.[2] For Marx the being of the state attests to the existence of a tension between the actual and the ideal, between the existing particularistic, interest-oriented social forces and the postulate of universality. This tension exists, according to Marx, because the modern political state exists as such only in one segment of real life, while all the other spheres of life lie open to the *bellum omnium contra omnes* of civil society. In an article in *Vorwärts* of 1844 Marx says that the more marked the existence of a separate political sphere, the farther is a society from realizing the true organizing principle of the state, i.e. universalism. In this respect the state resembles religion: the more intensive it is, the deeper the gap that it tries to cover.[3] Marx continues that the way to abolish this dualism cannot be found within the existing framework of the state as a separate, partial organization, since its partiality will always frustrate the attempts at universalism. The solution must be found beyond the state. The life of the individual can achieve universal content only after the framework of the state as a separate and distinct organization has disappeared, for the *separate* organization of a universal sphere (= the state) presupposes the existence of a particularistic, interest-oriented sphere.

[1] F. Engles, *Anti-Dühring*, 3rd English edition (Moscow, 1962), p. 385.
[2] Cf. R. Miliband, 'Marx and the State', *Socialist Register, 1965* (London), pp. 278–96.
[3] *Vorwärts*, 7 August 1844 (*Werke*, I, 402); Cf. *Early Writings*, p. 11.

Only the disappearance of a separate form of universality will make the realization of universality possible.

We have already seen in chapter 1 that in his *Critique of Hegel's Philosophy of Right* Marx makes the abolition of the state as a separate organization contingent upon universal suffrage. In realizing the determination of the political sphere by the whole public, universal suffrage abolishes the distinction between state and civil society and thus abolishes the state as a particular organ divorced from the totality of economic real life. That Marx viewed universal suffrage not as the mere realization of a radical democratic political vision but as the true *Aufhebung* of the state is evident also from notes he prepared in 1845 for a book on the modern state. Its last chapter would have been entitled: 'Suffrage, the fight for the abolition [*Aufhebung*] of the state and of civil society.'[1] The *Aufhebung* of the state is thus made possible only after the political structure has utilized all of its potentialities. Consequently, the form of the state, always partial, on becoming identical with its universal content also ceases to be mere form. The universality underlying Hegelian political philosophy will thus be realized only when the state itself will be *aufgehoben*—abolished, transcended, preserved. Realization of the Hegelian philosophy of the state is made possible only through the abolition of the state.[2]

Such an interpretation may give systematic substance to the closing paragraphs of the second chapter of *The Communist Manifesto*, where Marx details proletarian rule. Marx does not use the term 'dictatorship of the proletariat' in this context: he does not use the term more than two or three times in his life, and then always in what is basically a private communication.[3] In the *Manifesto*, proletarian rule is connected with the attainment of universal suffrage: 'The first step in the revolution of the working class is to raise the proletariat to the position of ruling class, to win the battle

---

[1] *The German Ideology*, p. 655.   [2] *The Poverty of Philosophy*, p. 197.
[3] *Critique of the Gotha Programme, Selected Works*, II, 33; Letter to Weydemeyer, 5 March 1852 (*ibid.* II, 452). Indirectly also Speech of 25 September 1871 (*Werke*, XVII, 433). The much-quoted reference to the 'dictatorship of the proletariat' in *The Civil War in France* does not represent Marx's own programme: once the reference is to slogans that appeared in Paris during the June 1848 insurrection, and once to the theories of Blanqui's (*Selected Works*, I, 162, 223).   [4] *Selected Works*, I, 53.

of democracy' (*die Erkämpfung der Demokratie*).[4] After enumerating the various steps undertaken by the proletarian regime, some of them, as we shall see, brutally interfering with property relations, Marx concludes that:

When, in the course of development, class distinctions have disappeared, and all production has been concentrated in the hands of a vast association of the whole nation, the public power will lose its political character. . .

In place of the old civil society, with its classes and class antagonisms, we shall have an association, in which the free development of each is the condition for the free development of all.[1]

The detailed plan leading to this result is extremely interesting in itself, and it should be quoted in full since it is one of the few instances where Marx gives some idea about the concrete steps to be undertaken by a proletarian government:

The proletariat will use its political supremacy to wrest, by degrees, all capital from the bourgeoisie, to centralise all instruments of production in the hands of the State, i.e. of the producers organised as the ruling class; and to increase the total of productive forces as rapidly as possible.

Of course, in the beginning, this cannot be effected except by means of despotic inroads on the rights of property, and on the conditions of bourgeois production; by means of measures, therefore, which appear economically insufficient and untenable, but which, in the course of the movement, outstrip themselves, necessitate further inroads upon the old social order, and are unavoidable as a means of entirely revolutionising the mode of production.

These measures will of course be different in different countries.

Nevertheless in the most advanced countries, the following will be pretty generally applicable.

1. Abolition of property in land and application of all rents of land to public purposes.

2. A heavy progressive or graduated income tax.

3. Abolition of all rights of inheritance.

4. Confiscation of the property of all emigrants and rebels.

5. Centralisation of credit in the hands of the State, by means of a national bank with State capital and an exclusive monopoly.

6. Centralisation of the means of communication and transport in the hands of the State.

7. Extension of factories and instruments of production owned by the

---

[1] *Ibid.* p. 54.

State; the bringing into cultivation of waste-lands, and the improvement of the soil generally in accordance with a common plan.

8. Equal liability of all to labour. Establishment of industrial armies, especially for agriculture.

9. Combination of agriculture with manufacturing industries; gradual abolition of the distinction between town and country, by a more equable distribution of the population over the country.

10. Free education for all children in public schools. Abolition of children's factory labour in its present form. Combination of education with industrial production, &c., &c.[1]

Despite its appearance as a haphazard list of regulations aimed at changing the structure of society, this is a sophisticated plan of action and legislation. Not only is it undoctrinaire and flexible, its approach is pluralistic in its clear assertion that the arrangements will have to vary considerably from one country to another. *But its most amazing feature is that it does not include nationalization of industry as such*: it suggests nationalization of land, but not of industry. The means of production are not to be taken away from their private owners by a political *fiat* which, according to Marx, might result in economic chaos, outright political opposition and sabotage and serious dislocation of production. Private industry will be allowed to continue to exist surrounded by such a climate of economic and political arrangements that it will slowly, in as peaceful and orderly a fashion as possible, have to transform itself. High progressive taxes, the abolition of inheritance, competition from the public sector which will no doubt be favoured by the state monopoly of banking and transport—all these will slowly ease private industry out. Not through one-sided political means, but by gradually creating the economic conditions which will make the further existence of private industry economically unviable.

Two more aspects characterize this list of Ten Regulations. First, this seemingly eclectic programme has one trait which underlies all the steps suggested here: all involve the wielding of state power for the attainment of universal goals. By applying this policy the proletarian state will be the first state in history to use political power for universal and not partial ends. This programme thus realizes the

[1] *Selected Works*, I, 53–4.

Hegelian postulate about the universality of the state. Dialectically, the state that would really carry out its universal potential must end with communism and consequently with its own abolition, since 'public power will lose its political character'. The ultimate realization of the Hegelian idea of the state as universal power implies, according to Marx, that, once the state is truly universal, it ceases to exist as a differentiated organism.

Secondly, none of the steps suggested here by Marx is by itself novel or revolutionary. All intensify and further develop trends already working within the capitalist system and gradually changing it. Proletarian rule will thus only accelerate the pace of this development and make dominant traits still marginal or secondary in existing society. Certainly the disappearance of ground rent characterizes capitalist society, but even progressive taxation on income (and not on consumption), introduced into England a few years before the writing of the *Manifesto*, was sometimes considered a dangerous assault on the rights of private property; so were slowly emerging death duties, the newly created monopoly of the Bank of England in note circulation and the prohibition to private banks against issuing negotiable notes. The most revolutionary development of the nineteenth century—railroad construction—could have been carried out only at the expense of severely infringing the rights of private property, both by recourse to expropriation and compulsory purchase of vast tracts of land necessary for the railroads, and by public guarantee of the stock and debentures floated by the railway companies. Thus capitalist society creates the tools of its own transformation, since it cannot continue to function unless it abolishes its own premises. It is this dialectical development which causes Marx to reflect that the transformation of capitalist society is immanently determined. The Ten Regulations of the *Manifesto* are nothing but such a dialectical realization and abolition of the processes already working within capitalist society. But the first act of the state as a state—i.e. as a universally oriented organization—will also be its last act as such. Once the proletariat submits the egoism of civil society to the universalism of the state the traditional dichotomies between state and civil society will disappear.

This dialectical attitude towards the state, to be realized and abolished at the same time, explains Marx's views on the various anarchistic theories of the state. For Marx the *Aufhebung* of the state realizes the content implied in the idea of the state, since his concept of the state remains tied to its Hegelian origins and is thus always slightly ambivalent. The anarchists, on the other hand, whose intellectual genealogy goes back to the basically individualist Natural Law theories, see in the state only its coercive, evil side. Marx never loses sight of this coercive element in all political institutions, but his argument implies that this element derives from circumstances which made the historical state dependent upon civil society. Once this dependence upon civil society disappears with civil society itself, coercion will automatically disappear as well. This disappearance of civil society can be achieved only through a prior wielding of state power for truly universal ends; in this way the potential universality immanent in the Hegelian theory of the state would become an actuality and not a merely abstract postulate.

Some of this attitude comes through in Marx's comments on Bakunin's exploits in Lyons in 1870:

As to Lyons, I have received letters not fit for publication...A revolutionary Government was at once established—*La Commune*—composed partly of workmen belonging to the 'International', partly of Radical middle-class Republicans...But the asses, Bakunin and Cluseret, arrived at Lyons and spoiled everything. Belonging both to the 'International', they had, unfortunately, influence enough to mislead our friends. The Hotel de Ville was seized—for a short time—and most foolish decrees on the *abolition de l'état* and similar nonsense were issued...[1]

For the anarchist the 'abolition' of the state is a political act, decreed by law and carried out by force. For Marx, *Aufhebung* of the state is the ultimate outcome of a lengthy process of economic and social transformations, introduced and sustained by political power. Marx sees the state as *aufgehoben* when its universal content has been realized. Bakunin wants the state abolished because he sees in it only coercion. According to Marx, *Aufhebung* is the consequence of a social *praxis* creating a new reality. For Bakunin it is a declaratory act. Marx argues that such a view of the state influenced the anarchists' disregard for political action and trade union activity. In

[1] Marx to Beesly, 19 October 1870 (*Selected Correspondence*, p. 304).

Universal suffrage

Marx's own language, the anarchists are estranged from 'tout movement d'ensemble'.[1]

Seen thus, the Paris Commune was for Marx an attempt to replace the illusory universality of a partial state by an association truly universally oriented. Based on universal suffrage, the Commune approached the stage at which the distinctions between state and civil society begin to disappear. The traditional state apparatus, the institutionalization of illusory universality, was smashed by the Commune. In the draft manuscript of *The Civil War in France* Marx says:

> The Commune—the reabsorption of the State power by society as its own living forces instead of as forces controlling and subduing it, by the popular masses themselves, forming their own force instead of the organised force of their suppression—the political form of their emancipation, instead of the artificial force (appropriated by their oppressors)... of society wielded for their oppression by their enemies.[2]

Consequently the elected magistracy of the Commune is to Marx something quite different from a bureaucracy. The fact that public servants were elected and dismissed by the electorate and were paid a worker's wage—all these arrangements of the Commune Marx praised not because they represented direct democracy or egalitarian principles. For Marx the emergence of such a public magistracy means the gradual disappearance of the distinction between state and civil society and protection against the re-emergence of a new *separate* sphere concerned with general, public affairs. Marx similarly refers to the Commune transferring to local, i.e. social, government what had previously been the separate realm of central, hierarchic government. Government is thus emptied of that kind of power that made it into an force independent *vis-à-vis* society.[3]

[1] *Recueil*, II, 284.   [2] *Archiv Marksa i Engelsa* (III), pp. 326–8.
[3] *Selected Works*, I, 520–1. How much the orthodox interpretation of Marx failed to grasp the dialectical implications of his thought on the *Aufhebung* of the state appears in the otherwise most intelligent study of H. Cunow, *Die Marxsche Geschichts-, Gesellschafts- und Staatstheorie* (Berlin, 1920) where the author says (I, 334) that the Commune abolished the coercive elements of the political structure while preserving the other element of political power and thus 'created a new state, based on self-government'. Lenin (*State and Revolution*, pp. 103 f.) shows a similar disregard for the dialectical element involved, but in this he only follows Engels who said in 1875

The new society

Thé principles underlying Marx's *The Civil War in France* are thus identical with the consequences implied by his 1843 *Critique* in discussing bureaucracy, universal suffrage and the dialectical abolition of the state. In both cases *Aufhebung* is connected with universal suffrage, whose effective existence implies the dialectical overcoming and disappearance of the state as a distinct organism. This vision is not, however, identical with the so-called 'reformist' tradition in Social Democracy which suggested that the workers can achieve their aims *through* universal suffrage. Such an attitude again fails to take into account the dialectical relationship between ends and means. For Marx universal suffrage *per se* stands for the end of the political state as previously known and introduces new conditions that do not preserve the alienation between state and civil society. For the 'reformist' Social Democrats, universal suffrage is just a means to attain specific aims.

This difference also implies that the later controversy among socialists about parliamentarism approaches the issue from an angle different from that of Marx. Marx never really identified universal suffrage with parliamentarism, which rather signified the bourgeois limited suffrage; the term 'parliamentary democracy' (current in later Marxist literature) never occurs in Marx's own writings. For Marx parliamentarism is the limited parliamentary rule of the mid-nineteenth century, socially and functionally almost a total antithesis of the universality implied in universal suffrage. Socially, because property qualifications make it class rule, the right to vote being directly determined by considerations drawn from the particularistic spheres of civil society; functionally, because under the (individualistic) doctrine of separation of powers, parliament's merely legislative powers alienate it from the decision-making executive power—a point already discussed by Marx in his 1843 *Critique*.

According to Marx, universal suffrage, bound to make the representative assembly represent all society, will also emancipate it from its limitations as a merely legislative body. In the published

that 'so long as the proletariat still *uses* the state, it does not use it in the interests of freedom but in order to hold down its adversaries' (*Selected Works*, ii, 42). The Ten Regulations of the *Manifesto* clearly show that the proletariat uses the state for entirely different aims.

version of *The Civil War in France* the implications of universal suffrage are described as follows:

Instead of deciding once in three or six years which member of the ruling class was to misrepresent the people in Parliament, universal suffrage was to serve the people, constituted in Communes, as individual suffrage serves every other employer in the search for the workmen and managers in his business. And it is well known that companies, like individuals, in matters of real business, generally know how to put the right man in the right place, and, if they for once make a mistake, to redress it promptly. On the other hand, nothing could be more foreign to the spirit of the Commune than to supersede universal suffrage by hierarchical investiture.[1]

The trans-political nature of universal suffrage is underlined by Marx in another fashion in the manuscript draft of the essay: 'General suffrage, till now abused either for parliamentary sanction of the Holy State Power, or a play in the hands of the ruling classes only employed by the people to sanction parliamentary class rule once in many years adapted [now] to its real purposes, to choose by the communes their own functionaries of administration and initiation.'[2]

This connection between universal suffrage and the *Aufhebung* of the state gives additional weight to those passages in Marx's work where he links the achievement of socialism in the West to the introduction of universal suffrage.

We have already seen that *The Communist Manifesto* makes the victory of the proletariat synonymous with winning the battle of democracy. The universal postulates of the state, implied in the Ten Regulations, would be implemented since political decision is now reached universally; form and content are united. These Ten Regulations are expressly limited by Marx to the more developed countries, because only there has the modern state differentiated itself sufficiently from the other spheres of life to be *aufgehoben*.

These Ten Regulations have a practical corollary: a few weeks

---

[1] *Selected Works*, I, 520–1. Marx further remarks that elections would be indirect. Ramm, *op. cit.*, points to the similarity between this indirect method of elections endorsed by Marx and the system of indirect elections introduced by Marx into the *League of Communists*. No Rousseauist overtones of direct democracy can be traced in Marx's description of the Commune.

[2] *Archiv Marksa i Engelsa* (III), p. 328.

after the publication of the *Manifesto*, Marx and Engels drew up—
on the outbreak of the 1848 revolution—a list of communist demands
for Germany. The list, published as a pamphlet by the *League of
Communists*, reiterates the Ten Regulations of the *Manifesto*, and
demands the establishment of a united German republic. Title II
of the list demands universal suffrage for every male citizen over
twenty-one years of age, and Title III demands the payment of an
adequate salary to all elected representatives.[1] These are not the
demands of communists 'in the bourgeois revolution', as the later
jargon would have had it, since all these demands seek to convert and
transform the (partially or fully developed) bourgeois society into a
socialist one. With universal suffrage bourgeois society transcends
itself. This is the basic prerequisite for the establishment of a
universally oriented state power dialectically bound to seek its own
disappearance. The abolition of universal suffrage in a revolutionary
situation, according to Marx, means reversion to a partial, illusory
universalism with one segment of society declaring itself the voice
of all society. For Marx such a *pars pro toto*, bourgeois or, for that
matter, Leninist, would never be able to carry out the universal
postulates inherent in the state, and abolish the state. On the contrary, such a narrow political view of revolution would only tend to
make the revolutionaries into a new 'political', i.e. partial group or
class.

Negatively Marx shows that universal suffrage leads to communism and the *Aufhebung* of the state in *The Class Struggles in France
1848–1850*. Here Marx analyses the impact of universal suffrage as it
functioned in the Second Republic. He argues against the radical
republicans, who saw in universal suffrage *per se*, disregarding the
conditions under which it was introduced, a universal panacea. The
difference between Marx's attitude and that of the radical democrats
is obvious. For the latter universal suffrage represents the ultimate
institutional form of political organization; for Marx it is just the
self-transforming vehicle that supersedes and abolishes politics itself.
Secondly, Marx points out that under the Second Republic universal suffrage has not been introduced in order to promote communism and the abolition of the state. Rather it was promulgated

[1] *Forderungen der kommunistischen Partei in Deutschland, Werke*, V, 3.

out of what Marx calls the radical illusions which thought that universal suffrage could co-exist with a bourgeois society. For Marx, these two are incompatible. If they exist simultaneously in any particular society they create a perpetual tension between the political constitution and the existing social forces. By itself universal suffrage would ultimately lead to communism. Since this was not the intention of the French legislators, every attempt was made to frustrate the necessary consequences of this legislation. Napoleon III is the hybrid product of this tension which wrote a structural conflict, an endemic civil war and the *putsch* into the French constitution. Bourgeois society will do anything—even prostrate itself before Louis Bonaparte—to prevent universal suffrage from achieving its ends:

The comprehensive contradiction of this constitution, however, consists in the following: the classes whose social slavery the constitution is to perpetuate, proletariat, peasantry, petty bourgeoisie, it puts in possession of political power through universal suffrage. And from the class whose old social power it sanctions, the bourgeoisie, it withdraws the political guarantees of this power. It forces the political rule of the bourgeoisie into democratic conditions, which at every moment help the hostile classes to victory and jeopardise the very foundations of bourgeois society. From the ones it demands that they should not go forward from political to social emancipation; from the others that they should not go back from social to political restoration.[1]

Marx uses similar criteria in his argument against Lassalle's agitation for universal suffrage in Bismarckian Prussia. Marx's doubts about these Lassallean demands mainly centre on the argument that, under the present conditions in Prussia, universal suffrage could be achieved only as a grant from the Junker, monarchic régime. It could not be wielded to establish communism. Only the social context of universal suffrage makes it a vehicle of revolution, and Marx has no doubt that the effort to use universal suffrage for this purpose in conservative Prussia would only precipitate a *putsch* by the Court and the aristocratic, reactionary establishment. Subsequent historical development confirmed Marx's fears, since Bismarck's *Sozialistengesetzte* demonstrated the régime's

[1] *Selected Works*, I, 172.

213

The new society

unwillingness to abide by the rules of the game. When it felt threatened, the Prussian state did not hesitate to use measures repugnant to the spirit of universal suffrage. Marx asserts that the relatively weak German proletariat would be a captive of its own slogans and of the Prussian monarchy if universal suffrage were granted by a royal *ukase*. As in France, universal suffrage might also make the conservative peasantry the ultimate arbiter of politics. To this one should add the fact that the Prussian monarch would have granted universal suffrage only to annihilate the parliamentary power of the liberal bourgeoisie, whose strength comes precisely from a limited suffrage dependent on property qualifications. Such a weakening of the bourgeoisie and of emergent capitalism in Germany would also, according to Marx, frustrate the development of capitalism toward its own internal *Aufhebung*.[1]

After the consideration of the possible perversion of universal suffrage for conservative ends, Marx's views of its legitimate use in the West should be discussed. Marx's first explicit statement about universal suffrage introducing working-class rule appears in an article called 'The Chartists' published in *The New York Daily Tribune* of 25 August 1852. After pointing to the differences between Continental and British conditions, he says:

We now come to the *Chartists*, the politically active portion of the British *working class*. The six points of the Charter which they contend for contain nothing but the demand of *Universal Suffrage*, and of the conditions without which Universal Suffrage would be illusory for the working class; such as the ballot, payment of members, annual general elections. But Universal Suffrage is the equivalent of political power for the working class of England, where the proletariat forms the large majority of the population, where, in a long, though underground civil war, it has gained a clear consciousness of its position as a class, and where even the rural districts know no longer any peasants, but only landlords, industrial capitalists (farmers) and hired labourers. The carrying of Universal Suffrage in England would, therefore, be a far more socialistic measure than anything which has been honoured with that name on the Continent.

Its inevitable result, here, is *the political supremacy of the working class*.[2]

[1] *Critique of the Gotha Programme, Selected Works*, II, 32–3.
[2] *On Britain* (Moscow, 1962), p. 361.

214

Universal suffrage

The revolutionary consequences of the introduction of universal suffrage into England are explicitly related by Marx to the socio-economic context of contemporary English society. We have already seen that Marx considers English society to be undergoing a profound internal change through the introduction of factory laws and other social legislation pointing toward post-*laissez-faire* economy:

In England the process of social upheaval [*Umwälzungsprozess*] is palpable. When it has reached a certain point, it must re-act on the Continent. There it will take a form more brutal or more humane, according to the degree of development of the working class itself. Apart from higher motives, their own most important motives dictate to the classes that are for the nonce the ruling ones, the removal of all legally removable hindrances to the free development of the working class. For this reason, as well as others I have given so large a space in this volume to the history, the details, and the results of English factory legislation. One nation can and should learn from another. And even when a society has got upon the right track for the discovery of the natural laws of its movement...it can neither clear by bold leaps, nor remove by legal enactments, the obstacles offered by the successive phases of its normal development. But it can shorten and lessen the birth pangs.[1]

This was written in 1867, when the Second Reform Bill introduced a considerable part of the British working class to parliamentary suffrage. Marx comes back to the same subject on another occasion during the same year. In a speech commemorating the fourth anniversary of the Polish insurrection, Marx says on 22 January 1867: 'It is possible that the struggle between the workers and the capitalists will be less terrible and less bloody than the struggle between the feudal lords and the bourgeoisie in England and France. Let us hope so.'[2]

In an interview published in an American journal in 1871, Marx again says that the working class in England does not need a violent revolution in order to achieve political power: 'In England, for example, the way is open for the working class to develop their political power. In a place where they can achieve their goal more

---

[1] *Capital*, I, 9–10.
[2] This speech was published in the Polish emigré paper *Głos Wolny* on 2 February 1867 (*Werke*, XVI, 204).

quickly and more securely through peaceful propaganda, insurrection would be a folly.'[1]

Less than a year later Marx again envisages the possibility that the British labour class might achieve power through universal suffrage. This time he adds the United States, and tentatively the Netherlands, to the list of countries where such a transformation may be possible. In his speech at Amsterdam on 18 September 1872 summing up the Hague Congress of the International, Marx says:

> The workers must one day conquer political supremacy in order to establish the new organisation of labour...But we do not assert that the attainment of this end requires identical means. We know that one has to take into consideration the institutions, mores, and traditions of the different countries, and we do not deny that there are countries like England and America and if I am familiar with your institutions, Holland, where labour may attain its goal by peaceful means.[2]

The caution of this statement demands caution in discussion. Since Marx determinedly refused to prophesy about the way revolution would occur in any particular country, he only sketches those possibilities more likely to happen than others. Moreover, his explicit reference to the different elements of political culture worthy of consideration clearly exhibits his pluralistic attitude, never limited to a mechanistic analysis of economic aspects. Marx adds an interesting reservation to a similar statement made about the same time in a conversation with Hyndman, the founder of the Social Democratic Federation of Great Britain. In his memoirs Hyndman writes that in the 'seventies Marx once remarked that 'England is the one country in which a peaceful revolution is possible; but—he added after a pause—history does not tell us so. You English like the Romans in many things are most like them in

[1] *Woodhull & Claflin's Weekly*, 12 August 1871. About a month later Marx says that England is the only country developed enough to allow the working class to turn universal suffrage towards its true end (see *New Politics*, II, no. 3, p. 131).

[2] *The First International: Minutes of the Hague Congress of 1872*, ed. H. Gerth (Madison, 1958), p. 236. One of the last survivors of the First International present at Marx's speech at Amsterdam could not remember in 1932 what Marx had said there (T. Cuno, 'Reminiscences', in *Reminiscences of Marx and Engels*, p. 212). Whether this was due to old age or to the unwillingness of Cuno, who was pro-Soviet, to embarrass the Marx-Engels-Lenin Institute to which he submitted his testimony is difficult to decide.

your ignorance of your own history.'[1] That the future is open to a variety of possibilities although the dominant tendency in England is working-class power through universal suffrage is again the theme of a letter from Marx to Hyndman, dated 8 December 1880: 'If the unavoidable evolution turn into a revolution, it would not only be the fault of the ruling class, but also of the working class.'[2]

This need not imply that Marx gradually shifted from a 're-volutionary' to an 'evolutionary' position,[3] since the connection between universal suffrage and *Aufhebung* of the state runs through all his writings. Marx never visualized a violent revolution in England even in his earlier writings; nor should it be overlooked that in the Amsterdam speech he explicitly says that the development on the Continent may not be peaceful at all.

This may also explain why Marx says so little about violence in the forthcoming revolution. In the context of Marx's thought the revolution is never an act of violence using physical power for ends that transcend physical power. A view of revolution based on such a relationship between means and ends will ultimately substitute the means for the end. For Marx the dilemma of revolution cannot be thus reduced to what later became known as the 'evolutionary' versus the 'revolutionary' view. From Marx's point of view the transformation of society is always revolutionary, since it implies the transformation of the determined into the determining and vice versa. This transformation in its turn implies a revolution in human consciousness, i.e. in human *praxis*. The exact circumstances in which the revolution will be carried out cannot therefore be pre-determined, because such a prediction would mean that man can will the future. Marx, envisaging a broad spectrum of possibilities, maintains an undoctrinaire attitude: gradualism may be possible in

---

[1] H. M. Hyndman, *The Record of an Adventurous Life* (London, 1911), p. 273.
[2] *Ibid.* p. 283. In his later years Engels tended to adopt a wholly evolutionary attitude. In his 1891 remarks to the Erfurt Programme he envisages the possibility of peaceful evolution in 'democratic republics like France and the U.S.A. and monarchies like England'—but not in Germany (*Werke*, XXII, 235–6). In his 1895 Introduction to *The Class Struggles in France* Engels is so overwhelmed by the SPD's success at the polls that he bases all his hopes on universal suffrage and even explains the military hopelessness of barricade war under modern technology and communication (*Selected Works*, I, 132–6).
[3] This has recently been most forcefully argued by Lichtheim, *Marxism*, pp. 223–30.

the Anglo-Saxon countries, whereas more radical means will probably have to be applied on the Continent. *The Communist Manifesto* itself, for all its aggressive language, is singularly silent about the way in which the revolution would occur. Marx can talk simultaneously in the *Manifesto* about winning the battle of democracy and about 'despotic inroads on the rights of property'. Even a revolution sustained by universal suffrage will have to expropriate certain forms of private property, although selectively as implied in the Ten Regulations. Expropriation, of course, may necessitate violence or threats of violence, and Marx is aware that an act may be 'despotic' with regard to an individual person even if it is sanctioned by a majority. The question of violent versus peaceful revolution thus resolves itself into the question whether the recourse to violence will occur prior to its legitimization by majority decision or after such legitimization. For Marx, this question is trivial, since it emphasizes the accepted bourgeois modes of legitimization and divorces legitimacy from social *praxis*. Marx envisions the revolution occurring in the more developed countries through universal suffrage, not because he insists on a democratic form of legitimization, but because he sees in universal suffrage the resolution of the conflict between state and civil society. Those who—justly—point to Marx's passages about universal suffrage should be careful not to confuse them with a commitment to democratic values.

We have already seen in the preceding chapter that Marx's attitude to physical force is determined also by his critique of the French Revolution as a merely political revolution. To Marx the wielding of power as a distinct political means admits that circumstances (and consciousness as one of their components) are yet unripe for change. Where, however, power is applied not through a distinct political structure, it is mostly superfluous, as socio-economic development itself has already caught up with the trends now being realized through the dialectics of internal change. The ends of social action are thus achieved without recourse to the threat of physical power. One can summarize Marx's position by saying that for Marx physical power will either fail or prove to be superfluous. By itself physical power achieves nothing.

Marx relates the chances of revolution to its geographical setting.

218

Universal suffrage

Here again an intensification of Marx's views caused a shift in emphasis. We have already noted that at the outset of his intellectual career Marx saw Germany as more fit than any nation for a radical revolution, mainly because its backwardness makes the gap between the realities of life and their theoretical reflection more pronounced. In 1843 Marx writes that 'the struggle against the political present of the Germans is a struggle against the past of modern nations' and that 'in politics the Germans have thought what other nations have done'.[1] Therefore, he argues, Germany is readier for a radical revolution, since Germany's backwardness confronts most glaringly the ideal she has embraced and finds herself unable to emulate. Further, since Germany has no strong middle class that can identify itself with the general will, a 1789 is just impossible in Germany and would lead directly to a proletarian revolution. In 1847 Marx observes that Germany's economic backwardness makes her bourgeoisie start defending itself against the proletariat before finishing its war against feudalism: 'the bourgeoisie is fighting the proletariat before it succeeded in establishing itself as a class'.[2]

The vulnerability of the German socio-economic structure is again discussed in *The Communist Manifesto*. For all it says about the contradictions of the more developed capitalist countries, the *Manifesto* does not expect the revolution to start there; on the contrary:

The Communists turn their attention chiefly to Germany, because that country is on the eve of a bourgeois revolution that is bound to be carried out under more advanced conditions of European civilisation, and with a much more developed proletariat, than that of England was in the seventeenth century, and of France in the eighteenth century, and because the bourgeois revolution in Germany will be but the prelude to an immediately following proletarian revolution.[3]

Later developments changed the position of Germany, and 1848 proved to Marx that weakness made the German bourgeoisie far readier than anyone supposed to come to terms with the feudal

---

[1] *Early Writings*, pp. 47, 51. Hess also felt that the Germans only contemplated what the Western nations actually did (Hess to Marx, 17 January 1845, in Hess, *Briefwechsel*, p. 105).
[2] *Deutsche Brüsseler Zeitung*, 18 November 1847 (*Werke*, IV, 351).
[3] *Selected Works*, I, 65.

classes and the absolute monarchy. Yet Marx envisages in the 1880s a revolution in Russia that might become 'a signal for a proletarian revolution in the West',[1] because Russia was then undergoing that kind of a late accelerated industrial development which Germany had experienced two decades earlier.

Where the introduction of universal suffrage implies, as in the Anglo-Saxon countries, the closing of the gap between state and civil society, it may, according to Marx, become the lever for proletarian revolution. In countries with a strong authoritarian tradition, a huge, docile peasantry and a late industrial development, universal suffrage may have limited, if not outright perverse, significance. Marx is aware that not only economic development counts in the effort to assess the chances of revolution and change. It is rather the relative development of the socio-political structure *vis-à-vis* the economic background that creates both the tensions and the chances for change. Paradoxically this historicism may be the most disappointing element in Marx's thought. Though it helps to emancipate Marx's thought from a naïve, linear theory of automatic and general progress, it creates another marked complication. For Marx's theory of revolution is based on universal criteria, yet its realization ultimately depends on historical circumstances that by nature vary from one place to another. This tension lends to Marx's analysis its sharp realistic edge, but it may, on the other hand, frustrate attempts to achieve his universalistic postulates. The historical and philosophical may not, after all, be so permanently united.

THE STAGES OF SOCIALISM

It has been frequently pointed out that Marx's sketches of future society are few and fragmentary. In addition to *The Civil War in France*, which deals mainly with the political aspects of the transition to socialism, only two texts deal in some detail with socialist society. They include one of Marx's earliest writings and one of his latest: a section of the 1844 *Manuscripts* called 'Private Property and Communism' and the *Critique of the Gotha Programme* (1875). Both texts are unfinished sketches, not intended for publication, and, as

[1] Preface to the Russian edition of the *Manifesto* (1882), *Selected Works*, I, 24.

a result, fragmentary. Despite this and the thirty years between them, they are similar in their description of future society and in a marked reticence about going into detail.

Systematically, it is significant that even in these two texts Marx says nothing about the way in which the transformation will occur. This limitation is imposed on Marx by his own epistemological premises. Though it may sometimes irritate anyone looking for precise eschatological prophecies in Marx, it cannot be divorced from his basic philosophy. Since the future is not as yet an existing reality, any discussion of it reverts to philosophical idealism in discussing objects which exist only in the consciousness of the thinking subject. Marx's discussions of future society are therefore most austere and restrained. He never tried to rival those socialists whom he called utopian by construing detailed blue-prints for a communist society, since for him communist society will be determined by the specific conditions under which it is established, and these conditions cannot be predicted in advance. One can only attempt to delineate some of the dominant features of future society, and even this is very cautiously and tentatively done.[1]

Since Marx attempts, in the *Manuscripts* and in the *Critique of the Gotha Programme*, the description of the unfolding of existing historical forces, he must describe the development of communism as a set of stages. In both texts Marx distinguishes at least two main stages. If these stages represented different degrees of the gradual perfection of communism, they would be a dispensable, arbitrary device, only complicating an already complicated picture. But these stages are necessary for the dialectical unfolding of the principles of *existing* society. Each represents a further *Aufhebung* of these principles. The description of future society becomes a posthumous analysis of the passing of the bourgeois world: the historicity of Marx's description of communism is thus strongly emphasized against the *a priori* 'systems' of the so-called utopian socialists. In

---

[1] In the *Critique of the Gotha Programme* Marx says (*Selected Works*, II, 23): 'What we have to deal with here is a communist society, not as it has *developed* on its own foundations, but, on the contrary, just as it *emerges* from capitalist society.' A similar statement occurs in *The Civil War in France* (*ibid*. I, 523): '[The working class] have no ideals to realise, but to set free the elements of the new society with which the old collapsing bourgeois society itself is pregnant.'

221

The new society

The German Ideology Marx expresses this idea by saying that 'Communism is for us not a *state of affairs* which is to be established, an *ideal* to which reality will have to adjust itself. We call communism the *real* movement which abolishes the present state of things.'[1] Or, as he puts it in the *Manuscripts*, 'Communism is the necessary form and the dynamic principle of the immediate future, but communism is not itself the goal of human development—the form of human society.'[2]

The methodological approaches adopted by Marx in both works are identical: both descriptions bring present actuality to its ultimate conclusions and try to project an image of future society from the internal tensions of existing society, implying that, at the outset, communist society would perfect and universalize those elements in existing society that can be universalized. In the *Manuscripts* Marx adds a further dimension, making the stages of development of communism parallel the stages of the development of communist ideas. The less sophisticated stage of communism seems also to correspond to a less sophisticated and more primitive socialist theory. This enables Marx to acknowledge the immense contribution of the first and more primitive theories of socialism while demonstrating their utter insufficiency. He can even point to their dialectical necessity for the full emergence of his own synthesis, but this implies that by themselves they are unsatisfactory.

To Marx the main defect of these socialist theories, and the main defect of the first stage of socialist society, is that they see the abolition of private property only objectively. Proudhon advocates the abolition of private property as capital 'as such', while other critics propose only the abolition of certain forms of property. Fourier, following the Physiocrats, sees only agricultural labour as useful and non-alienating, whereas Saint-Simon ascribes these attributes to industrial labour alone. Each would like to preserve only that kind of property related to the type of labour and production he favoured.[3] Marx argues that at this stage the subjective aspect of property (i.e. its status as objectified human labour) has not yet been grasped and cannot therefore be transcended and abolished.

[1] *The German Ideology*, p. 47. [2] *Early Writings*, p. 167.
[3] *Ibid.* p. 152.

The stages of socialism

Consequently in its first stage, socialism will appear as follows: private property will be abolished, but only through turning it into universal property, the property of all. In the *Manuscripts* Marx calls this stage of the new society 'crude communism': it is both the ultimate realization of the principles of civil society and their initial abolition. Therefore this stage will retain some of the more unfortunate characteristics of capitalist society. At this stage man's emancipation from property resides in the nationalization of property, i.e. in its universalization, in everyone's becoming an employee of society and in a strict equality of wages. This is a crude, vulgar, philistine and materialistic communism, centred on material goods and values, not yet aware that goods are mere projections of human labour; this communism overlooks all those values which cannot be turned into objects of common ownership. This society, despite its progress beyond capitalism, barbarizes culture and its underlying egalitarian ethos is basically a narrow-minded jealousy. It may perhaps come as a surprise to find Marx saying the following about the first stage of communist society:

Finally, communism is the positive expression of the abolition of private property, and in the first place of universal private property. In taking this relation in its universal aspect communism is, in its first form, only the generalisation and fulfilment of the relation. As such it appears in a double form; the domination of material property looms so large that it aims to destroy everything which is incapable of being possessed by everyone as private property. It wishes to eliminate talent, etc. by force. Immediate physical possession seems to it the unique goal of life and existence. The role of the worker is not abolished, but is extended to all men. The relation of private property remains the relation of the community to the world of things. Finally, this tendency to oppose general private property to private property is expressed in an animal form; marriage (which is incontestably a form of exclusive private property) is contrasted with the community of women, in which women become communal and common property. One may say that this idea of the community of women is the open secret of this entirely crude and unreflective communism. Just as women are to pass from marriage to universal prostitution, so the whole world of wealth (i.e. the objective being of man) is to pass from the relation of exclusive marriage with the private owner to the relation of universal prostitution with the community. This communism, which negates the personality of

223

man in every sphere, is only the logical expression of private property, which is this negation. Universal envy settling itself as a power is only a camouflaged form of cupidity which re-establishes itself in a different way. The thoughts of every individual private property are at least directed against any wealthier private property, in the form of envy and the desire to reduce everything to a common level; so that this envy and levelling in fact constitute the essence of competition. Crude communism is only the culmination of such envy and levelling-down on the basis of a preconceived minimum.[1]

This, then, is a distributive communism, a communism based on a 'minimum', still imagining that the world of products is finite and objectively determined. It still sees its relationship to property as a relation to an object. This communism tries to regulate consumption without solving the riddle of production and without understanding that production is nothing but the endless unfolding of human creative potentialities. According to Marx such a communism is necessarily driven to asceticism, to making a virtue of its low standard of living. It reduces human needs to the bare existential minimum. In such a society communism means only the community of work and wages, not the mutuality of common life. The relationship to capital as an object of possession remains very much the same as in capitalist society, though possession is now collective and not individual. Society emerges, according to Marx, as a universal capitalist, not abolishing but universalizing the wage system. Working for a wage is, then, the universal principle of this crude communism, which preserves the most distinct elements of alienation:

How little this abolition of private property represents a genuine appropriation is shown by the abstract negation of the whole world of culture and civilisation, and the regression to the unnatural simplicity of the poor and wantless individual who has not only not surpassed private property but has not yet even attained it.

The community is only a community of work and of equality of wages paid out by the communal capital, by the community as universal

---

[1] *Early Writings*, pp. 152–3. Cf. *The Communist Manifesto, Selected Works*, I, 61: 'The revolutionary literature that accompanied these first movements of the proletariat had necessarily a reactionary character. It inculcated universal asceticism and social levelling in its crudest form.'

capitalist. The two sides of the relation are raised to a supposed universality; labour as a condition in which everyone is placed, and capitalism as the acknowledged universality and power of the community.[1]

How far this description provides an insight into some of the elements of present Soviet society depends, of course, on one's private view about the nature of Communist Russia; elaboration would therefore be outside the scope of this study.

Marx's description of the first stage of future society in the *Critique of the Gotha Programme* closely resembles the account given in the *Manuscripts*, though his language is more restrained and his thought is economically rather than speculatively oriented. Again the major characteristic of this first stage of communism is the socialization of the means of production which makes society into the only employer. Wage labour continues to exist; it becomes the sole and universal mode of labour, though surplus value is diverted to investment in economic growth and social services and not to private consumption. Though wages are not egalitarian (and in this respect this description varies from the *Manuscripts*) but depend on production, the principle underlying wage differentials ('to each according to his work') remains egalitarian and preserves the bourgeois element of property rights related to commodities as objects of consumption. Therefore, the system of social distribution cannot take into account the uniqueness of each individual and his specific needs and wants. This much-quoted passage is cited here *in extenso* to show how much it draws on the basic ideas of the *Manuscripts* and how much understanding its tone depends on reading the earlier sketch:

What we have to deal with here is a communist society...which is thus in every respect, economically, morally and intellectually, still stamped with the birth marks of the old society from whose womb it emerges. Accordingly, the individual producer receives back from society—after the deductions have been made—exactly what he gives to it...The same

---

[1] *Early Writings*, pp. 153–4. This description of 'crude communism' very strongly recalls Heinrich Heine's condemnation of communism in his *Lutetia*. But, whereas Heine saw in this vulgar communism the last stage communism could ever reach, for Marx it was merely a dialectically necessary step towards a better world. Cf. W. Victor, *Marx und Heine* (Berlin, 1953), pp. 78–91.

amount of labour which he has given to society in one form he receives back in another.

Here obviously the same principle prevails as that which regulates the exchange of commodities, as far as this is exchange of equal values. Content and form are changed, because under the altered circumstances no one can give anything except his labour, and because, on the other hand, nothing can pass to the ownership of individuals except individual means of consumption...

Hence, *equal right* here is still in principle—*bourgeois right*, although principle and practice are no longer at loggerheads...

In spite of this advance, this *equal right* is still constantly stigmatised by a bourgeois limitation. The right of the producers is *proportional* to the labour they supply; the equality consists in the fact that the measurement is made with an *equal standard*, labour.

But one man is superior to another physically or mentally and so supplies more labour in the same time, or can labour for a longer time; and labour, to serve as a measure, must be defined by its duration or intensity; otherwise it ceases to be a standard of measurement. It recognises no class differences, because everyone is only a worker like everyone else; but it tacitly recognises unequal individual endowment and thus productive capacity as natural privileges. *It is, therefore, a right of inequality, in its content, like every right.* Right by its very nature can consist only in the application of an equal standard; but unequal individuals (and they would not be different individuals if they were not unequal) are measurable only by an equal standard in so far as they are brought under an equal point of view, are taken from one *definite* side only, for instance, in the present case, are regarded *only as workers* and nothing more is seen in them, everything else being ignored. Further, one worker is married, another not; one has more children than another, and so on and so forth...

But these defects are inevitable in the first phase of communist society as it is when it has just emerged after prolonged birth pangs from capitalist society.[1]

Here again the first stage of communist society merely universalizes the principles of bourgeois society.

The transition to the second stage, no longer circumscribed by the limitations of capitalist society, is free from the birth pangs of the new society. Much of Marx's criticism of the other socialist schools can be reduced to the contention that they usually see the first stage

---

[1] *Selected Works*, II, 23-4.

of socialism as the last and ultimate one, and present a vulgar and barbarian society as the apotheosis of human development. For Marx this stage, only transitory, epitomizes the basic shortcomings of capitalist society only in order to radicalize and overcome them: 'No social order ever perishes before all the productive forces for which there is room in it have developed; and new, higher relations of production never appear before the material conditions of their existence have matured in the womb of the old society itself.'[1]

The 1844 *Manuscripts* maintain that the positive *Aufhebung* of property in the second stage of future society implies the end of man's domination by the objective forces he created. Similarly, the dichotomies that divided and alienated man's life in civil society disappear. Man's relationship to his fellow men ceases to be competitive. He no longer achieves his goals at the expense of his fellow man, since competition was the natural corollary of a world which conceived the quantity of its objects and products as finite and given. In the new society man becomes conscious that the products are human artifacts. As such their quantity is not limited but depends upon the proper organization of man's creative powers.[2]

Under such a system man's relation to nature ceases to be determined by objective necessity: man, now conscious of his mastery over his own nature, creates it. Finally, the process of human creativity is no longer accompanied by alienation: the creation of objects becomes man's specific activity, no longer limited by the objective necessity of creating for mere survival. Thus Marx can see the solution of man's economic existence as the resolution of the traditional dilemmas of philosophical speculation:

Communism is the positive abolition of private property, of human self-alienation, and thus the real appropriation of human nature through and for man. It is, therefore, the return of man to himself as a social, i.e. really human, being, a complete and conscious return which assimilates all the wealth of previous development. Communism as fully developed naturalism is humanism and as fully developed humanism is naturalism. It is the definitive resolution of the antagonism between man and nature, and between man and man. It is the true solution of the conflict between

---

[1] *Ibid.* I, 363.
[2] For this see Marx's interesting remarks in his notes on James Mill, *MEGA*, I, 3, pp. 543-7.

existence and essence, between objectification and self-affirmation, between freedom and necessity, between individual and species. It is the solution of the riddle of history and knows itself to be this solution.[1]

This radical transformation, the essential content of the revolution envisaged by Marx, will enable man to discover properties not related to him possessively, as mere external objects. Man, according to Marx, will be able to develop a new kind of appropriation which will not imply a hedonistic attitude towards the world that reduces it to possession and consumption. This new relationship will enhance the analogy between man's free, creative activity and artistic creation. As the pleasure derived from a work of art re-creates it for the observer without diminishing another's share of pleasure in it, so the many-sided relationship of man to his product will now give rise to a many-sided relationship between man and man:

Just as private property is only the sensuous expression of the fact that man is at the same time an objective fact for himself and becomes an alien and non-human object for himself; just as his manifestation of life is also his alienation of life and his self-realisation is a loss of reality, the emergence of an alien reality; so the positive supersession [*Aufhebung*] of private property, i.e. the sensuous appropriation of the human essence and of human life, of objective man and of human creations, by and for man, should not be taken only in the sense of immediate, exclusive enjoyment, or only in the sense of possession or having. Man appropriates his manifold being in an all-inclusive way, and thus as a whole man. All his human relations to the world—seeing, hearing, smelling, tasting, touching, thinking, observing, feeling, desiring, acting, loving—in short, all the organs of his individuality, like the organs which are directly communal in form, are in their objective action...the appropriation of this object, the appropriation of human reality. The way in which they react to the object is the confirmation of human reality.

Private property has made us so stupid and partial that an object is only ours when we have it, when it exists for us as capital or when it is directly eaten, drunk, worn, inhabited, etc., in short, utilised in some way.[2]

The true nature of consciousness thus becomes apparent. Consciousness determines not only the recognizing subject but also the recognized object which thus ceases to be a passive object and be-

[1] *Early Writings*, p. 155.   [2] *Ibid.* p. 159.

comes for man an objectification of subjective force. The curtain which has till now divided man and the universe can be raised by a humanization of the universe. The 'natural substratum' does not disappear, but is revealed in its true light emerging from the reciprocal process that turns it into a human object. This is the new consciousness, liberated from the falsifications and inversions of the alienated world. The universe is thus conceived as a projection of human activity, and dialectically the vision of philosophical idealism can finally be realized through a philosophy whose premises are an *Aufhebung* of idealism itself. This realization does not imply a retreat from the world or resignation and withdrawal into the inner self. On the contrary it is action-oriented, conscious of man's shaping of his world:

As we have seen, it is only when the object becomes a human object, or objective humanity, that man does not become lost in it. This is only possible when man himself becomes a social object; when he himself becomes a social being and society becomes a being for him in this object.

On the one hand, it is only when objective reality everywhere becomes for man in society the reality of human faculties, human reality, and thus the reality of his own faculties, that all objects become for him the objectification of himself. The objects then confirm and realise his individuality, they are his own objects...The object is not the same for the eye as for the ear, for the ear as for the eye...Man's musical sense is only awakened by music. The most beautiful music has no meaning for the non-musical ear' is not an object for it...For this reason the senses of social man are different from those of non-social man...[1]

This new human association will thus be able consciously to control man's conditions of life instead of allowing man's consciousness to be determined by his circumstances as if they were objective, external forces. Marx's view of socialism at this stage is unique in that it consciously overturns existing reality, when this reality is understood as a product of human activity and creativity.

[1] *Ibid.* pp. 160–1. Cf. *The German Ideology*, pp. 48–9. These passages clearly indicate that Engels' later remark about socialism as domination over things and not over people fails to grasp the philosophical significance of Marx's analysis of labour, since 'things' are objectified human labour. This mechanistic attitude is also evident in Engels' conviction that authority in industry will have to be retained even in socialist society, since it is immanent in the industrial system itself. For Marx, of course, the question poses itself in a wholly different manner.

The new society

The determination of man by his economic circumstances means his determination by his own historical products. Man can liberate himself from this master who is himself. Since this cannot be achieved by individuals alone (because they can individually emancipate themselves only by subjecting someone else to this yoke), this emancipation of man must be social. Through it man will become conscious of himself as the prime mover of history as well as its product:

Communism differs from all previous movements in that it overturns the basis of all earlier relations of production and intercourse, and for the first time treats all natural premises as the creatures of hitherto existing men, strips them of their natural character and subjugates them to the power of the united individuals. Its organisation is, therefore, essentially economic, the material production of the conditions of this unity; it turns existing conditions into conditions of unity. The reality, which communism is creating, is precisely the true basis for rendering it impossible that anything should exist independently of individuals, insofar as reality is only a product of the preceding intercourse of individuals themselves.[1]

Thus communism as a movement in capitalist society, and communism as a future organizing principle of the new society, are two different modes of the same principle: communism as a movement is the microcosmos of future communist society.

In the *Critique of the Gotha Programme* the second stage of future society is also characterized by the disappearance of the social division of labour.[2] In the *Manuscripts* this element appears only negatively in Marx's critique of Adam Smith's theory of division of labour as a rational allocation of different sorts of labour to people already different from each other. Marx contends that only the division of labour gave rise to human types different from each other in capacities, faculties and potentialities, and only the perpetuation of this system creates the notion that people differed fundamentally before the emergence of division of labour.[3]

In *The German Ideology* the abolition of the division of labour

---

[1] *The German Ideology*, pp. 86–7; Cf. *Early Writings*, p. 166: 'Since, however, for socialist man, the whole of what is called world history is nothing else but the creation of man by human labour, and the emergence of nature for man, he, therefore, has the evident and irrefutable proof of his self-creation, of his own origins.'
[2] The later distinction, which called the first stage 'socialism' and the second 'communism', has no foundation in Marx's own writings.
[3] *Early Writings*, pp. 181 f.

appears for the first time as a major characteristic of future society. Abolishing the division of labour means, according to Marx, abolishing the subsumption of man under the conditions of his work. Hence it means the emancipation of man from the narrowness and partiality imposed upon him by the conditions of alienated labour:

As long as man remains in natural society, that is, as long as a cleavage exists between the particular and the common interest, as long, therefore, as activity is not voluntarily, but naturally, divided, man's own deed becomes an alien power opposed to him, which enslaves him instead of being controlled by him. For as soon as the distribution of labour comes into being, each man has a particular, exclusive sphere of activity, which is forced upon him and from which he cannot escape. He is a hunter, a fisherman, a shepherd, or a critical critic, and must remain so if he does not want to lose his means of livelihood; while in communist society, where nobody has one exclusive sphere of activity but each can become accomplished in any branch he wishes, society regulates the general production and thus makes it possible for me to do one thing today and another tomorrow, to hunt in the morning, to fish in the afternoon, rear cattle in the evening, criticise after dinner, just as I have a mind, without ever becoming hunter, fisherman, shepherd or critic. This fixation of social activity, this consolidation of what we ourselves produce into an objective power above us, growing out of our control, thwarting our expectations, bringing to naught our calculations, is one of the chief factors in the historical development up till now.[1]

How these pastoral, bucolic occupations can serve as models for the abolition of the division of labour in a sophisticated, industrial society is, of course, a question to which an answer might have been expected, but an answer is not forthcoming in this or in any other of Marx's writings. Marx's choice of such idyllic examples may indicate that he has sensed the internal difficulty of the relevance of his argument for a modern society. Yet if one accepts Marx's model of man as an other-directed being, a *Gattungswesen*, then one can envisage how the occupation of one individual can engender satisfaction in another, since each is now conceived as a moment of the other's social being and not as an external, even potentially dangerous, competitor. The paradigm of the lovers, used by Marx in

[1] *The German Ideology*, pp. 44–5.

231

the *Manuscripts*, can illustrate the other-oriented possibilities in man, as can family solidarity. Thus even if a division of labour will after all be necessary, one man can find joy and satisfaction in another's occupation, provided the social structure is oriented toward such possibilities.[1]

It has sometimes been argued that in his later writings Marx ceased to look at labour as the positive content of human life and adopted a view of labour as a necessary evil, to be minimized as much as possible. Some evidence to the contrary comes, surprisingly enough, from those passages in Marx's later writings which deal with child labour. From them it appears that Marx still thinks that labour, which makes man, is the main constituent of the human personality. While strongly objecting, of course, to child labour as practised under the appalling conditions of mid-nineteenth-century Britain, Marx still thinks that education through work is indispensable. In *The Communist Manifesto* he calls for the abolition of child labour 'in its present form', but accompanies this by a call for a combination of education with industrial production.'[2] In the *Critique of the Gotha Programme* this is made even more explicit:

A *general prohibition* of child labour is incompatible with the existence of large-scale industry and hence an empty, pious wish. Its realisation—if it were possible—would be reactionary, since, with a strict regulation of the working time according to the different age groups and other safety measures for the protection of children, an early combination of productive labour with education is one of the most potent means for the transformation of present-day society.[3]

The argument is therefore not merely utilitarian or historicist. The combination of production and education is essential to the new man. Incarcerating the child in an unproductive scholastic ivory tower may be the first step toward alienation experienced once the child steps out into real life. In *Das Kapital* Marx characteristically points out that this educational aspect of child labour is already apparent in capitalist society. Future society will have to perfect the rough tools provided it by capitalism and emancipate them from their alienating aspects:

[1] *The Poverty of Philosophy*, p. 161.
[2] *Selected Works*, I, 54.   [3] *Ibid.* II, 36.

The stages of socialism

From the Factory System budded, as Robert Owen has shown us in detail, the germ of the education of the future, an education that will, in case of every child over a given age, combine productive labour with instruction and gymnastics, not only as one of the methods adding to the efficiency of production, but as the only method of producing fully developed human beings...

One step already spontaneously taken towards effecting this revolution is the establishment of technical and agricultural schools, and of the 'écoles d'enseignement professionel', in which the children of working-men receive some little instruction in technology and in the practical handling of the various implements of labour. Though the Factory Act, that first and meagre concession wrung from capital, is limited to combining elementary education with work in the factory, there can be no doubt that when the working-class comes into power, as inevitably it must, technical instruction, both theoretical and practical, will take its place in the working-class schools.[1]

The importance of education through work is emphasized again in the same passage when Marx refers to the need for a rounded human being, instead of the partial man of capitalist society: future society will have 'to replace the detail-worker of today...reduced to a mere fragment of a man, by the fully developed individual, fit for a variety of labours...to whom the different social functions...are but so many modes of giving free scope to his own natural powers'.[2] The language of *Das Kapital* is thus identical with that of the *Manuscripts*.

In the *Critique of the Gotha Programme* the ultimate consequences of this development are revealed: not only will the form of labour be changed, but so will its place in human existence. This *locus classicus* can be adequately understood only if considered in the context of Marx's earlier thoughts on this subject. These give substance to the epigrammatic description of the second phase of communist society, in which every phrase seems to telescope whole chapters of earlier writings:

In a higher phase of communist society, after the enslaving subordination of the individual to the division of labour, and therewith also the antithesis between mental and physical labour, have vanished; after labour has

---

[1] *Capital*, i, 483, 488. This section contains some extremely interesting insights into the sociology of education.   [2] *Ibid.* p. 488.

become not only a means of life but life's primary want; after the productive forces have also increased with the all-round development of the individual, and all the springs of co-operative wealth flow more abundantly—only then can the narrow horizon of bourgeois right be crossed in its entirety and society inscribe on its banners: 'From each according to his ability, to each according to his needs'.[1]

The closing sentence (actually of Saint Simonian origins) of course became an empty slogan long ago. Yet it has a definite meaning within Marx's theoretical premises: a man's needs are not a quantity determined *a priori* to be set down by a central authority that will thus become the supreme regulator of social rewards. Such an arrangement would only perpetuate political institutions under a different name. Marx's meaning is totally different: since work will now constantly unfold each individual's potentialities, each man's contribution will accord with his faculties, just as his rewards (which now include work itself, 'life's prime want') will be adequate to his needs. In socialist society, as in any other society, the needs of men are historically determined by the circumstances in which men live. Communist society will be the first, Marx argues, in which the satisfaction of needs will be adequate to their very production. Capitalist society too, because of its universal ethos, creates universal needs; but the limitations of capitalist production enable it to satisfy those needs only with regard to some and not all members of society. In socialist society, the creation of needs will simultaneously also create the means to ensure their satisfaction. Thus the equilibrium between production and consumption postulated by Ricardo will finally be achieved in socialist society, since the system of production will no longer be separate from the system of consumption.

This discussion necessarily leads to a consideration of the length of the working day in future society, since this cannot be automatically determined by labour's ceasing to be mere wage labour.[2] Again, Marx proposes a view that may seem surprising: there is no assurance, he says, that the working day in future society will be in all cases much shorter than it is now. Even if surplus value be diverted to investment and social services, any shortening of the working day

---

[1] *Selected Works*, II, 24.
[2] This is Marx's view not only in the *Manuscripts*, but also in the *Grundrisse* (p. 506).

would imply a distinct reduction in society's standard of living, unless the reduction in the working day be compensated by the better organization and larger expansion of the socialist economy. Since the needs of man in future society will increase despite higher productivity, the working day may have to remain at something like its present level to ensure the ability to meet the ever increasing needs of society:

Only by suppressing the capitalist form of production could the length of the working-day be reduced to the necessary labour time. But, even in that case, the latter would extend its limits. On the one hand, because the notion of 'means of subsistence' would considerably expand, and the labourer would lay claim to an altogether different standard of life. On the other hand, because a part of what is now surplus-labour, would then count as necessary labour...[1]

Improved technology can of course create more material goods in a shorter time, but nowhere does Marx explicitly say that the increase in future wants could be fully compensated by technological innovation. He does hint that in future society 'there would be a very different scope for the employment of machinery than there can be in a bourgeois society';[2] but does not spell out the nature of this transformation.

Labour discipline is another aspect of future society that Marx touches on. Some of Engels' later writings have shifted the emphasis elsewhere. During the anti-Anarchist controversy, Engels said that authoritarian discipline is an immanent ingredient of large-scale industry; it exists in autonomy of productive relations and will not disappear when social control of production is changed. Engels calls it a despotism independent of the form of social organization.[3] Such an analysis is, of course, at variance with Marx's basic premise about production determining the forms of social organization. Engels' view of the autonomy of technology *vis-à-vis* social relations is, though, quite characteristic of the technological bent of his thought. It poses another question: Engels conceives of man facing the natural objects of material production as if they were

---

[1] *Capital*, I, 530.   [2] *Ibid*. p. 393.
[3] F. Engels, *On Authority, Selected Works*, I, 636–9.

totally alien to him, as if something in the relations of production in modern industry could not be reduced to directable human action. Since Marx does not view technology as an objective, external force, he would have expressed his opinions differently. Indeed in volume III of *Das Kapital* Marx clearly says that future society will not require authoritarian industrial discipline. In present society, he argues, discipline is ensured through the worker's drill and through the discipline enforced by the capitalists on the labour force at large. This discipline 'will become superfluous under a socialistic system in which the labourers work for their own accord, as it has already become practically superfluous in piece-work'.[1] Again, the parallel with modes of payment in capitalist society may be surprising, but Marx has the internal structure, and not the form, of piece-work in mind. He can project from a phenomenon present in capitalistic society the possibilities of the future. The implications are definitely different from Engels' in *On Authority*.

In volume III of *Das Kapital* Marx's discussion of labour has caused speculation about whether he did not, after all, change views about labour as the sphere of man's spontaneous activity:

In fact, that realm of freedom actually begins only where labour which is determined by necessity and mundane considerations ceases; thus in the very nature of things it lies beyond the sphere of actual material production. Just as the savage must wrestle with Nature to satisfy his wants, to maintain and reproduce life, so must civilised man, and he must do so in all social formations and under all possible modes of production. With his development this realm of physical necessity expands as a result of his wants; but, at the same time, the forces of production which satisfy these wants also increase. Freedom in this field can consist in socialised man, the associated producers, rationally regulating their interchange with Nature, bringing it under their common control, instead of being ruled by it as by the blind forces of Nature; and achieving this with the least expenditure of energy and under conditions most favourable to, and worthy of, their human nature. But it nonetheless remains a realm of necessity. Beyond it begins that development of human energy which is an end in itself, the true realm of freedom, which, however, can blossom forth only with this realm of necessity as its basis. The shortening of the working-day is its basic prerequisite.[2]

[1] *Capital*, III, 83.   [2] *Ibid.* pp. 799–800. Cf. Ramm, *op. cit.* p. 104.

The stages of socialism

Carefully analysed, this passage does not contradict Marx's earlier view on the subject. The dialectical relation between freedom and necessity only accentuates this. That labour needs to master the 'natural substratum' of human existence is difficult to deny, nor has it ever been denied by Marx himself. Even in the pastoral idyll of *The German Ideology* most of man's free activity (hunting, fishing, raising cattle) is oriented towards the satisfaction of these needs. Man can never emancipate himself from this basic existential need, but he can emancipate himself from the process that makes the satisfaction of these needs into a dehumanizing drudgery.

This may give some further insight into the transformation of the conditions of human life in future society. To Marx socialism will not emancipate man as he is from external limitations, but will bridge the gap between existing man and the potentialities inherent in his activity as an historical being. This *praxis* implies a reciprocal relation between man and his circumstances. Hence 'in revolutionary activity the changing of oneself coincides with the changing of circumstances'.[1] Such a view tends, of course, to limit the possibilities of projecting the future, though one can point to the principles that are likely to determine its general outline. Marx's vision of perfect society is never static, and here his thought differs from both the Platonic and the Hegelian tradition. Marx never denies that further developments may occur under socialism, and therefore he never believes in a static, absolutizing blue-print for *the* socialist society. He contends only that, once the distinct political element has been abolished, the disturbing effects of further development could be neutralized in class terms so that no new tension between the content of social life and its form would arise: 'It is only in an order of things in which there are no more classes and class antagonisms that *social evolutions* will cease to be *political revolutions*.'[2]

A related issue became part of a long and protracted struggle within the labour movement. During the controversy with the Bakuninists in the 1870s, Marx's followers were labelled by their opponents 'authoritarians'. The term originated in Marx's insistence upon the authority of the General Council of the International over the various federations affiliated with it; later it came to connote Marx's attitude

---

[1] *The German Ideology*, p. 230.   [2] *The Poverty of Philosophy*, p. 197.

toward future society in general (Engels' *On Authority* helped to drive this home). Yet so far as the argument between Marx and Bakunin revolved around the nature of future society, it was Marx who consistently pointed out that both the tactics and the ideology of Bakunin lead in an authoritarian—today we would say totalitarian—direction. Marx's disgust with the methods of organization and intimidation developed by Bakunin and Nechaev expressed his fear about the possible impact of such methods on future society. Marx's theory of *praxis* easily suggested to him that such a revolutionary *praxis* will substantially determine the nature of future society. A revolutionary movement based on terror, intimidation and blackmail will ultimately produce a society based on these methods as well.

In 1874/5 Marx wrote a running commentary on Bakunin's *Étatism and Anarchy*. In this book Bakunin had attributed to Marx étatist tendencies originating in the German philosophical background of his thought. Bakunin's book clearly showed how unfamiliar Bakunin was with the German, and specifically Hegelian, philosophical tradition. When he said that the background of Marx's authoritarianism must be traced to his being a German, a Hegelian and a Jew, the level of argument had indeed slipped considerably. Marx's commentary on the book brings out not only the philosophical ignorance of Bakunin, but also the strong authoritarian traits in his thought.[1] In an anti-Bakunin pamphlet of the same period, Marx confronts the principles of anarchism with Bakunin's description of strong social control in future society. This Bakuninist centralized authority will be, according to Marx, an instrument in the hands of a political organization that retains all the characteristics of the political state. The anarchists' abolition of the state by decree is thus just an empty gesture. Marx quotes extensively from the Bakuninist *Principle Bases for the Social Order of the Future*, and adds:

What a wonderful example of barracks-communism! Everything is here: common pots and dormitories, control commissioners and *comptoirs*, the regulation of education, production, consumption—in one word, of all social activity; and at the top, *our Committee*, anonymous and unknown, as supreme direction. Surely, this is most pure anti-authoritarianism![2]

[1] *Werke*, XVIII, 601 f.   [2] *Recueil*, II, 445.

The stages of socialism

Elsewhere Marx directs the same kind of criticism against August Comte's system. In an interview published in an American newspaper Marx says that Comte's theory replaces an old hierarchy with a new one.[1] The criterion common to Marx's criticism of Bakunin and Comte is simple: for Marx, both perpetuate a political structure not identical with universality of social life. Marx aims his critique of the Bakuninist modes of action at more than their terroristic aspect. He argues that, as a result of the anarchist abstention from political action and trade union activity, the Bakuninist élitist approach divorces a small group of workers from their wider social context. The élite of the proletariat is cut off from the proletariat, and Marx sees this separation as a reversion to the particularism of the earlier socialist sects, which failed to consider the universalistic aspects of proletarian activity.[2]

Marx's critique of Bakunin's revolutionary activity is thus directly derived from his views about the dialectical tension between political power and social structure. Because it overlooks the universal postulates concealed in the concept of the state, Bakunin's view of future society never emancipates itself from its particularism and its separate, distinctly political organization. Anarchism may be able to decree the state out of existence (*abschaffen*), but this will be merely a mechanistic act of destruction, not a dialectical abolition-cum-realization. Hence its ultimate outcome may imply that the state will be destroyed, but political power and institutions survive in a separate political apparatus minutely controlling every aspect of society. Bakunin's anarchistic communism will remain, according to Marx, *un communisme de caserne*.

THE PARIS COMMUNE: THE NECESSARY FAILURE

Marx's attitude to the Paris Commune before its establishment, during its short life and after its brutal defeat is so complex that it has sometimes led observers to conclude that Marx was swept by circumstances into positions which he initially opposed and that he changed his views about the subject more than once. We have already seen that, although Marx gallantly defended the record of the

[1] *Woodhull & Claflin's Weekly*, 12 August 1871 (*Werke*, XVII, 643).
[2] *Recueil*, II, 445–6, 284.

Commune in *The Civil War in France*, he tried to intervene in September 1870 to prevent an insurrection, and his letter of 1881 to Domela-Nieuwenhuis says that the Commune was 'in no way socialist, nor could it be'.

These contradictions may disappear if one distinguishes between Marx's attitude toward the insurrection itself and toward the significance of what the Commune tried to do politically and socially. Though he strongly opposed, on a multitude of levels, the attempt at insurrection, he still thought that the Commune, though doomed to failure, introduced some elements of revolutionary significance for the development of future society. Therefore, albeit the Commune had according to Marx no chance to survive, its historical significance may transcend the subjective folly of initiators totally unaware of the utter hopelessness of their heroic but futile endeavour. Some of the Commune's political arrangements could therefore be viewed as anticipations of future society, though the historical failure of the Commune limited the significance of the experience. Though Marx never actually called the Commune the dictatorship of the proletariat (Engels said this in his 1891 Introduction to a new edition of *The Civil War in France*),[1] he still thought of it as an epoch-making breakthrough in political organization. Prescription and analysis thus supplement each other in Marx's discussion of the Commune.

A textual criticism of *The Civil War in France* would show that what Marx saw in the Commune as a model for the future were not the actual, concrete arrangements it instituted, but a projection of the potentialities of these arrangements onto the future. Only this projection gives the Commune its historical significance. Marx, then, does not discuss the Commune as it actually was, but as it could be, not *in actu* but *in potentia*. He elevates the Commune's *possible* enactments and its *potential* arrangements to a paradigm of future society. It is not the Paris Commune of 1871 that provides the

---

[1] *Selected Works*, I, 485; 'Of late, the Social-Democratic philistine has once more been filled with wholesome terror at the words: Dictatorship of the Proletariat. Well and good, gentlemen, do you want to know what this dictatorship looks like? Look at the Paris Commune. That was the Dictatorship of the Proletariat.' This statement was made by Engels for internal SPD consumption in the 'nineties, but it became inseparable from Marx's own views, into which it was projected.

model for future society, but the immanent reason Marx saw in it *had* it survived (though he was sure that it would not). Only such a projection allows Marx, in his 1881 letter, to criticize the historical Commune for not nationalizing the *Banque de France*, and to praise the potential Commune for an intention to abolish private property. Most of the relevant passage in *The Civil War in France* is phrased conditionally: despite its superficial appearance as a narrative of the Commune's achievements, it actually considers the significance of what it would have done had it managed to survive. The following, written originally by Marx in English, brings this out clearly (italics supplied):

The Paris Commune *was*, of course, *to serve* as a model to all the great industrial centres of France. The communal regime once established in Paris and the secondary cities, the old centralised Government *would* in the provinces, too, have to give way to the self-government of the producers. In a rough sketch of national organisation which the Commune had no time to develop, it states clearly that the Commune *was to be* the political form of even the smallest country hamlet, and that in the rural districts the standing army *was to be replaced* by a national militia, with an extremely short term of service. The rural communes of every district *were to administer* their common affairs by an assembly of delegates in the central town, and these district assemblies *were again to send* deputies to the National Delegation in Paris, each delegate *to be at any time revocable and bound* by the mandat impératif (formal instruction) of his constituents. The few but important functions which still would remain for a central government *were not to be suppressed*, as has been intentionally mis-stated, but *were to be discharged* by Communal, and therefore strictly responsible agents. The unity of the nation *was not to be broken*, but, on the contrary, *to be organised* by the Communal Constitution and *to become* a reality...[1]

This extremely cautious and sophisticated language enables Marx to show how the Commune could have overcome the tension between state and civil society—yet preserve at the same time a critical attitude towards the historical phenomenon of the Commune itself. Thus Marx's sole reference to the Commune's communist elements occurs in a strongly future-oriented context.[2] He calls communist not the

[1] *Selected Works*, I, 520.
[2] *Ibid.* p. 523. The name *Commune de Paris* had of course nothing to do with communism or communists but happened to be the historical name of municipal

Commune but the unfolding of principles hidden in it and sometimes imperceptible to the Communards themselves. These fine distinctions between the historical Commune and the principles of the Commune may have also helped Marx in a difficult situation to formulate his own position in a language that might mean different things to different people.

If this explanation that Marx evaluates the Commune on two distinct levels is correct, no contradiction remains between Marx's various private and public statements concerning the Commune. Historically, the whole issue received different proportions and perspectives once the publication of *The Civil War in France* put the International—and Marx—in the forefront of the battle of words waged in the aftermath of the Commune. Undoubtedly this publicity helped to perpetuate the image held by the right wing and by later socialists as well—that the Commune was initiated by the International and the 'Red Doctor' heading it. The origins of this rumour seem to go back to the publication in the extreme right-wing Versailles paper, *Journal de Paris*, of 19 March 1871, of a story about an alleged letter by Marx to his supporters in Paris, instructing them in detail to start an insurrection. This forgery was probably a brainwave of one of the German advisers in Versailles, Stieber, who twenty years earlier was one of the chief prosecutors of the League of Communists in post-1848 Prussia. This might have been a belated, yet effective, revenge on Marx who had frustrated Stieber's efforts in the notorious Cologne trial of the early 'fifties. Most of the Continental, as well as the British press, took up this story, and on 6 June 1871 Thiers' Foreign Minister, Jules Favre, circulated a note to all Powers making the International responsible for the insurrection of the Commune. As the International was most active at that time helping the Commune refugees financially and revealing the horrible vengeance taken by the French government on the Communards, the connection became creditable. Ironically, Marx's name thus became world-famous almost overnight not through his works and writings, but in connection with an insurrection which he opposed, whose downfall he foresaw and predicted, whose initiators

government in France. But the easily suggested link between Commune and Communism has been a forceful instrument in the creation of the myth of the Commune as a communist insurrection.

were not his disciples, and which, according to him, was not and could not be socialist. After the rumour concerning his responsibility for the Commune took hold, Marx wrote dozens of letters to numerous papers on the Continent and in Britain trying to explain his position, but it was difficult to undo the image already created in the public consciousness.[1]

The tension between the evaluation of the Commune as an historical phenomenon and the potential seeds of future development inherent in it also emphasizes the dialectical relationship between the abolition of the state (towards which the Commune would have developed had it survived) and the fact that the Commune itself was still an expression of political power. Only the Commune of the future, described by Marx in the conditional, futuristic language of the passage quoted above, would be the positive *Aufhebung* of the state, creating an unalienated social solidarity. The concrete, historical Commune, as it existed and as it was defeated, was a mere prolegomenon, a still political organ. In this sense the partial, 'political' Commune attempted to accomplish what Marx preached in the *Manifesto*: the wielding of political power, supported by universal suffrage, towards universal ends, making the state a truly universal organ, and thus abolishing it not by minimizing state activity but by a maximizing of it which would be self-*aufhebend*.

The background to Marx's opposition to a merely political insurrection of the proletariat has already been discussed in chapter 7. In the late 'sixties Marx actively sought to minimize the impact of the Jacobin-oriented French peripheral groups on the International. His attempt was far from successful, since these traditions went deep into the historical myth of the left wing in France and created an a-historical image of the future by making the Left in France a prisoner of its own revolutionary historical nostalgia. It was in this

---

[1] For Marx's numerous letters to the Press on this, see *Werke*, XVII, 295–302, 366–405, 474–82. He seems, however, to have enjoyed the gratuitous fame bestowed upon him: 'I have the honour to be at this moment the best calumniated and most menaced man of London. That really does one good after a tedious twenty years' idyll in my den', he writes to Kugelmann on 18 June 1871 (*Letters to Kugelmann*, p. 126). This myth of Marx as the initiator of the Commune tends to persist: cf. R. Postgate, *Revolution from 1789 to 1906* (London, 1920), p. 281. The episode has recently been documented by Jeanine Verdès, 'Marx vu par la police française 1871–1883', *Cahiers de l'ISEA*, série S, no. 10 (August 1966), pp. 83–120.

context that the *Commune de Paris* became a battle cry of the Jacobins and Blanquists, and in a letter of 1868 Marx refers to it: 'The twelve ragamuffins of the so-called French Branch [of the International] have again staged on Tuesday a public meeting presided by Pyat, who read out one of his revolutionary proclamations... [Among the points] was a vote of support for a manifesto, read by Pyat and concocted by him, of a *Commune de Paris* existing on the moon...'[1]

Marx's views on the Commune were thus largely determined by the circumstances of the Franco-Prussian War and the internal confrontations within the International. On 23 July 1870 the International published its first address on the war. In it Marx explains that the proletariat as such has no stake in the war and condemns it. Marx accepts the German version of the immediate causes of the outbreak of the war in this *Address*, not (as has sometimes been suggested) because of his German background, but because this was also the generally accepted view in England at this time. No one seemed to doubt that Napoleon III was to be blamed for the war. Nevertheless the *Address* adds two reservations: though the war has been waged by Prussia in self-defence, the conduct of foreign affairs by Bismarck made such a course imperative. Another Prussian foreign policy could have steered, at an earlier stage, a totally different course. Marx hopes that a Prussian victory will crush the hybrid régime of Napoleon III and bring about German unification—not for its own sake, but because so long as Germany is divided the national issue overshadows all social antagonisms and paralyses the emergence of proletarian class consciousness. Nevertheless, the International warns Prussia not to turn the war against Napoleon III into a war against the French people. In case of such a development, the *Address* implies that the International will have to reconsider its position.[2]

A few days later Marx supplements this by remarking, in a letter to his daughter Laura and his son-in-law Paul Lafargue, that the

[1] Marx to Engels, 24 October 1868 (*Briefwechsel*, IV, 141; the word 'ragamuffins' appears in English in the German text). In a letter to Marx of 6 July 1869 (*ibid.* p. 244), Engels doubts the viability of an isolated revolutionary dictatorship in Paris: 'This is really a comic view that supposes that the dictatorship of Paris over France, at which the first revolution foundered, could be repeated just like that today with any success.' [2] *Selected Works*, I, 486–90.

downfall of Napoleon III in France can open the way for tremendous political and social progress in France, whereas a German defeat will, by toppling Bismarck, throw Prussia back into a medievalizing, *ständisch* romanticism.[1] Marx is not anticipating an outbreak of a revolution in Paris, but a peaceful development towards republicanism. A revolutionary régime in Paris might be crushed by the twin pressures of external war and internal class antagonisms. Writing to Engels early in August 1870, Marx says: 'If a revolution breaks out in Paris, then one has to ask oneself whether it will have both the means and the leaders to offer serious resistance to the Prussians. One cannot deny that 20 years of Bonapartist farce have been enormously demoralising. One cannot expect revolutionary heroism. What do you think?'[2] Marx's doubts, then, were not limited to the war situation only. The structure of French society, and of the French working class, makes the outcome of a possible revolutionary attempt appear unpromising to him.

The internal consistency of Marx's attitude is well illustrated by his change of opinion on the relative merits of the French and German cases for the war after the abdication of Napoleon III and the establishment of the Provisional Government under Thiers. Once Napoleon was out, Prussia could no longer claim to wage a war of defence. Prussia's continuation of the war turned this, for Marx, into a war against the French people. True to his view in the *First Address*, in the *Second Address*, written on 9 September 1870, he condemns Bismarck for waging an aggressive war, announces the opposition of the *International* to the German plans for the annexation of Alsace-Lorraine and calls upon the workers of France to support the Provisional Government. Marx admonishes the workers 'not to be deluded by the souvenirs of 1792' and urges them 'calmly and resolutely improve the opportunities of Republican liberty for the work of their own class organisation'.[3]

The prognosis is clear: an insurrection points to delusions about Robespierrist revolutionary *grandeur*. Such attempts are doomed to fail by the lack of organization of the French working class—the legacy of Bonapartism. Only years of patient organizational work,

[1] Marx to Laura and Paul Lafargue, 28 July 1870 (*Annali*, 1958, pp. 177–8).
[2] Marx to Engels, 8 August 1870 (*Briefwechsel*, IV, 430).
[3] *Selected Works*, I, 497.

under republican liberty, could help the French proletariat make up for two decades of Bonapartist demoralization.

The *Second Address* was written against the background of the euphoria and enthusiasm which spread among the French radical exiles in London. They took the abdication of the Emperor as the sign to stage a proletarian coup. We have already seen that at the beginning of September Marx sent Seraillier, one of his French supporters, to Paris to stop the Blanquists and Jacobins from 'doing all kinds of follies in the name of the International...bring down the Provisional Government, establish a *Commune de Paris*...'[1] The capitulation of Thiers' government eliminated Marx's objection to insurrection during national war; yet his basic opposition to an insurrection originates in his assessment of the weakness of the social structure of the French working class, and these considerations remained relevant even after Thiers' change of policy.[2]

This attitude also explains Marx's view of the social structure of the Commune, once the insurrection broke out. On 27 April 1871 the Public Works Commissioner of the Commune, Leo Fränckel (the only member of the *International* among the leaders of the Commune) wrote to Marx to ask his advice about the steps he should undertake in his post. What could be more tempting than to plunge into social planning and produce a blue-print for a new society? Yet Marx does nothing of the sort. His letter, not written until 13 May, is extremely cool and reserved. He totally disregards the request for advice about public works and employment. Instead, he lectures Fränckel about the dangers to the Commune from the non-

---

[1] Marx to Engels, 6 September 1870 (*Briefwechsel*, IV, 453). At this time, September 1870, Engels moved to his new house in Regent's Park in London after selling his share in the Ermen and Engels partnership in Manchester. This ended the voluminous Marx–Engels correspondence, since the two were now to see each other almost every day in London. Thus we lack, for the period of the Commune, the detailed background story of Marx's views which was supplied till then through his correspondence with Engels.

[2] In a letter to Sorge of 5 January 1880 (*Selected Correspondence*, pp. 404–5), Marx hails the founding of the French socialist party by Guesde and Lafargue as the emergence of the first real working-class party in France: 'To my mind, this is the first real labour movement in France. Up to the present time only sects existed there, which naturally received their slogans from the founder of the sect, whereas the mass of the proletariat followed the radical or pseudo-radical bourgeois and fought for them on the decisive day, only to be slaughtered, deported, etc., the very next day by the fellows they had hoisted into the saddle.' The implications of this for Marx's views of the Commune are obvious.

proletarian elements influencing its course.[1] Marx does not go into the details of the question directed to him because he thought that the Commune would be defeated anyway. He was sure that the non-proletarian elements in the Commune could make any universally oriented policy impossible.

The social composition of the Commune, still a rather moot question, is not as important for this discussion as Marx's view on the subject. This view, whether false or correct, determined his attitude to the Commune. The various drafts of *The Civil War in France* offer clear evidence that Marx considered the Commune not a working-class affair, but a petty-bourgeois, democratic-radical émeute. He never explicitly states this in the final, published version of the essay, though he hints in this direction. After all, a eulogy is not the right moment for an autopsy.

The analysis of the class structure of the Commune in the draft manuscripts of *The Civil War in France* is extremely interesting. In tracing the origins of the insurrection, Marx reveals that some of its social background was far from working-class in character. Marx mentions very prominently the moratorium introduced by the Thiers government in September 1870: this ordinance deferred all outstanding bills of payment and rents for the last months of 1870 till 13 March 1871. In this way the Thiers government secured the support of the Paris petty bourgeoisie of shopkeepers and small artisans, the chief beneficiaries of this moratorium. When the moratorium was about the expire, the Paris lower middle classes pressed Versailles for a further extension, but Thiers refused. Between 13 and 18 March more than 150,000 claims for payment of bills and rents were lodged, a terrible financial blow for the lower middle classes. The insurrection of the Commune on 18 March, though directly engendered by a different issue, came to a head because of strong resentment against Thiers among the plebeian petty bourgeoisie of Paris. Marx points out that, consequently, a characteristic measure of the Commune was the further extension of his moratorium.[2]

With this social background of the Commune in mind, Marx is

---

[1] Marx to Fränckel and Varlin, 13 May 1871 (*Selected Correspondence*, p. 321). Fränckel's letter to Marx has been published in *Die Neue Zeit* (1911), p. 793.

[2] *Archiv Marksa i Engelsa* (III), pp. 304, 342. Cf. also *Werke*, XVII, n. 222 on p. 708.

not surprised that most of its legislation would not be working class in nature. Actually, there is nothing proletarian in the social legislation of the Commune except its abolition of night baking. In the section of the draft dealing with legislation affecting the working class Marx cannot show more than a few laws against prostitution and the abolition of some payments which were remnants of feudal legislation. On the other hand, he devotes much more space to the sub-chapter called 'Measures for the working class but mostly for the middle classes'.[1] He goes on to articulate the result: 'The principal measures taken by the Commune are taken for the advantage of the middle class.'[2]

Since the Commune became after its demise a symbol for proletarian solidarity, Marx did not include these passages in the final draft, though obliquely he refers to this issue in a most characteristic passage. A main difference between June 1848 and the Commune was, according to Marx, the shift in the behaviour of the lower middle classes. In 1848 they joined the bourgeosie and helped to slaughter the workers. During the Commune, they joined the workers against the bouregoisie.[3] This seems an adequate explanation: what Marx does not explicitly say here is that the Commune's whole initiative was also petty-bourgeois in origin.

This ambivalent attitude towards the Commune also characterized Marx's views in later years. At the Hague Congress of the International in 1872 the Commune was hardly discussed or mentioned. Marx's Amsterdam Speech limits itself to the statement that the Commune collapsed because no parallel revolutions in the other capitals of Europe followed.[4] Marx could have added that, according to his own views, no such revolutions could follow under the given circumstances. Hence also the derogatory tone in the letter to Domela-Nieuwenhuis, in which Marx says that the Commune should have come to terms with Versailles.[5]

Thus the failure of the Commune did not represent the failure of the working class or the failure of the ideas that guided the working class. It represented rather the failure of the social structure of the

---

[1] *Archiv Marksa i Engelsa* (III), p. 304.   [2] *Ibid.* p. 342.
[3] *Selected Works*, I, 522–3. Marx also obliquely refers here to the 'multiplicity of interests' at work in the Commune.
[4] *Werke*, XVIII, 161.   [5] *Selected Correspondence*, p. 410.

movement that carried it. This movement was basically non-proletarian in composition, despite socialist ideologies sometimes popular among some leaders. It was also suffering from the traditional French left-wing illusion of trying to re-enact 1793 all over again. Much as the Commune's ultimate development might have followed socialist lines, its revolutionary *praxis* could not be emancipated from the social and political backwardness into which France—once the pioneer nation of social progress—was thrown by the *Bas Empire* of Napoleon III. It is not enough, then, for thought to strive to realize itself: reality must also strive towards thought.[1]

[1] *Early Writings*, p. 54.

EPILOGUE: THE ESCHATOLOGY
OF THE PRESENT

It seems that the intellectual achievement of Marx's thought is also its main weakness in precisely that sphere in which Marx considered his theory to have achieved a major breakthrough towards historical realization. Marx arrives at the philosophical meaning of the revolution by confronting Hegel's philosophy with the contemporary reality which it sought to justify and legitimize. This strategy distinguishes Marx's theory of revolution from most other nineteenth-century revolutionary theories, for they either deduced the revolution from *a priori* principles whose relation to reality was based on a mere negation of it, or limited themselves to merely empirical analysis of contemporary reality. Marx's breakthrough from philosophical theory to a *praxis* possessing a social, historical subject whose legitimacy it justifies in terms of the theory is doubtless a turning point in nineteenth-century history. Wedding socialism to the proletariat, it gave historical meaning to the conscious social organization of the working class. The lot of the proletarians thus ceased to be the affair of the workers themselves and forced its way into world history.

Precisely here the internal weakness of Marx's thought is most evident. Turning the possibility of human redemption into an historical phenomenon about to be realized here and now secularizes the Hegelian synthesis that saw the dialectical tensions resolving themselves in the present generation and finding their *Aufhebung* in an apotheosis through which the historical process would achieve its ultimate height. It is immaterial that whereas Hegel called this act the culmination of history, Marx sees it as the beginning of true history; the implications are the same. From a systematic point of view the difference between Marx and Hegel in this respect can be reduced to Marx's rejection of the Hegelian postulate about the existence of a super-historical essence, Absolute Spirit, and to his contention that the process of the *Aufhebung* of the antagonisms has yet to occur, while Hegel thought that it had already occurred. Endowing the present generation with such an eschatological significance was common to Marx and Hegel—despite the conservative, quietistic implications of Hegel's philosophy and the revolutionary and activist implications of Marx's. The radical element in Hegel, like the passivist, 'objectivist' interpretations of Marx, points to the internal tensions of a system that combines eschatology and dialectics.

The implications of Marx's theory called for a proletarian movement. But the intellectual achievements of Marx's philosophy cannot provide without modifications an ideological basis for a political movement possessing organizational continuity and experiencing the normal ups and downs of political life. The vulgarization of Marx's theory thus becomes a necessary component in the make-up of those historical movements brought to life by Marx's own philosophical speculation and historical analysis. It is therefore more than a mere side effect of Marx's theory that the various Marxist movements, social democratic or communist, had to emancipate themselves from many of the most outstanding and most brilliant of Marx's intellectual achievements and replace them by simplified vulgarizations and a wholly uncritical reverence towards the founding fathers of the movement. Thus a popularizing emasculation of his theory went hand in hand with an idolatrous attitude towards a mythical image of the person of Marx. Kautsky and Bebel were guilty of this not less than Lenin and Stalin, though the methods of course differed. Marxist parties may thus become the grave diggers of Marxism, and Marx's theory may thus be denied by the very historical processes he foresaw. A main target of historical research into Marxism may therefore be to rescue Marx from the hands of his disciples, whatever their affiliation.

Marx's career reveals throughout an implicit tension between his conviction that the revolution is imminent and his disinclination to be implicated in a coup that would try violently to usher in the millennium. This tension between eschatology and dialectics implies that Marx sees the political activity of the proletariat creating the conditions that would facilitate the realization of the revolutionary objectives so that the proletariat would be ready when circumstances would make this realization unavoidable. For Marx such an attitude toward conscious intervention in the historical process tries to avoid

Epilogue

the twin dangers of subjectivist wishful thinking and quietistic objectivism. The sophistication of such an attitude could be hardly followed by leaders of mass movements, both parliamentary or revolutionary.

Contrary to what has sometimes been claimed, it is not true that Marx adopted this view only after 1848. In September 1847 Marx says in a draft speech on Free Trade that only unlimited total Free Trade will bring the productive forces of capitalist society to their full development and thus introduce the possibility of further change and transformation.[1] Even on the immediate eve of the revolution of 1848 Marx does not anticipate violent upheavals. *The Communist Manifesto* has been presented sometimes as a prelude to 1848, but it is nothing of this sort. Its concluding chapter indicates very clearly that Marx looked forward to a lengthy process of change rather than to a violent imminent revolution, and that he was oriented far more toward organizational political work than toward revolutionary conspiracy.[2] As late as 9 January 1848 Marx tells the Democratic Association in Brussels that Free Trade is the main vehicle for change. The adherence of some workers' groups to the Anti-Corn-Law League he considers a step in the right direction, since the repeal of the Corn Laws gave protectionism a death blow and thus paved the way for the internal change of capitalism: 'Free Trade dissolves the hitherto existing nationalities and pushes to its climax the tension between proletariat and bourgeoisie. In one word, the system of free trade precipitates the social revolution.'[3]

This view prevails in Marx's thought in the post-1848 years. We have already seen that, despite the radical language of the March 1850 *Address*, Marx insists in September 1850 that it would take '15, 20, 50 years' for the workers to be fit for power.[4] And in an article of October 1850 he says:

With all this universal boom, with the productive forces of civil society developing in such a luxurious way...there is no chance for a real re-volution...The numerous quarrels in which the representatives of the various factions of the continental party of order get involved are far from giving a new impetus to revolution; on the contrary, they are themselves

---

[1] *Werke*, IV, 308. [2] *Selected Works*, I, 64–5.
[3] *Werke*, IV, 457–8. [4] *Ibid.* VIII, 598.

252

possible only because the basis of momentary conditions is so secure and (what the reaction does not know) so *bourgeois*. Against this bastion there will crush all the reactionary attempts to stop bourgeois progress as well as all moral indignation and the enthusiastic proclamations of the Democrats.[1]

Marx's aloofness from all different conspiratorial and revolutionary groups of exiles in London is a direct corollary of this attitude. In 1860 he writes to Freiligrath:

Let me state, to begin with, that after the League [of Communists] had been dissolved, at *my instance*, in November 1852, I *never* again belonged, and do not now belong, to any *secret* or *public* society; that therefore the *Party* in this wholly ephemeral sense ceased to exist for me eight years ago. The lectures on political economy which I delivered after the appearance of my work (autumn, 1859) to a few selected workers, including some *former* League members, had nothing in common with a closed society.[2]

Marx's pre-1848 and post-1848 attitudes differ only with regard to the scope of capitalist development. Prior to 1848 Marx felt that capitalist society was quickly reaching its maturity, but the debacle of 1848 probably convinced him that capitalism was still far removed from such a maturity. The Preface to *Das Kapital* nevertheless shows that Marx thought that at least in England capitalist development had already reached its climax and was slowly changing capitalism internally.

These considerations cause Marx to oppose any attempt at revolution. In a letter to Adolph Cluss, a German friend who emigrated to the United States, Marx says in 1852 that the present economic prosperity, which seems to him bound to last for a long time, prevents a revolution.[3] In a letter to Engels, also of the same year, Marx comments painfully on the attempts of Mazzini and Kossuth to stage another 1848. These revolutionaries do not understand that under prevailing conditions their attempt stands no chance, because their subjectivist Jacobin attitude to merely political revolutions makes them unable to perceive his.[4] In his

[1] *Ibid.* VII, 440.
[2] Marx to Freiligrath, 29 February 1860 (*Selected Correspondence*, pp. 146–7).
[3] Marx to Cluss, 22 April 1852 (*Werke*, XXVIII, 515).
[4] Marx to Engels, 6 May 1852 (*Briefwechsel*, I, 424).

typically brutal style Engels remarks that some of these revolutionary adventurers, who time and again fail in their coups, should be caught and executed, so that this folly would stop.[1] The concentration of Marx's energy on the study of economic growth of the capitalist system results from his conviction that in this process lies the key to revolution in Europe; his pre-1848 Free Trade speeches pointed in the same direction. Because of the universality of capitalism, the riddle of revolution cannot be solved within Europe alone, and Marx turns his attention to the processes of change in the non-European countries. He even suggests that these non-European conditions may ultimately determine the chances of revolution in Europe itself:

It may seem a very strange and paradoxical assertion that the next uprising of the people of Europe, and their next movement for republican freedom and economy of government, may depend more probably on what is now passing in the Celestial Empire—the very opposite of Europe—than on any other political cause that now exists...Now, England having brought about the revolution of China, the question is how that revolution will in time react on England, and through England on Europe.[2]

The impact of the Crimean War on British society caused Marx to speculate that under certain conditions the established political forces in England may become so finely balanced against each other as to leave the door open for an independent political action by the working class which may tip the scales.[3] The somewhat violent working-class demonstrations of 1855 impress Marx very deeply and he visualizes the possibility of their turning into uncontrolled riots.[4] Palmerston's victory and the economic crisis of 1857-8 again encourage Marx to hope that a revolution is possible in the foreseeable future, since the period of expansion and internal prosperity may be over.[5] In 1858 Marx writes to Lassalle that: 'All in all, the

[1] Engels to Marx, 7 May 1852 (*Briefwechsel*, I, 426: 'Es wäre den Chefs, die das Ding leiten sollen, zu wünschen, dass sie sämtlich gefangen und füsiliert würden'.
[2] 'Revolution in China and in Europe', *New York Daily Tribune*, 14 June 1853 (*On Colonialism*, pp. 15, 17).
[3] *New York Daily Tribune*, 27 April 1855 (*Werke*, XI, 178-83).
[4] Marx to Engels, 3 and 26 June 1855 (*Briefwechsel*, II, 114, 116).
[5] Marx to Engels, 31 March 1857 (*ibid.* p. 222). In *Herr Vogt* Marx again says that no new revolutionary wave could have been conceived before 1857-8 (*Werke*, XIV, 452).

present period is pleasant. History is evidently bracing itself to take
again a new start, and the signs of decomposition everywhere are
delightful for every mind not bent upon the conservation of things
as they are.'[1]

Though the crisis was well over by the end of 1858, Marx gets
some consolation from internal developments in Russia. Writing to
Engels he says that 'it is at least consoling that in Russia the
revolution has begun'.[2] The radicalization of the German political
scene in 1862 again gives rise to the hope that revolution may break
out there. In a letter to Kugelmann, Marx says: 'I should be very
pleased if you would occasionally write to me on the situation at
home. We are obviously approaching a revolution—which I have
never doubted since 1850. The first act will include a by no means
refreshing repetition of the stupidities of '48–'49. However, that is
the way of world history, and one has to take it as it is.'[3]

The ever-deepening crisis of Prussian politics in 1863 prompts
Marx to write to Engels that 'we shall soon have a revolution'.[4]
In the same year he considers the Polish insurrection a prelude to a
European revolution in which 'hopefully the lava will flow this time
from East to West'.[5] Five years later, in 1868, Marx sees in the
revolutionary development in Spain the signal for a universal
transformation: 'I am completely of your opinion that the Spanish
revolution, having the same meaning as the Neapolitan one in 1848,
gives to European history a totally different turn...'[6]

The last time Marx directly anticipated revolution occurred in
1877, after the initial Russian defeats in the Russo-Turkish War.
In a letter to Sorge he explains the effects of these defeats on Russian
society:

This crisis is a *new turning point* in European history. Russia—and I have
studied conditions there from the original *Russian* sources, unofficial and
official...—has long been standing on the threshold of an upheaval; all
the elements of it are prepared. The gallant Turks have hastened the

[1] Marx to Lassalle, 31 May 1858 (*Werke*, XXIX, 561).
[2] Marx to Engels, 8 October 1858 (*Selected Correspondence*, p. 133).
[3] Marx to Kugelmann, 28 December 1862 (*Letters to Kugelmann*, p. 25).
[4] Marx to Engels, 21 February 1863 (*Briefwechsel*, III, 158).
[5] *Ibid.* 13 February 1863 (*ibid.* pp. 151–2).
[6] *Ibid.* 23 September 1868 (*ibid.* IV, 118).

explosion by years with the thrashing they have inflicted not merely on the Russian army and Russian finances, but on the very persons of the *dynasty commanding* the army (the Tsar, the heir to the throne, and six other Romanovs). The upheaval will begin *secundum artem* with some playing at constitutionalism, *et puis il y aura un beau tapage*. If Mother Nature is not particularly unfavourable towards us, we shall yet live to see the fun!

The stupid nonsense the Russian students are perpetrating is merely a symptom, worthless in itself. But it is a symptom. All sections of Russian society are in full decomposition economically, morally, and intellectually.

This time the revolution begins in the East, hitherto the unbroken bulwark and reserve army of the counter-revolution.[1]

Within a few weeks the whole picture was radically changed by the resounding Russian victory in the Balkans and the Treaty of San Stefano, and Marx's bold assertions looked like so much wishful thinking. Yet when the revolution did occur in Russia, it broke out in circumstances almost identical with those described here by Marx: military defeat, diminishing popularity of the Tsar, and 'some play at constitutionalism' preceding a radical revolution. This was forty years later, and though it is amusing to reflect that Marx was wrong by a few weeks but right in four decades, the time lag is still crucial. Any attempt to systematize Marx's various predictions may be quite confusing, if not outright senseless. Marx sees the revolution breaking out in England, in Spain, in Poland, in Russia. Every crisis that seems to shock the stability of the established order he projects into a portent and prelude to revolution. His philosophical system is quite unable to help him to greater discrimination about the precise location of the next revolutionary outburst. All that the philosophical system, with all its richness, insight, complexity and intellectual brilliance could offer him was the evangelical truth that the millennium was around the corner. The more concrete predictions Marx attempted he could not relate to his philosophical premises. They grew out of his ordinary socio-political intuition, which did not prove to be much superior to that of his contemporaries.

But once a revolution broke out in 1917 in Russia in conditions similar to those envisaged by Marx in 1877 in his letter to Sorge, Lenin had

[1] Marx to Sorge, 27 September 1877 (*Selected Correspondence*, p. 374).

at his disposal a political weapon to which Marx had always objected and which he had consistently opposed on principle—a tightly knit party organized as a conspiratorial and aggressive power. Since the early 'fifties Marx had consistently divorced himself from any connection with such political organizations. Even in 1848 he had never tried to turn the *League of Communists* into anything of this sort. We have also seen that Marx conceived the *International* as an organ for creating universal proletarian self-consciousness. His initiative in transferring the seat of the General Council of the *International* to New York in 1872 was doubtless motivated by his fear that the Bakuninist influences might make the *International* into a conspirational organization which may try to stage another coup, another ill-begotten Commune. Even during 1857–8, when he envisaged a possible radicalization that might lead to revolution, Marx did not try to prepare for it by forming or joining a revolutionary group. Quite the contrary: when he saw the gathering storm, he immersed himself with additional intensity in his economic studies, so that his Political Economy would be ready once the revolution broke out.[1] And Engels, who thought in 1866 that a revolution was imminent, urged Marx to finish at least volume I of *Das Kapital*: 'What will it help us...if even the first volume of your book will not be ready for publication when we shall be surprised by the events?'[2]

Even with regard to the German Social Democratic movement, Marx never saw himself as the guide and mentor of any of its groups, and his letter to Bracke accompanying the *Critique of the Gotha Programme* said that he did not in any way see himself as the leader of the Eisenachers.[3]

Leninism did not experience this internal difficulty. Lenin's view on the nature of revolutionary activity was far less beset by difficulties precisely because it lacked the dialectical insights of Marx's

---

[1] Marx to Cluss, 15 September 1853 (*Werke*, XXVIII, 592).
[2] Engels to Marx, 10 February 1866 (*Briefwechsel*, III, 368).
[3] Marx to Bracke, 5 May 1875 (*Selected Works*, II, 15: 'After the Unity Congress has been held, Engels and I will publish a short declaration to the effect that our position is altogether remote from the said programme of principles and that we have nothing to do with it. This is indispensable because the opinion—the entirely erroneous opinion—is held abroad, assiduously nurtured by the enemies of the party, that we secretly guide from here the movement of the so-called Eisenach Party').

philosophical speculation. Its linear, mechanistic attitude was far more straightforward, and its basic principle of action (though not of historical analysis) was far more akin to that voluntaristic Jacobin political tradition so much criticized by Marx himself. Soviet Communism may then be termed a combination of the Jacobin subjectivist view of political revolution with a somewhat mechanistic interpretation of history derived from Marx through Engels. That the outcome may have been similar to what Marx calls in the *Manuscripts* 'crude communism' should not be surprising.

Yet one must concede that, with all the differences between Marx and Soviet, Leninist Communism, Leninism would have been inconceivable without Marx. Ironically, it was in his various letters on Russia that Marx pointed out that historical developments are always open to several possibilities. Yet Marx disregarded the possibilities open to his own theory; and here lies his major intellectual blunder. Though he thought of open historical alternatives none the less determined by identifiable and explicable causes, he overlooked the possibility that one of the alternatives to which the future development of his own theory was open might be the combination of his philosophical and historical theory with the Jacobin tradition of merely political, subjectivist revolutionary action: Leninism embodied such a combination. Thus, if Marx's point of departure was Hegelian, so was his blind spot: like Hegel himself he did not subject his own theory to a dialectical critique.

BIBLIOGRAPHY

WORKS BY MARX AND ENGELS

Karl Marx/Friedrich Engels. *Historisch-kritische Gesamtausgabe* (*MEGA*), ed. D. Rjazanov/V. Adoratskij. Frankfurt-Berlin, 1927–32.

Karl Marx/Friedrich Engels. *Werke*, vols. I–XXXIX. Berlin, 1956– .

Karl Marx/Friedrich Engels. *Selected Works*, vols. I–II. Moscow, 1962.

Karl Marx. *Early Writings*, trans. T. B. Bottomore. London, 1963.

Karl Marx/Friedrich Engels. *The Holy Family*, trans. R. Dixon. Moscow, 1956.

Karl Marx/Friedrich Engels. *The German Ideology*, revised English trans. London, 1965.

Karl Marx. *The Poverty of Philosophy*. Moscow, n.d.

Karl Marx. *Capital*, vols. I–III. Moscow, n.d.

Karl Marx. *Grundrisse der Kritik der politischen Oekonomie* (*Grundrisse*). Berlin, 1953.

Karl Marx. *Pre-Capitalist Economic Formations*, ed. E. Hobsbawm. London, 1964.

Karl Marx/Friedrich Engels. *On Britain*. Moscow, 1962.

Karl Marx/Friedrich Engels. *On Colonialism*. Moscow, n.d.

Friedrich Engels. *Anti-Dühring*, 3rd English ed. Moscow, 1962.

Friedrich Engels. *Dialectics of Nature*, trans. C. Dutt. Moscow, 1954.

Karl Marx/Friedrich Engels. *Briefwechsel*, vols. I–IV. Berlin, 1949–50.

Karl Marx/Friedrich Engels. *Selected Correspondence*. Moscow, n.d.

Karl Marx. *Letters to Kugelmann*. London, 1936.

Karl Marx/Friedrich Engels. *Letters to Americans*. New York, 1953.

Marx-Engels-Archiv, ed. D. Rjazanov, vols. I–II. Frankfurt, 1927.

The General Council of the First International, vols. I–III. Moscow, n.d.

La Première Internationale: Recueil de documents (*Recueil*), ed. J. Freymond, vols. I–II. Genève, 1962.

The First International: Minutes of the Hague Conference of 1872, ed. H. Gerth. Madison, 1958.

OTHER WORKS

Acton, Harry Burrow. *The Illusion of the Epoch*. London, 1955.

Adler, Georg. 'Die Anfänge der Marxschen Sozialtheorie und ihre Beeinflussung durch Hegel, Feuerbach, Stein und Proudhon', *Festgabe für Adolf Wagner*. Leipzig, 1905.

259

Bibliography

Adler, Georg. *Die Grundlagen der Karl Marxschen Kritik der bestehenden Volkswirtschaft*. Tübingen, 1887.

Avineri, Shlomo. 'From Hoax to Dogma: A Footnote on Marx and Darwin', *Encounter* (March 1967), pp. 30–2.

—— 'Marx and the Intellectuals', *Journal of the History of Ideas*, XXVIII, no. 2 (April–June 1967).

Axelos, Kostas. *Marx penseur de la technique*. Paris, 1961.

Baader, Franz v. 'Über das dermalige Misverhältnis der Vermögen-losen, oder Proletairs, zu den Vermögen besitzenden Klassen der Sozietät', *Schriften zur Gesellschaftsphilosophie*, ed. J. Sauter. Jena, 1925.

Barion, Jakob. *Hegel und die marxistische Staatslehre*. Bonn, 1963.

Barzun, Jacques. *Darwin, Marx, Wagner*. Boston, 1946.

Bauer, Bruno. *Die bürgerliche Revolution in Deutschland*. Berlin, 1849.

Berlin, Isaiah. *Karl Marx*, 2nd ed. London, 1952.

—— *The Life and Opinions of Moses Hess*. Cambridge, 1959.

Bernstein, Eduard. *Evolutionary Socialism*, trans. E. C. Harvey. New York, 1909.

Beyer, Wilhelm R. 'Hegels Begriff der Praxis', *Deutsche Zeitschrift für Philosophie*, 6. Jhrg. (1958).

Blanc, Louis. *Histoire de la Révolution française*. Paris, 1866.

Blumenberg, Werner. 'Zur Geschichte des Bundes der Kommunisten', *International Review of Social History*, IX (1964), 81–121.

Bober, M. M., *Karl Marx's Interpretation of History*. Cambridge, Mass., 1950.

Böhm-Bawerk, E. v. *Karl Marx and the Close of His System*. New York, 1949.

Buber, Martin. *Paths in Utopia*. London, 1949.

Calvez, Jean-Yves. *La Pensée de Karl Marx*. Paris, 1956.

Cieszkowski, August v. *Prolegomena zur Historiosophie*. Berlin, 1838.

—— *De la pairie et de l'aristocratie moderne*. Paris, 1844.

—— *Notre Père*, French edition. Paris, 1904.

Collins, Henry and Abramsky, Chimen. *Karl Marx and the British Labour Movement*. London, 1965.

Conze, Wilhelm. *Staat und Gesellschaft im deutschen Vormarz*. Stuttgart, 1962.

Cornforth, M. *Dialectical Materialism*, vols. I–II. London, 1954.

Cornu, Auguste. *Karl Marx et Friedrich Engels: leur vie et leur œuvre*, vols. I–III. Paris, 1955–62.

—— *The Origins of Marxian Thought*. Springfield, Ill., 1957.

Bibliography

Cunow, H. *Die Marxsche Geschichts-, Gesellschafts- und Staatslehre.*
Berlin, 1920.

de Vries, J. *Die Erkenntnistheorie des dialektischen Materialismus.* Salzburg/München, 1958.

Dupré, Louis. *The Philosophical Foundations of Marxism.* New York, 1966.

Easton, Loyd D. 'August Willich, Marx and Left-Hegelian Socialism', *Cahiers de l'ISEA*, série S, no. 9 (1965), pp. 101–37.

Feuerbach, Ludwig. *Das Wesen des Christentums*, ed. H. Schmidt. Leipzig, 1909.

—— *Kleine philosophische Schriften.* Leipzig, 1950.

—— 'Vorläufige Thesen zur Reformation der Philosophie', *Anekdota zur neuesten deutschen Philosophie und Publizistik* vol. II. Zürich/Winterthur, 1843.

—— *Briefwechsel*, ed. W. Schuffenhauer. Leipzig, 1963.

Földes, B. *Das Problem Karl Marx–Lorenz Stein.* Jena, 1927.

Fromm, Erich. *Marx's Concept of Man.* New York, 1961.

—— (ed.). *Socialist Humanism.* Garden City, 1965.

Galbraith, John Kenneth. *The Affluent Society.* London, 1958.

Gebhardt, Jürgen. *Politik und Eschatologie.* München, 1963.

Gregor, A. James. *A Survey of Marxism.* New York, 1965.

Habermas, Jürgen. *Theorie und Praxis.* Neuwied am Rhein, 1963.

Hegel, G. F. W. *Early Theological Writings*, trans. T. M. Knox. Chicago, 1948.

—— *The Phenomenology of Mind*, trans. J. B. Baillie, 2nd ed. London, 1931.

—— *The Philosophy of Right*, trans. T. M. Knox. Oxford, 1942.

—— *Vernunft in der Geschichte*, ed. J. Hoffmeister. Hamburg, 1955.

—— *Enzyklopädie der philosophischen Wissenschaften*, ed. Nicolin and Pöggeler. Hamburg, 1959.

—— *Briefe von und an Hegel*, ed. J. Hoffmeister, vols. I–IV. Hamburg, 1952–60.

Hepner, Benoit P. 'History and the Future: The Vision of August Cieszkowski', *The Review of Politics*, XV, no. 3 (July 1953).

Hertz-Eichenrode, Dieter. 'Massenpsychologie bei den Junghegelianer', *International Review of Social History*, VII, no. 2 (1962).

Hess, Moses. *Die europäische Triarchie.* Leipzig, 1841.

—— *Philosophische und sozialistische Schriften*, ed. A. Cornu and W. Mönke. Berlin, 1961.

—— *Briefwechsel*, ed. E. Silberner. Haag, 1959.

Bibliography

Heusel, A. *Untersuchungen über das Erkenntnisobjekt bei Marx*. Jena, 1925.

Hilferding, Rudolf. *Böhm-Bawerk's Criticism of Marx*, ed. P. Sweezy. New York, 1949.

Hodges, Donald C. 'Engels' Contribution to Marxism', *Socialist Register*, 1965 (London), pp. 297–310.

Hommes, Jakob. *Der technische Eros*. Freiburg, 1955.

Hook, Sidney. *From Hegel to Marx*, new ed. Ann Arbor, 1962.

Hyndman, H. M. *The Record of an Adventurous Life*. London, 1911.

Hyppolite, Jean. *Études sur Marx et Hegel*. Paris, 1955.

Kamenka, Eugene. *The Ethical Foundations of Marxism*. London, 1962.

Kaufmann, Walter. *Hegel*. New York, 1965.

Kautsky, Karl. *Terrorism and Communism*. London, 1920.

Kindersley, R. *The First Russian Revisionists*. Oxford, 1962.

Kühne, W. *Graf August Cieszkowski, ein Schüler Hegels und des deutschen Geistes*. Leipzig, 1938.

Künzli, Arnold. *Karl Marx: Eine Pszychographie*. Wien, 1966.

Labedz, Leopold (ed.). *Revisionism*. London, 1962.

Lange, Oskar. *Problems of Political Economy of Socialism*. Calcutta, 1962.

Leff, Gordon. *The Tyranny of Concepts*. London, 1961.

Lenin, V. I. *Collected Works*, vols. I– . Moscow, 1960– .

Lessner, F. 'Before 1848 and After', *Reminiscences about Marx and Engels*. Moscow, n.d.

Lewis, John. *The Life and Thought of Karl Marx*. London, 1965.

Lichtheim, George. *Marxism*. London, 1961.

—— 'Marx and the Asiatic Mode of Production', *St Antony's Papers*, XIV (1963), 86–112.

—— 'Western Marxist Literature', *Survey*, no. 50 (January 1964), pp. 119–28.

—— 'The Origins of Marxism', *Journal of the History of Philosophy*, III, no. 1 (April 1965), 96–105.

Lindsay, A. D. *Karl Marx's 'Capital'*. London, 1925.

Lobkowicz, Nicholas (ed.). *Marx and the Western World*. Notre Dame, 1967.

Lossky, N. O. *Three Polish Messianists: Sigmund Krasinski, August Cieszkowski, W. Lutoslawski*. Prague, 1937.

Löwith, Karl. 'Max Weber und Karl Marx', *Archiv für Sozialwissenschaft und Sozialpolitik*, LXVII (1932).

—— *From Hegel to Nietzsche*. New York, 1964.

—— (ed.). *Die Hegelsche Linke*. Stuttgart, 1962.

Lukács, Georg. *Geschichte und Klassenbewusstsein*. Berlin, 1923.

Bibliography

Lukács, Georg. *Moses Hess und die Probleme der idealistischen Dialektik.* Leipzig, 1926.

—— *Der junge Hegel.* Wien, 1948.

—— 'Zur philosophischen Entwicklung des jungen Marx', *Deutsche Zeitschrift für Philosophie*, II, no. 2 (1954), 288 f.

Luxemburg, Rosa. *The Russian Revolution*, ed. Bertram D. Wolfe. Ann Arbor, 1961.

Marcuse, Herbert. *Reason and Revolution*, 2nd ed. New York, 1954.

Marxismusstudien, vols. I–IV, eds. E. Metzge and I. Fetscher. Tübingen, 1954–62.

Masaryk, Thomas G. *Die philosophischen und soziologischen Grundlagen des Marxismus.* Wien, 1899.

Mehring, Franz. *Karl Marx.* London, 1936.

Mengelberg, K. 'Lorenz v. Stein and His Contribution to Historical Sociology', *Journal of the History of Ideas*, XXII, no. 2 (1961).

Mészáros, István. 'Collettività e alienazione', *Nuova Presenza*, no. 5 (1962).

Meyer, Alfred G. *Marxism : The Unity of Theory and Praxis.* Cambridge, Mass., 1954.

Miliband, Ralph, 'Marx and the State', *Socialist Register*, 1965 (London), pp. 278–96.

Morgan, Roger P. *The German Social Democracy and the First International.* Cambridge, 1965.

Müller, Adam. 'Die heutige Wissenschaft der Nationalokonomie kurz und fasslich dargestellt', *Ausgewählte Abhandlungen*, ed. J. Baxa. Jena, 1921.

—— *Gesammelte Schriften.* München, 1839.

Na'aman, Shlomo. 'Zur Geschichte des Bundes der Kommunisten in der zweiter Phase seines Bestehens', *Archiv für Sozialgeschichte*, V (1965), 5–82.

Nicolaevsky, Boris and Maenchen-Helfen, O. *Karl Marx, Man and Fighter.* London, 1936.

O'Malley, Joseph J. 'History and Man's "Nature" in Marx', *The Review of Politics*, XXVIII, no. 4 (October 1966), 508–27.

Paul, G. A. 'Lenin's Theory of Perception', *Analysis*, V, no. 5 (1938), 65–73.

Postgate, R. *Revolution from 1789 to 1906.* London, 1920.

Plamenatz, John. *German Marxism and Russian Communism.* London, 1954.

Popper, Karl. *The Open Society and Its Enemies.* Princeton, 1950.

Bibliography

Riedel, Martin. *Theorie und Praxis im Denken Hegels.* Stuttgart, 1965.

Rotenstreich, Nathan. *Basic Problems of Marx's Philosophy.* Indianapolis/ New York, 1965.

Rubel, Maximilien. *Karl Marx : essai de biographie intellectuelle.* Paris, 1957.

—— 'Marx's Conception of Democracy', *New Politics*, I, no. 2 (1962), 78–90.

Ruge, Arnold. *Werke.* Mannheim, 1847.

Schmidt, Alfred. *Der Begriff der Natur in der Lehre von Marx.* Frankfurt, 1962.

Schuffenhauer, Werner. *Feuerbach und der junge Marx.* Berlin, 1965.

Silberner, Edmund. 'Beiträge zur literarischen und politischen Tätigkeit von Moses Hess, 1841–1843', *Annali dell'Istituto Giangiacomo Feltrinelli*, VI (1963), 387–437.

Sorel, Georges. *Les Polémiques sur l'interprétation du marxisme.* Paris, 1900.

Stuke, Horst. *Philosophie der Tat.* Stuttgart, 1963.

Talmon, J. L. *The Origins of Totalitarian Democracy.* London, 1952.

Tillich, Paul. *Der Mensch im Christentum und im Marxismus.* Stuttgart, 1952.

Tucker, Robert C. *Philosophy and Myth in Karl Marx.* Cambridge, 1961.

Venable, V. *Human Nature : The Marxian View.* London, 1946.

Verdès, Jeanine. 'Marx vu par la police française 1871–1883', *Cahiers de l'ISEA*, série S, no. 10 (August 1966), pp. 83–120.

Vico, Giambattista. *The New Science*, trans. T. G. Bergin and M. H. Fisch. New York, 1961.

Victor, W. *Marx und Heine.* Berlin, 1953.

Vogel, Paul. *Hegels Gesellschaftsbegriff und seine geschichtliche Fortbildung durch Lorenz Stein, Marx, Engels and Lassalle.* Berlin, 1925.

Weber, Max. 'Die "Objektivität" sozialwissenschaftlicher und sozialpolitischer Erkenntnisse', *Archiv für Sozialwissenschaft und Sozialpolitik*, XIX (1904), 22–87.

—— *Essays in Sociology*, trans. Gerth and Wright Mills. New York, 1946.

Weiss, J. 'Dialectical Idealism and the Work of Lorenz v. Stein', *International Review of Social History*, VII, no. 1 (1963).

Żółtowski, A. *Graf A. Cieszkowski's Philosophie der Tat.* Posen, 1904.

INDEX

Abramsky, C., 200
absolutism, 21, 49, 165, 183
Adler, G., 55 n.
agriculture, 112–13, 156, 169
alienation, 2, 10, 43–7, 86, 97, 105 ff., 133,
   163, 165, 179; Hegel, 96
Alsace-Lorraine, 245
anarchists, 208, 235, 238–9
Aristotle, 131
Aufhebung, 36–8, 84, 99, 105, 150, 160,
   179, 186, 202–4, 208–12, 221, 243, 250
Australia, 167
Axelos, K., 24 n.

Baader, F. v., 55–6
Baboeuf, F. N., 186, 191
Bagehot, W., 42
Bakunin, M., 144, 174, 182, 184, 192, 208,
   237–9, 257
Balance of Power, 43
Barzun, J., 66, 89
Bauer, B., 43, 54, 62, 132, 186; critical
   school, 100–1
Bebel, F. A., 251
Belgium, 54
Bismarck, O., 184, 213, 244–5
Blanc, Louis, 186, 196
Blanquists, 192, 194–6, 198, 200–1, 244,
   246
Blumenberg, W., 196
Bolshevism, 144
Bolte, F., 145
Bonapartism, 49–50, 245
Buonarroti, P-M., 186
bourgeoisie, 41, 44–5, 53, 60, 90–1, 159,
   162–3, 174–5, 247; civilizing role, 165;
   liberalism, 183; property, 83, 115; revo-
   lution, 186, 192
Bracke, W., 257
bureaucracy, 23–4, 26, 37, 48–52, 209
bürgerliche Gesellschaft, 13–14, 17–22, 36–
   7, 155
Burnham, J., 179

California, 167
Calvez, J.-Y., 68 n.
Calvinism, 157
Campanella, T., 43
capitalism, 150–6; change, 174–84; civi-
   lizing nature, 168; emergence, 11 4–15;

labour and, 119–22; universality, 162–74
cash nexus, 164
Chartists, 147, 214
China, 167, 254
Christianity, 35–6, 44, 56
Cieszkowski, August v., 124–8
'citizen', 44
class, 25–6, 145; abolition of, 59; lower-
   middle, 172, 247; relations, 164; rising
   and declining, 58
classless society, 31–40
Cluseret, 208
Cluss, A., 253, 257 n.
collectivism, 92, 95
Collins, H., 200
colonial expansion, 168
commodities, fetishism of, 30, 49, 117–23
Commune (Paris, 1871), 116, 193, 200,
   . 209, 211 n., 239–49
communism: crude, 223, 258; defined,
   61–2, 89, 222, 230, 234; distributive,
   224; practical, 141; republicanism and,
   187
Communists, League of, 63, 146, 242,
   253, 257; address to (1850), 196; demands, 212; split, 195; theoretical, 95
Comte, A., 239
concrete labour, class of, 26
Condorcet, Marquis de, 4
conservatism, 99
Considérant, V. P., 54, 62
co-operatives, 174–84
Copernicus, N., 43
Cornforth, M., 66 n.
Crimean War, 254
Cunning of Reason, 5
Cuno, T., 216 n.
Cunow, H., 209

Dark Ages, 4
Darwinism, 70
democracy, 20, 47, 217; battle of, 204;
   Social Democrats, 144, 210; true, 31–8
Democritus, 126
demystification, 162–3
despotism: military, 47; oriental, 113, 168
Domela-Nieuwenhuis, F., 200 n., 240,
   248

Easton, L. D., 196 n.

265

Index

education through work, 232–3
Eisenachers, 257
Engels, F., 13 n., 34 n., 39, 53, 77 n., 86, 93, 108 n., 125, 126 n., 143–4, 148 n., 164 n., 167 n., 176, 193 n., 200 n. 209 n., 229 n., 244 n., 254 n., 255; background, 3; dictatorship of proletariat, 240; evolutionary, 217 n.; influence, 2, 153; labour discipline, 235–6; materialism, 6, 65–9; move to London, 246 n.; state 'withering away', 202–3; Works: *Anti-Dühring*, 69, 202; *Dialectics of Nature*, 66; *Grundsätze des Kommunismus*, 153–4
England, 42, 256; Bank, 207; capitalism in, 159, 253; Corn Laws, 160–1, 167, 252; factories, 160, 215, 233; Glorious Revolution, 156; Levellers, 187; materialism, 67–8; proletariat, 141; Reform Bill, 215; Settlement (1660), 156; social criticism, 138–9; social upheaval, 160; suffrage, 215; taxation, 207; take-over, 49; working-class, 53, 55, 62, 214, 216; *see also*, Chartists, India
Enlightenment, the, 4
entailed estates, 27–9, 156
Epicurus, 126
epistemology; Hegel, 99; Marx, 69, 136, 148
exploitation, 120, 163

family, the, 28–9, 89–91, 163
Favre, J., 242
Ferguson, A., 4
feudalism, 20, 155–6, 162, 185
Feuerbach, L. A., 98, 101, 128, 133, 137, 139, 140; Hegel and, 10–12; materialism, 66–74; transformative method, 11, 14, 30, 49, 86, 97; *see also*, Marx: *Theses*
Fichte, J. G., 8 n., 43, 125
Földes, B., 53 n.
Fourier, F. M. C., 54, 130
France: bureaucracy, 49; Directoire, 185, 189; Enlightenment, 4; Franco-Prussian War, 244; International, 147–8; July Revolution (1830), 185; materialism, 6, 66–8; Napoleon I, 185; Orléanists, 199; peasantry, 214; proletariat, 141; Revolution of '48, 194; Second Empire, 50–1, 213; Second Republic, 212; social criticism, 138–9; socialism, 54, 246 n; workers, 199; *see also*, Commune, French Revolution,

Jacobinism, Napoleon III
Fränckel, L., 246
Free Trade, 163, 252
freedom, 92, 93 n.
Freiligrath, F., 253
French Revolution (1789), 21, 32, 45, 129 n., 218, 185–201; *see* Jacobinism, Robespierre, terrorism
Friedrich Wilhelm IV, 43

Galbraith, J. K., 81 n.
Gattungswesen, 84–5, 87–8, 231
Gebhardt, J., 124 n.
Gemeinwesen, 34, 57, 112, 114
Germany, 133, 151, 159, 255; call for republic, 212; Empire, 51; fit for revolution, 219; idealism, 139; labourers, 141; League of Communists, 196; liberalism, 137; proletariat, 214; rising of '48, 195, 219; social democrats, 67, 83, 257; workers, 51, 63 n., 197
Goethe, J. W., 111
Graeco-Roman, 19, 190
Gregor, A. J., 2
Grotius, H., 43
ground rent, 207
Grün, K., 54
Guesde, J., 246

Hecker, F., 195
Hegel, G. W. F.: Absolute Spirit, 128; alienation, 96–100; existence and actuality, 106; freedom, 92, 129; Feuerbach and, 10–12; history, view of, 4–5, 84, 250; idealism, 102; identity, 149; influence on Marx, 3–12; materialism, 65; political philosophy, 8–40; property, 109; role of philosophy, 135; *Stände*, 21–6; universal class, 57–8, 62; Works: *Logic*, 70; *Phenomenology of Mind*, 68, 96, 98, 100, 170 n., 189 n.; *Philosophy of History*, 19, 126; *Philosophy of Right*, 5, 13, 16, 22–3, 26 n., 27, 29, 39, 106 n., 128, 132, 188: quoted, 7, 124, 135; *see also*, Marx: *Critique of Hegel's Philosophy of Right*
Heine, H., 225 n.
Hepner, B. P., 125 n.
Hertz-Eichenrode, D., 62 n.
Hess, Moses, 17 n., 109, 124–5, 133
Heusel, A., 66 n.
history, interpretation of, 4–5, 79, 84, 95, 99, 127–8; world, 166

Index

Index

Index